BLOOD RUSH

BLOOD RUSH

THE DARK HISTORY OF A VITAL FLUID

JAN VERPLAETSE

Translated by Andy Brown

REAKTION BOOKS

Published by Reaktion Books Ltd
Unit 32, Waterside
44–48 Wharf Road
London N1 7UX, UK

www.reaktionbooks.co.uk

Bloedroes © 2016 by Jan Verplaetse
Originally published by Uitgeverij Nieuwezijds, Amsterdam,
The Netherlands, 2016
First published in English 2020
Copyright © Jan Verplaetse 2020
This book was published with the support of Flanders Literature
(flandersliterature.be)

**FLANDERS
LITERATURE**

Printed and bound in India
by Replika Press Pvt. Ltd

A catalogue record for this book is available from the British Library

ISBN 978 1 78914 196 2

CONTENTS

INTRODUCTION

I was a philosophy student, not quite twenty years old and still living at my parents' house, when I descended the steps to the cellar. I don't remember why I went down there, but what happened to me I would never forget. It would change my life and my way of thinking for ever. One day, I would start a book with it. Down there in the cellar hung a dead animal, head down, its hind legs skewered by a meat hook fixed to a water pipe. It was a fair-sized hare, and it had been skinned and its guts removed. That dead beast had already been hanging there for a few days, ageing in preparation for the family Christmas dinner. Although this one was new to me, I'd seen skinned hares in the cellar before. I knew the sour aroma and the almost purple colour of the marinade – a mixture of wine, vinegar, onion and cloves – in which the cuts of meat were soaked for several days. I remembered the smell of the firm, fleshy thighs frying in butter before they were put to simmer in the marinade. I knew about the ritual of crushing the liver and putting it through a sieve to bind the simmering liquid to a sauce. And I knew about the strange practice of adding fondant chocolate to the sauce to make it sweeter and darker. So I was familiar with the sight of a stripped hare. What affected me so intensely this time was not the hare itself, but the blood dripping so slowly out of its mouth and falling neatly into a white dish. There was a sheet of newspaper under the dish to keep the spatters of blood within the bounds of decency.

What did that blood do to me? The most surprising thing was that I felt absolutely no fear, revulsion or disgust. On the contrary, I wanted to touch it. To stick my finger into the dish and stir it.

To put my finger to my mouth and taste it. I wanted to smell it, feel it and savour it. Like a prehistoric cave painter, I wanted to draw figures on the white walls of the cellar with my red fingers. I felt excited and intoxicated. But above all, I experienced an endless fascination for this red bodily fluid that dripped from the hare's throat and formed a red puddle. Suddenly, I understood why blood has had such a seductive attraction for humankind throughout the centuries. Blood is at the centre of many rituals, from heathen offerings to the Christian mass, where the priest drinks the blood of Christ – even though it is, of course, only wine. Blood is also a major factor in hunting wild animals and slaughtering their domesticated counterparts. Hunting, breeding animals and eating meat are impossible without spilling blood. Blood is spilled during wars and other acts of violence. Blood calls for revenge and revenge calls for blood. In that moment I realized that, without blood, these things had no meaning. That it was blood that gave them their emotional charge and a deep significance. The blood rush I had experienced on the cellar steps immediately explained why people could be so absorbed by religion, hunting, violence, games or gastronomy. Because blood intoxicates us, we seek it out and want more of it. It makes us happy. The deeper meaning of blood revealed itself to me. It was, by analogy with the cellar story by Argentine writer Jorge Luis Borges, my Aleph, my mystical cellar experience – where deep insight came not from a crystal ball that enabled you to see the entire universe, but from a skinned hare from which the blood dripped into a dish, like water from a leaking tap.

The blood had a strange effect on me – emotionally and intellectually. It befuddled me and, at the same time, gave me insight into things that I had previously not fully understood. It shed more light on the darker side of our human nature, our more irrational impulses. But it also has the same effect on others. I was by no means the only one to experience blood rush. I later came to realize that the number of artists fascinated by blood and who work with blood is beyond count.[1] The German artist Joseph Beuys perhaps understood my cellar experience best: he used dried hare's blood for his drawings and dead hares in his performances, and always carried a small triangular plastic bag containing hare's blood.[2] If I were to consider myself more of an artist than a philosopher, I would undoubtedly have done the same. Scientists, too, have noted this effect of blood. More than fifteen years after my blood rush, I read a report by Swiss criminologist Rodolphe Archibald Reiss, one of the founding fathers of forensic science, on atrocities committed by Austro-Hungarian soldiers in a Serbian village at the outbreak of the First World War. In the report, I found the following fragment: 'But at the sight of blood, the phenomenon took place which I have often had occasion to observe: man was transformed into a bloodthirsty brute. A positive access of collective Sadic frenzy seized upon the troops.'[3] I have since read many accounts of this phenomenon, known as bloodlust – a blood rush that turns into aggression, cruelty and destruction – but Reiss's description was the first. It was then that it became clear to me that blood rush is not a phenomenon that occurs only in a certain period or location, let alone in a cellar in Belgium. These stories extend from ancient times to the modern era, from the south of Greece to the north of Germany – and that is only if we restrict ourselves to Europe. Tales of the powerful effect of contact with blood are to be found everywhere and at all times. I also quickly realized that bloodlust is not something that occurs only in times of war. I have heard stories of the exhilarating effect of blood during hunting parties, in abattoirs, while practising – and watching – combat sports, and during mass events that get out of hand. At times of conflict and violence, blood rush turns into bloodlust, and people become frenzied through their contact with blood. It arouses them to such an extent that they turn into wild animals who take delight in excessive violence and yearn to spill more blood. The comparison with animals can be taken literally: bloodlust is not restricted to humans. There are accounts of horses, cattle, dogs, leopards, chimpanzees, sharks, wolves, bears, elephants and even iguanas running amok on contact with blood. Once they have tasted the blood of a human or another animal, they yearn for more and will attack to get it. Animals, too, are not indifferent to blood. It excites them and makes them aggressive.

HEALTHY SCEPTICISM

The effect that the blood had on me in the cellar was not exceptional. Blood rush has frequently been observed, and there are countless stories about it. But stories prove nothing if they are unreliable, if they make claims that are not supported by argument. Despite his undisputed expertise, Reiss had not witnessed the atrocities at first hand. He had not seen with his own eyes in Serbia how the sight of blood had aroused bloodlust and provoked collective sadism. Perhaps he had heard about it or assumed that bloodlust would have occurred in such circumstances. He went to the site of the horrific bloodbath after it had taken place. Whether it was the blood that had caused the frenzy was not proven. It may just have been something he wanted to believe.

There is much scepticism about bloodlust. It is significant that two prominent historians start their books with descriptions of bloodlust, and that one finds the phenomenon credible while the other dismisses it as pure fiction. *The Cultivation of Hatred* (1993), by American psychoanalytical historian Peter Gay, begins with an eyewitness account by English humorist Jerome K. Jerome, who witnessed a *Mensur* in Germany around 1990. A *Mensur* was a kind of fencing practised by German students, which could get quite bloody. The combatants not only crossed swords, but their sharp rapiers often cut through each other's flesh, causing wounds and scars that they later wore as a badge of pride. Jerome described one of these contests in an overheated student hall, where the beer flowed profusely, noting:

As the blood began to flow, and nerves and muscles to be laid bare, I experienced a mingling of disgust and pity. But with the second duel, I must confess, my finer feelings began to disappear; and by the time the third was well upon its way, and the room heavy with the curious hot odour of blood, I began, as the American expression is, to see things red. I wanted more. I looked from face to face surrounding me, and in most of them I found reflected undoubtedly my own sensations. If it be a good thing to excite this blood thirst in the modern man, then the *Mensur* is a useful institution.[4]

Gay is delighted with this testimony, exclaiming 'This is an extraordinary confession.' It is surprising because it is so open and uncensored. Finally, someone dares to say that blood has an exhilarating effect that intoxicates people and makes them bloodthirsty. Such a glimpse of man's bestial nature is rare, Gay must have thought, so rare that it was worth starting a book with it. The bestial unconscious immediately grabs the reader's attention. No Freudian lets a chance like that go by.

The Origins of Crowd Psychology (1975) by American historian Robert A. Nye, about French pioneer of mass psychology Gustave Le Bon, begins completely differently. Nye opens with an eyewitness description by the French prime minister Georges Clemenceau of an extremely violent moment during the Paris Commune in 1871. At one point in this short but fierce civil war, revolutionaries took generals Lecomte and Thomas captive in Montmartre, where they were horrifically murdered a few days later by an angry mob. Clemenceau, then mayor of Montmartre, had the following to report on the lynch party: 'All were shrieking like wild beasts without realizing what there were doing. I observed then that pathological phenomenon which might be called bloodlust.'[5]

After killing the generals, the mob mutilated their bodies. Nye derides this description of bloodlust, which appears in every biography of Clemenceau and every popular historical account of the Paris Commune. What the reader is not aware of is that Clemenceau was a friend of Le Bon, who studied the psychology of masses because he was extremely afraid of the power of the mob. For him, anything that brought a protesting or rebellious crowd into disrepute was like a red rag to a bull. It suited him only too well to describe how collective protest turned individuals into a brainless rabble that acted en masse according to their animal instincts. Such bloodthirsty beasts did not deserve to be taken seriously. If you wanted to avoid a bloodbath, you simply had to ban them from protesting. According to Nye, this description of bloodlust is a rhetorical cliché based on a dangerous fiction. Anyone who sees people as predatory animals will eventually hunt them down.

AN UNMODERN FLUID

So is the effect of blood imaginary? As a student, I was not a young innocent. Blood gave me something that modernity did not. In Goethe's words, 'Blut ist ein ganz besonderer Saft' (blood is a very special fluid).[6] It was a gateway to another world, a world that not only consisted of the atoms and molecules that science unravelled – and technology replicated – but which gave them a deeper meaning. Modernity has been ruthless with blood. It has taken away its magical powers. While pre-modern healing was all about blood, even to the extent that a physician could not diagnose or heal a single disease without bloodletting, in modern medicine it plays only a very humble role. Blood is no longer the carrier of our genetic material; that role has been taken over by DNA. We no longer see sperm as aroused blood. Blood does not make you pregnant, as French researcher François Magendie still believed in the first half of the nineteenth century – but he did not exclude the possibility that women could become pregnant from sperm injected into their veins.[7] Menstrual blood is no longer accorded toxic properties: it will not cause flowers to wilt or mayonnaise to fail. Medical science set these beliefs aside as superstition. Almost everything that was formerly alleged about blood is now considered wrong. The modern perspective on blood is rational, objective and disapproving. In contemporary society, blood has lost its romance. In the economy, animal blood has become a residual product used for a wide range of industrial applications. In political terms, blood is a reminder of fanatical times, of 'blood and soil' ideologies that we never wanted to see again after the Second World War. Modern society was built on rational abstractions like human rights, not on romantic sentiments. For modern bodies, contact with blood is a portent of medical disaster. High blood pressure, clogged-up blood vessels, streaks of blood in our stools: we don't like blood any more.

Blood is an unmodern fluid. Anyone ill at ease with demystified modernity feels nostalgic for the time when blood was still something special. As a student of philosophy I was touched by that malaise. It was what held schools of thought like phenomenology, existentialism, *Lebensphilosophie* and psychoanalysis together. The new wave and postpunk of The Cure, Echo and the Bunnymen, The Sound and the Sisters of Mercy expressed that cultural pessimism in an atmosphere of melancholy. Raving and dancing, I became receptive to the effect that dripping hare's blood had on me. I was certain to be overcome by a blood rush sooner or later, and my parents' house provided the ideal decor. I had spent my youth in a house built in the atmosphere of post-war optimism and unprecedented prosperity, and its gleaming tidiness was the most tangible evidence of the victory of modernity. Old demons were given no opportunity to nestle in filth. The maid, who came every Tuesday and Friday, even blew the fine dust from the wine bottles in the cellar. From attic to cellar, everything was as bright and clean as new. If I think of my mother during my childhood, I see her in an apron, with a vacuum cleaner, a frothing bucket of soapy water, a dustpan or a scrubbing brush in her hands. Or with a cigarette in her mouth. Cleaning was a modernistic struggle against the appeal of the animal and the irrational. The more you cleaned and the neater everything was, the clearer the boundary became between the rational human being and the irrational beast, and the smaller the risk of pleasure to be found in something that was dirty, loathsome or scary. Bleach was the best way to drive out intoxication and lust.

But it didn't work with me. Despite – or perhaps because of – the whole house smelling so fresh and gleaming with tidiness, I was enthralled by that bleeding animal which struck such a harsh contrast with all that hygienic modernity. The contrast between its skinned body and the whitewashed walls was enormous. Every drop of blood threatened to destroy the cleanliness with a spatter or a stain. That animal had everything the modern house lacked. It had been wild and untameable. The smell of dirt lingered on the skin around its legs. It still inspired fear, because hunters had riddled its head and chest with shot. Its death had not been clean. But above all, that hare's blood had something mysterious. It did not clot, while you would expect blood to do so. Was hare's blood somehow different? Had Aristotle been right when he had claimed that the blood of wild animals did not coagulate?[8] I now know better, but back then I found that liquid hare's blood mysterious and inexplicable.

IN SEARCH OF AN EXPLANATION

That's how I saw it then, as a student of philosophy. Several decades have now passed. My blood-rush experience has stayed with me, that much is clear, but time has also made me more critical. Many questions have come bubbling to the surface and I have explored many answers. I have conducted a great deal of research, of which this book is the result. Many years have passed between my original experience and the book's publication. That is partly due to the enormous quantity of literature on the subject, but is also partly down to the personal dimension of the theme. Because it affected me so deeply, blood became an autobiographical topic. It fed my identity and my happiness and the way I gave meaning to my life.

This book is about blood rush, a fascination for blood that can invoke an intoxicating feeling on contact with blood. If this intoxication fuels aggression and leads to violence, or even killing and destruction, it is called bloodlust. This book is not about bloodlust as a metaphor for the urge to kill. That requires actual physical contact with blood. Nor is it restricted to a vampire-like desire for more blood. Here, we use bloodlust in a more general sense. Is this intoxicating effect of blood real or only fantasy? That's the central topic of this book. If blood rush and bloodlust are real how can we explain them? If they are imaginary, where do these fantasies come from? Natural scientists are primarily interested in whether bloodlust really occurs and in identifying its material causes – chemicals in the blood, for example. That question is fascinating, but too limited for a full understanding of the phenomenon. The conclusions that I offer in this book go beyond natural scientific explanations, though I do discuss those too. Even if blood rush is a figment of our imagination, it is still interesting to know why we are so keen to believe in it.

I will elaborate on these explanations later. But first, in this introduction, I want to take a look at a number of possibilities that seem convincing at first glance, but which prove inadequate on closer examination. They are fast and simple, but provide no real answers. The English *fin-de-siècle* psychiatrist Henry Havelock Ellis once wrote 'There is scarcely any natural object with so profoundly emotional an effect as blood', to which he immediately added 'and it is very easy to understand why this should be so'.[9] I wish I could have shared Ellis's simple insight. I found it more difficult to discover why blood has this overwhelming effect.

One overly simple medical explanation for bloodlust is that it occurs in people suffering from congenital erythropoietic porphyria (CEP). Porphyria is the collective name for rare hereditary diseases in which a deficit of haem causes a wide range of health problems. Haem is an important substance for the production of haemoglobin in our red blood cells. The name 'porphyria' comes from the Greek *porphyra*, meaning purple. One typical symptom of porphyria is that urine turns the colour of red wine in daylight. The deficit of an enzyme causes overproduction of a large number of chemicals, including this purple pigment. CEP also causes hypersensitivity to light, leading to painful skin complaints. In addition, the teeth colour slightly fluorescent red when exposed to ultraviolet light and there is a risk of anaemia because the purple pigment destroys blood cells. These symptoms have led to CEP and other variants of porphyria being associated with vampires and vampirism since Bram Stoker's *Dracula* was published in 1897.[10] Speculation that CEP patients cure themselves by drinking haem-rich blood and that the disease was particularly prevalent in Transylvania is persistent. A medical explanation for bloodlust is then only a small step. It becomes a desperate act by CEP sufferers looking for haem-rich blood to alleviate their painful symptoms. When I called veterinary doctors to learn more about the rumour that the blood of slaughtered animals made abattoir employees aggressive, they were completely dumbfounded. None had ever heard the story before. But one of them was certain that, if it did ever occur, it would be due to CEP.

Whether CEP can be treated by drinking blood is doubtful. Haem would have to be a strong molecule to survive the stomach's juices and find its way into the bloodstream. Blood transfusions are administered to CEP patients, but to alleviate anaemia caused by the loss of blood cells, not to add more haem to the blood. Moreover, bloodletting and centrifuging blood are just as common in treating CEP. Transfusions bring the risk of a surplus of iron in the blood. There is no simple treatment – the disease is too complex. If CEP could be treated with haem from dried blood, it would have been done long ago. But it is not that simple.

The greatest misconception, however, is that CEP explains bloodlust. Bloodlust occurs in large masses of people during fighting and hunting, and in slaughterhouses, and not among people suffering from a rare genetic disease – approximately one in a million – who avoid daylight and tire quickly because of anaemia. People in perfect health experience bloodlust, and not individually but in groups, in the right circumstances. Furthermore, satisfying the desire does not always result in pleasure. Why should we become intoxicated by the thought of drinking someone's blood, even if it can reputedly save our lives? I don't know of anyone who is aroused by seeing or smelling medicine, even when it is necessary for their survival. And no one would be overly keen to drink a cup of urine, even if it had been proved to have an equally therapeutic effect. Fresh blood is by no means a delicious or refreshing drink, and it never has been. We have always had a *horror cruoris*, an aversion to blood. In certain circumstances we can overcome it, and contact with blood can even be exhilarating, but suffering from a disease like CEP is not one such circumstance.

Overly simple explanations do not tell us where that exhilaration comes from, thereby failing to consider an essential element of bloodlust. The same applies to the explanation that blood symbolizes life and the life force. That association attributes all kinds of phenomena to contact with blood, including a lust for life. There is undeniably a tradition that associates blood with life and the life force, based on the observable role that blood plays in life and death. If you lose a lot of blood, you die. Dead people turn pale and lose the pinkness of their cheeks. Dead bodies no longer bleed, because the heart no longer beats and the blood seeks the lowest point – usually the back or stomach – where it decomposes. New human life used to seem impossible without menstrual blood. Young girls are not fertile until they start to menstruate. When they become pregnant, the menstrual cycle stops. When menstruation stops for good, a woman is no longer fertile. For those ignorant of the biological processes that lead to pregnancy, it seems logical that new human life is created from this female blood and the male seed. Without blood, there is no life, only death. The Old Testament repeats this over and over again. Leviticus 17:14 tells us twice that 'the life of all flesh is the blood thereof', while Deuteronomy 12:23 is short and to the point: 'the blood is the life'. For many Jews, the association between blood and life is enough to prevent them from consuming the blood of any animal. Jews do not eat blood sausage. When Jews slaughter an animal, the blood should flow away into the sand. Whether this is the real historical reason why Jews are forbidden to consume blood is unlikely but, either way, the association is very old.

Conversely, the same notion has led to blood being used as a medicine to combat a wide variety of ailments. Human blood was reputed to help cure epilepsy, goat's blood a pale complexion and dried frog's blood was used to stop bleeding. Men who wanted a son were advised to rub their penises with hare's blood before having sex.[11] This was not the first thing that came to mind when I saw that hare hanging in our cellar.

The association between blood, life and the life force may be ancient and strong, but it does not explain the phenomenon of blood rush, or why it has such an exhilarating effect. Blood brings life and gives us vitality and energy, but that is not the same as excitement, intoxication and ecstasy. Being full of life cannot be compared with the feeling of being drunk, especially when bloodlust has aggressive or even lethal consequences. Collective sadism, a thirst for blood, desecration of corpses

– such bloodlust is aimed not at the life of others, but at their death. It is a life force that sows death and destruction, a state of intoxication in which the wish to see more blood flow and an insatiable desire to kill is experienced. If you feel bloodlust, you want blood that brings not life, but death and pain. The destructive power of bloodlust stands in complete opposition to the vital force of blood. Bloodlust belongs to the darker side of humankind and not to its more optimistic, light-hearted side. Anyone who sees bloodlust as something vital cannot explain why it is so life destroying.

THREE EXPLANATIONS

In this book, I propose three plausible explanations for bloodlust and blood rush. They divide the book into three parts and ten chapters. Working chronologically, I start with the oldest: the supernatural explanation of 'blood magic', which sees blood as a magical fluid because it is the point of contact with a super-natural world. This is the realm of gods, spirits, demons and the dead. It is a cosmos of superpowers that have an inexplicable yet direct and tangible impact on human activity. By using blood in rituals, you can curry favour with that influential supernatural world. Blood rituals are a way to avert disaster for yourself or to bring it down on others. Blood magic is not without its dangers. The dialogue between the earthly and the supernatural world does not always go as we wish. Instead of bringing protection, healing, prediction or whatever else you ask by practising blood magic, the demons you summon during blood rituals can drive you out of your mind. As they demand more and more blood for smaller and smaller favours, you become obsessed by it. In this supernatural explanation, blood rush has nothing animal or bestial, but is elevating and spiritual. Blood does not bring you into contact with your lower animal instincts, but with the powerful realm of immortal spirits and occult life forces.

The supernatural explanation offers a good insight into our fascination with blood. It explains the special meaning of blood and explains why contact with it can be exhilarating, even drive you out of your mind. I am not asking the modern reader to believe in magic. I don't believe in it myself, nor is it necessary to. In itself, the explanation holds water, even though it is implausible to most of us. The point is that there were sufficient people who did believe in it in the past and, for them, blood magic explained bloodlust. Belief in blood magic has proved tenacious in the modern age, too – not only in dying superstition, but in medical science. The idea that blood is a special fluid whose secrets will never be completely unravelled has survived for many centuries. For a long time there was no question at all of blood being demystified, and certainly not among those who had difficulties adapting to modernity. Demystification is now approaching – as the first drops of artificial blood start flowing through our veins, it will be clear that blood holds no more secrets than, for example, urine – but we haven't quite reached that point yet.

The second explanation is the bestial, or naturalistic, explanation – 'blood thirst' – which will probably be of most interest to those curious about the natural sciences. Here, bloodlust is a remnant of, or a return to, a primitive and bestial state in which humans, like beasts of prey, had an aggressive instinct – an instinct to hunt or kill – that helped them to capture prey or dispose violently of other members of their species. Bloodlust is a prehistoric remnant of a wild time and a wild environment. The pleasure that comes from contact with blood meant that the aggression was enjoyable. Sadism helped with survival. Just as sexual lust encourages reproduction, bloodlust urges the attack of hostile animals and humans. Something we would not do spontaneously, because blood revolts us or because we are afraid of being injured or killed, is made easier by bloodlust. I will go into this in more detail later but, in general terms, this is the essence of the second explanation. It is built around factual claims that have been tested scientifically. It contains no elements of magic. In this second part of the book, I will discuss what science has to say about bloodlust. Can we smell blood? Do we get aggressive or excited by contact with blood? How does the colour red affect how we behave? What is its effect on animals?

The final explanation for bloodlust is the 'aesthetic' one. Bloodlust is all in our minds. A certain belief or psychological mechanism can be enough to trigger blood rush. Blood rush goes back to the dynamics of repulsion and attraction referred to in aesthetics as the sublime, which is linked historically to Romanticism. Blood inspires fear and revulsion. In the last part of the book, I discuss those who faint at the sight of blood, who suffer from blood phobia and who derive no pleasure at all from contact with blood. And yet everything that is repulsive and frightening can also be attractive – for those who can stomach it and are sufficiently distanced from it. Think of the pleasure we derive from watching horror films. Blood and bloodlust – like that of vampires, for example – can scare us in a pleasurable way. Where that paradoxical attraction comes from is not clear. There are many theories to explain it. According to one that appeals to me – although I cannot claim that it explains all cases of attraction to blood – the exhilaration comes from a deeper insight. No matter how repulsive and terrifying blood is, contact with it touches something far below our surface. It confirms a philosophical belief that enraptures us. I already suspected as a student that my malaise with modernity was in some way connected to my blood-rush experience. Apparently I was open to the aesthetics of the sublime and the sensibilities of Romanticism. The fear and revulsion that unmodern blood invoked raised questions about the modernist ideal that we can control and shape the world we live in. That doubt about the power of the Enlightenment and of modernity appealed to me very strongly back then. The contrast between the clean cellar and the dripping blood of the wild animal set the dynamics of the sublime in motion. The horror-aesthetic explanation brings all these elements together. The core of this explanation is that it is not blood itself that gives us the blood rush, but our perceptions of it. The thought that blood has something about it that has escaped modernity exhilarates us.

IN SEARCH OF THE MEANING OF BLOODLUST

My primary aim is to explain where bloodlust comes from. That is why I am exploring the three explanations and all the stories that back them up. But this theme is too personal to limit myself to that. I not only want to know where that blood experience came from, I want to find out what it means. Does the feeling of ecstasy I experienced have any foundation? Was there anything to be exhilarated about? That is my philosophical objective. Throughout the book, I will return to my blood experience at regular intervals to try and unravel its meaning.

I do not wish to reveal that meaning here in the Introduction. Nor have I devoted a separate chapter to it. It closely follows the explanations because, though explanation and meaning do not fully coincide, they are closely connected in two ways. First of all, each explanation gives substance to the meaning. The three explanations outline three forms of philosophical happiness. The supernatural explanation sees ultimate happiness as establishing contact with a world that transcends the material one. Blood is the point of contact with a spiritual cosmos, and blood rush is the exhilaration that comes from communicating with a higher world. The naturalistic explanation finds deep happiness in the notion that a primitive past still haunts our civilized world. It does not deny that there is only a material world, but suggests that blood is the link between the present and a distant past, and thus offers the prospect of a trans-historical experience. Bloodlust is a wild remnant of that past which no civilization, no matter how sophisticated, can tame. Lastly, the horror-aesthetic explanation experiences beauty in the horrific. This paradoxical happiness lies in the philosophical awareness that the belief on which the Enlightenment and modernity are founded – that we can control and shape the world in which we live – is an exaggerated illusion. Dark forces are always stronger than enlightened ideals. From a suitable distance, blood can offer a sublime experience. Blood rush exhilarates us by showing that the Enlightenment was wrong.

These three meanings share in the strengths and weaknesses of the three explanations. Although the latter are good explanations for bloodlust, the principles they are founded on can be strong or weak. Accepting or rejecting the principles means accepting or rejecting the meanings. If blood still confronts us with a number of unanswerable questions, that could justify its magical meaning. If blood proves to contain chemicals that can exhilarate us, that is something different to bloodlust as romantic self-deception. But even a romantic fantasy can be philosophically defensible – at least, as long as it has no unacceptable moral consequences. In short, each explanation includes claims that are crucial to the philosophical justification of my experience. I will test those claims and, if the results are negative, the consequences will be clear. Happiness has no foundation. There is no deeper meaning, or not one that can be defended. Here, too, my ambiguous attitude towards modernity forms the backdrop. What happiness does modernity still permit? What forms of happiness must we relinquish? Is blood rush not an experience from a hopelessly obsolete world? Is there any future for that unmodern happiness in our society? That, in essence, is what this book is about.

To retain control over the material, I have imposed certain limits on myself. My starting point is our fascination, even obsession, with blood, not blood itself. I do not offer a comprehensive history of thought on blood: given the enormous quantity of literature on all facets of the subject, that would be impossible.[12] It is only possible to write histories of specific themes relating to blood. Consequently, many others are not addressed. I do not discuss the role of blood in virginity or circumcision, about blood relationships and incest, or about flagellants or blood doping. Nevertheless, I do address a wide variety of themes – vampires, blood transfusions, sacrifice, bloodletting and blood medicines – and I do give a broad outline of the history of thought on blood, which does make this book a history of blood, of sorts. But I approach these themes from my focus on bloodlust and blood rush. These two main themes bring all the others together. In addition, I limit myself to the European continent and European cultural history with, by way of exception, short detours to discuss the Jews and Christians in the Levant, and to Japan. There are no American, African or Islamic stories in this book, no Aztec human sacrifices, nothing about the Islamic ritual of Hijama (a religious variant of bloodletting) and no visits to animal sacrifices still practised in Cuba, Nepal and India. Interesting as they are, they fall beyond the scope of the limitations I have set for myself. My approach is unavoidably Western and European, but that was also my explicit intention. This book is a reflection on the role of blood in our culture. Where does that fascination come from and what remains of it in a rapidly changing world?

PART ONE
BLOOD MAGIC

BLOOD MIST

In a brilliant article published in 1934 in the encyclopaedia series *Antike und Christentum*, which he himself initiated, Franz Joseph Dölger listed a number of reasons why early Christians were accused of infanticide.[1] Dölger was a respected Catholic theologian and religious historian, who later had an institute of religious research in Bonn named after him. His accusations were shocking, to say the least. During a nocturnal initiation ritual, Christians were alleged to kill a baby, retain its blood in a receptacle, throw morsels of bread into the blood and then eat it with relish. This gruesome dish was supposed to give them access to eternal life. Once this basic rumour took hold, all kinds of hideous details were added. Some sources left no doubts at all that parts of the baby were also eaten, and preferably the bloodiest organs, such as the heart, liver and lungs.[2] Other sources had the infant covered in flour, ready to make into blood-bread rolls. Yet other accounts claimed that this cannibalistic feast degenerated into a decadent orgy of incestuous sex. The horrific ritual ended theatrically with trained dogs knocking over large candleholders with burning candles. The rumours lasted not a few months or years, but several decades. All Greek and Latin apologists between AD 150 and 200 recounted these rumours, emphatically denying they were true. Perhaps the best known of all these denials is that of Tertullian in his *Apology*. The claims are less common in pagan and Jewish sources, but a letter from Pliny the Younger to Emperor Trajan from AD 110, stating that Christians in Bithynia (in Asia Minor) came together to eat and that the food was perfectly normal and not harmful, can be interpreted as an early pagan reference to this accusation. The most recent reference was by the theologian Origen, who wrote around AD 240 that pagans had finally agreed that the rumours were all scandalmongering.

In his article, Dölger gave a number of explanations for these stubborn allegations. The first was a logical one: a literal interpretation of the Eucharist, where Christians eat the body and drink the blood of Christ in the form of bread and wine. As St John's Gospel (6:53–5) tells us:

> Verily, verily, I say unto you, Except ye eat the flesh of the Son of man, and drink his blood, ye have no life in you. Whoso eateth my flesh, and drinketh my blood, hath eternal life; and I will raise him up at the last day. For my flesh is meat indeed, and my blood is drink indeed.

Dölger's second explanation was more controversial. He believed that the allegations were not entirely based on fabrication. There is no smoke without fire. Although a Catholic theologian like Dölger would find it difficult to believe that infanticide, cannibalism and promiscuous sex were compulsory rights of initiation in 'orthodox' church communities, he did not exclude the possibility that such outrages could have been committed by libertine sects in Syria and Egypt. Montanist and Gnostic groups in particular had bad reputations. What Christian authors considered unthinkable in their own communities, they attributed to groups with illustrious names like Marcionites, Carpocratians, Borborians and Phibionites. Of this latter group of Gnostics, the Cypriot Epiphanius of Salamis wrote in his *Panarion* (AD 375) that, for their gruesome feast, they first aborted the unborn child from the mother's womb, then cut it into pieces and crushed it in a bowl that served as a large mortar and seasoned it with honey, pepper and other spices, using a lot of incense to disguise the disgusting smell. Each participant at this Easter feast had to eat a piece of the baby with their fingers. According to Epiphanius, they also drank menstrual blood or poured it over their bodies, uttering the sacred words 'This is the blood of Christ.'[3]

Dölger thus believed that, in some ancient communities, Easter was not only celebrated with an Easter lamb or Easter eggs. And he was not the only one; many later researchers also believed in these horrific practices.[4] Epiphanius was apparently a reliable chronicler with an eye for detail which proved that he had experienced everything at first hand. Furthermore, he knew the Gnostic groups in Alexandria and read their pamphlets, in which they described their rituals in gory detail. This made the implausible allegations against the Christians more understandable. It is not unfeasible to assume that pagans who mistrusted Christianity as an alien and persistent religion easily picked up on a rumour about the ritual of a marginalized group and generalized it, accusing all Christians of practising it on a regular basis. Uninformed outsiders often make no distinction between the criminal wrongdoings of a minority and the harmless rituals of the majority. They could have projected what they heard about Syrian or Egyptian sects onto all Christian communities in the Roman and Byzantine empires. Current commentators no longer share these opinions. They are astounded that, while no one believes the original allegations about Christians, they were considered well-founded in relation to heretical groups.[5] Why were stories about Gnostic atrocities considered to be true, while those about Christian cruelty were based on scandalous lies? The venom with which the pagans wanted to condemn the Christians was matched by the hatred of the orthodox Christians for renegade heretics. In both cases, the allegations were propaganda aimed at showing the opponent in a bad light. Accusing hostile groups of bloody atrocities is as old as human history.

Whether the accusations were slanderous or not, they do not adequately explain bloodlust. That such atrocities happened is one thing, but why they happened is another. Why did fanatical adherents or those who spread slander explicitly choose this horrific ritual in which blood played the leading role? Why was the murder of a baby not enough? The initiate had to consume the baby's blood, and the bloodiest flesh. What made it so macabre was not the murder of the infant, as such, but the gruesome details of ritual cannibalism and the drinking of human blood.

Dölger's third explanation is of the most interest to us here: 'The heathen reproach that, during their nocturnal worship, Christians slaughtered children, ate their flesh and drank their blood, is not exceptional. It is a common accusation aimed at evil magic in general.'[6] Spilling the blood of innocent children was a magic ritual. The hands of magicians were stained with children's flesh and blood. Christians were therefore not just child killers, they indulged in black magic, too. That inspired not only aversion, but fear.

Practising evil magic was strictly forbidden in both the Roman Empire and Jewish Israel, and anyone found guilty of such practices faced exceptionally severe punishment. They would be thrown to the wild beasts or crucified. Magicians were burned alive. Who exactly qualified as practising magic was never defined, but a collection of laws from the third and early fourth centuries, the *Pauli sententiae*, referred explicitly to 'people who have performed wicked or nocturnal rites', 'sacrificed a man' or 'obtained omens from his blood'.[7] In short, the kinds of obscure practices of which Christians were accused. Dölger substantiated his statement with many analogies in which children are killed for magical purposes. Emperor Domitian (AD 51–96) accused the eccentric philosopher Apollonius of Tyana of slaughtering a young boy to inspect the organs for omens. Apollonius' biographer, Philostratus the Elder, added that Apollonius also ate the child's flesh, an absurd accusation considering that the philosopher was a vegetarian who abhorred animal sacrifices.[8] For their part, Roman emperors were accused of practising the same gruesome magic. The more sadistic their reigns of terror – as with Didius Julianus, Elagabalus, Valerian and Maxentius – the greater the probability of such accusations being made. Of Elagabalus, the adolescent emperor from Syria, the *Historia Augusta* (The Augustan History), a collection of biographies of doubtful historical reliability, said: 'Elagabalus also sacrificed human victims, and for this purpose he collected from the whole of Italy children of noble birth and beautiful appearance, whose fathers and mothers were alive, intending, I suppose, that the sorrow, if suffered by two parents, should be all the greater.'[9]

Once the children were dead, he would inspect their organs to predict the future of his reign, which proved to be very short. It must be said, however, that the wildest of claims were made about Elagabalus' behaviour.

More tangible evidence of the use of child's blood and flesh for magical purposes can be found in old books of magic, like the great magical papyrus of Paris, part of the Greek Magical Papyri.[10] The papyrus contains a supplication to the moon goddess, which speaks of 'a gruesome incense offering with blood, suet and the filth of a dappled goat, menstrual blood from a virgin, the heart of a premature child, magical material from a dead dog and a female embryo'.[11] You could use this magical spell to destroy your enemies from a great distance. The papyrus also recommends blood for less aggressive purposes, such as bewitching an unwilling woman. This ritual went as follows:

> Leave a bit of the bread which you eat; break it up and shape it into seven bite-size pieces. And go to the place where heroes and gladiators and those who have died a violent death were slain. Say the spell to the pieces of bread and toss them. And pick up some polluted dirt from the place where you perform the rite and throw it inside the house of the woman whom you desire.[12]

There is probably no need to add that it is better not to tell the woman in question who threw the dirty scraps covered in blood and mud into her house. Other magic books offered spells requiring a little more effort for lovers desperate to achieve the same objective. The biography of sixth-century patriarch Severus of Antioch by Zacharias of Mytilene relates the story of an Egyptian who studied law in Beirut but who primarily collected books of magic. In love with a woman who was firmly attached to her chastity, he consulted one of his magic books, which advised him to sacrifice a woman by night. His African slave was the obvious choice. His gruesome plan failed, however, when his friends became suspicious and the slave girl resisted so furiously that neighbours and passers-by sounded the alarm.[13]

The most tangible proof of the magical use of the blood and flesh of sacrificed children is found on the inscription on an urn discovered at a Roman burial site, now kept in the Museo Lapidario Maffeiano in Verona. It is the urn of a four-year-old boy, and his obituary reads as follows: 'I was still a child in my fourth year when fate took me and death crushed me, while I brought such joy to my father and mother. The hand of a sorceress [*saga manus crudelis*] who raged cruelly at this place tore me away, while she lived further on earth and caused harm with her arts.'[14]

THIS BRINGS us much closer to the stories of Horace, Lucanus and Petronius about witches (*strigae*), poisoners and sorceresses who kidnapped children, sacrificed them and used their blood and organs for magical ends. With trembling hands, they wrote of witches like Erichtho, who – although she preferred to eat corpses – did not shy away from killing babies, or Canidia, who buried young men up to their mouths to starve them and then cut out their bone marrow and shrivelled livers to make love potions. When Roman heathens thought of magic and magical rituals, these heinous deeds are what came to mind. A good example is

Pliny the Elder, who ruthlessly condemned magic in his *Natural History* (AD 77–9), despite the work itself being shot through with superstition. He praised the total ban on magical practices by the Romans, including in the annexed territories, saying, 'It is beyond calculation how great is the debt owed to the Romans, who swept away the monstrous rites, in which to kill a man was the highest religious duty and for him to be eaten a passport to health.'[15] That even the emperor Nero rejected black magic proved the falsity of this discipline, which stood at the crossroads of medicine, astrology and religion. Those who agreed with Pliny and believed the malicious rumours about Christians murdering children presented Christianity as a lethal magical religion.

BLOOD VAPOUR

What gave blood its magical power? Why not the saliva or urine of the murdered child? Dölger's article does not answer this question. The answer is given by one of his followers. As early as 1930, Franz Rüsche published *Blut, Leben und Seele* (Blood, Life and Soul), a voluminous study of the significance of blood for Greek, Jewish and Christian theologians, philosophers and physicians, as well as for the uneducated masses. The book remains an astoundingly detailed encyclopaedic work. Rüsche's starting point was the same as that of anyone who has wondered where our fascination with blood comes from: blood contains our life force. That fascination needs to be put into context. There is no evidence at all to suggest, for example, that blood – of people or animals – was used in prehistoric art.[16] The sensual desire to smear the walls with blood that overcame me in that cellar was unknown to the prehistoric artist. And yet the association of blood with the life force is widespread – though not universal. This is not so surprising. I have already mentioned that this symbolic view of blood is founded on its role in life and death. An animal that loses enough blood will die, and a woman who stops menstruating becomes pregnant and later brings a child into the world, an event also involving much blood. That blood has something to do with life and death was always abundantly clear. But what gives blood its life force? What is in blood that makes it so powerful and magical?

Rüsche added something to this cliché that made it clearer. Homer knew that when blood escapes from the body in large quantities – through damage to the arteries – it releases vapour. Rüsche called this *Blutrauch* or *Blutdunst*, blood vapour or mist.[17] During the bloodbaths of Odysseus and the murder of Agamemnon, the floor not only dripped with blood, but steamed with the vapour of the fresh blood pouring from the victims' slashed arteries.[18] Anyone not familiar with slaughter and battle-fields – most of us, fortunately – will not have experienced blood vapour at first hand. Yet I was told at slaughterhouses that it is not a fabrication. When a large volume of blood escapes from the body of an animal, its temperature will be that of the body and, on contact with a colder environment like the slaughterhouse floor, condensation will form, creating a kind of mist around the carcass. Although this vapour evaporates quickly, it gives the impression that something volatile is escaping from the blood. Greek soldiers who attacked their enemies with swords, spears and knives had the same experience. During such frequent man-to-man fighting, a lot of blood would flow from the dead bodies, releasing a light mist over the cold battlefield. As the mist disappeared, the victims stopped breathing. Blood that came bubbling out of wounded bodies and then came to a standstill, steaming vapour that rose into the air and wheezing bodies taking their final breath – for Homer it was clear that something vital escaped from the blood at death, something that gave a healthy body its life force and life's breath.

Blood vapour bound us to the supernatural world of spiritual beings and spectral shades. Blood was not just an earthly substance but contained all kinds of spiritual elements (*spiritus*), the higher forms of which returned to their supernatural habitat after the body expired. The blood vapour thus returned home, while the blood that remained behind ceased to move and coagulated. Blood vapour was to blood what the soul was to the human body. During life, blood was a combination of material and form, but once death had occurred, the two separated into mortal fluid and immortal *spiritus*. Blood thus contained the key to the supernatural realm populated by the souls of the dead, and by demons, demigods and gods. The ethereal properties of blood made contact with the supernatural a possibility. Who knows – perhaps it was possible to send messages via the airwaves of the blood vapour. It was taken for granted that the spiritual world had control over our existence. After all, eternal spirits were more powerful than mortal bodies. Nevertheless, a normal mortal could send suggestions to these higher powers. With its volatile vapour, blood was the perfect means of communication, especially when it became clear that the higher powers were enamoured of that warm bodily fluid.

MAGIC BLOOD RITUALS

Rüsche described fascinating rituals that went back to this supernatural blood contact. A somewhat foolhardy example is feeding blood to the shades of the underworld (*haimakouria*), who roamed around like zombies and were addicted to this red energy drink, which brought back memories of their earthly adventures.[19] Homer gave us the most literary description of this ritual. During his travels, Odysseus came to a city shrouded in mist, which the light of the sun or the stars never penetrated. Deathly night hung permanently over its unfortunate people. The city offered access to the misty world of the dead where Hades ruled. Because Odysseus wanted to talk to the blind prophet Tiresias about the future, he lured the phantoms with sacrificial blood:

Thus to assuage the nations of the dead I pledged these
rites, then slashed the lamb and ewe, letting their black
blood stream into the wellpit. Now the souls gathered,
stirring out of Erebos, brides and young men, and men
grown old in pain, and tender girls whose hearts were
new to grief; many were there, too, torn by brazen lance-
heads, battle-slain, bearing still their bloody gear. From
every side they came and sought the pit with rustling
cries; and I grew sick with fear.[20]

Odysseus kept the wispy but bloodthirsty shades at a distance
with his sword until he had spoken to Tiresias, who could not
predict anything without a pool of sheep's blood. Odysseus
would even see his own mother begging for a few drops of blood.
The *haimakouria* undoubtedly existed, at least from an earthly
perspective. Plutarch and Pindar had seen this bloody meal of the
dead in Plataea and by the Alfeiós during the annual celebration
of the dead.[21] 'But blood has also flowed for normal mortals,'
Rüsche assured us, 'although it hardly occurs during the centuries that lie behind us in the clear light of recorded history.'[22]
According to Plutarch, Solon banned the slaughter of oxen at
graveyards in Athens in the sixth century BC.[23]

The most bizarre blood ritual that Rüsche reported was a
kind of pharmaceutical *haimakouria* that healed the sick.[24] We
do not even have to go back to antiquity to find it. It took place
seventy years before the publication in 1930 of *Blut, Leben und
Seele*, in the German city of Göttingen, where an eyewitness of
the public execution of criminals sentenced to death wrote the
following:

On an open terrain near to the city, a scaffold had been
erected that could be seen from afar. On the scaffold
stood not only the condemned prisoners, but also the
executioner and his assistants, a few constables, and a

number of other spectators. I, too, stood at this spot, from where I could follow the events clearly. On the gallows mound around the scaffold, a crowd of many hundreds of people had gathered . . . A constable read out the sentence, which had been confirmed by the King, and, according to traditional custom, broke the staff above the heads of the condemned . . . After the heads and eyes of the condemned had been covered with hoods, the executioner took his large, broad, sharp, smooth sword from beneath his cloak and stood on the left side of the condemned. He then swung the sword, separating their heads from their bodies . . . Two streams of blood spouted from the wounds half a metre into the air, receded again, and then welled out a few more times as the heartbeat of the dead men grew fainter. A number of epileptics who had lined up close to the scaffold handed glasses to the executioner and his assistants. The latter filled the glasses with the spouting blood and gave them back to the epileptics, who quickly drunk them dry. It was believed at that time that the blood of the condemned, if drunk fresh, could cure epilepsy.[25]

This blood cure was still practised in the twentieth century. In 1908, during the execution of a murderess in Freiburg, Germany, an old woman begged for the fresh blood of the condemned prisoner to help a young epileptic girl. This macabre medicinal practice dated back many centuries. Various sources from the first century AD onwards contain reports of epileptics waiting to drink the fresh blood of dead gladiators in the Roman arenas. The sources differ in some details. Physician Scribonius Largus informs us that a single dose was not enough. The treatment had to be repeated three, nine or thirty times. Others claimed that the afflicted not only drank the gladiators' blood, but ate their livers raw. Anyone who did not have access to the real thing could make do with the liver of a stag, as long as it had been killed with a gladiator's sword. Caelius Aurelianus, a physician practising a few centuries later, also knew of the use of human livers as a treatment for epilepsy around AD 400. Because gladiator fights had become a rarity by then, executed criminals offered a good alternative – their blood or livers worked just as well. As Largus had already pointed out, the donors did not always have to be human. The blood of turtles or pigeons, the raw heart of a cormorant or weasel, even the brains of a vulture, all had a beneficial effect on the disease. But nothing could beat the healing power of human blood and organs. According to Byzantine physician Alexander of Tralles, who lived in the sixth century AD, anyone who found it difficult to drink human blood was advised to mix it with wine. No physician of the time doubted that this blood cure was abhorrent. Only desperation could drive people to drink human blood and eat raw human livers. Serious doctors would keep their distance from such nonsense.

Where did that nonsense come from? At first glance, using the blood of people who have just been killed is an example of *similia similibus curentur* therapy, treating a disease with something that resembles it. Since the spasms of a dying gladiator are similar to those of an epileptic suffering from a grand mal seizure, the convulsing body is seen as possessing the power to heal epilepsy. But this homeopathic explanation does not clarify why blood or the liver is required. Why not some other bodily fluid or organ? Why blood again?

For Rüsche, this blood therapy had its roots in the belief that blood is the point of contact between the physical world and the spiritual soul, between body and mind. When the *spiritus* escaped from the jugular veins of beheaded criminals, the life force left the mortal body. The soul that resided in the blood returned to its ethereal homeland. When epileptics fell senseless, that point of contact was disrupted. Dead spirits and demons plagued the consciousness, causing it to stop functioning. The body would then start to convulse to kick-start it again. In folklore, epilepsy was known as the 'sacred disease' because it had no known physical cause. Spiritual forces neutralized the consciousness of epileptics so that they seemed dead, insane or possessed. After some time, the victim would return to normal consciousness. From this perspective, the symptoms of epilepsy pointed to an unstable quantity of life force in the blood, which could be remedied by an extra dose of blood. The blood had to be as fresh as possible, so that the patient could inhale the blood vapour. Besides victims murdered specifically for this purpose – about which there have always been rumours – freshly killed gladiators or criminals were ideal donors. Their bodies were young and strong, their blood was fresh and warm, and their deaths were irrevocable. Dölger, who devoted a separate article to this blood cure, endorsed this explanation.[26] Blood was the seat of life and consciousness, and epilepsy a disruption of it.

The explanation is, however, not conclusive and it remains an enigma that this blood therapy continued to be practised for so long. Official medicine never believed in it. Until the end of the nineteenth century, doctors continued to swear by the opposite form of blood treatment – bloodletting. Rather than receiving the blood of others to restore the balance of their humours, epileptics lost their own. Although blood retained its magical aura in medical circles, no one believed in the special power of blood vapour or mist any more. If there were such a thing as blood magic, it worked in a much more subtle way. The Christian faith, too, was staunchly opposed to this 'heathen' blood practice. In his defence against the charges of infanticide, Tertullian asked himself rhetorically 'Again those who, when a show is given in the arena, with greedy thirst have caught the fresh blood of the guilty slain, as it pours fresh from their throats, and carry it off as a cure for their epilepsy . . . how far are you from those Christian banquets?'[27] Christians do not drink blood, not even – as Clement of Alexandria recounted – when they are lost in the desert and only have the blood of their camels to quench their thirst.[28] With such resolute opposition, it seems very surprising that this form of blood cure survived for so long. Until medical science eradicated it for good, there was a tradition of popular healing that ignored religious and medical disapproval and held on strongly to magic and superstition.

Rüsche's argument fails to explain the origins of this blood cure. If it were founded on the life force and blood vapour – ideas that were already present in Homer – you would expect the therapy to be older than surviving accounts of its use. But the oldest known report is by Aulus Cornelius Celsus, who wrote his *De Medicina* around AD 40, and not a single source mentions the cure in any context other than the gladiator games. Beheaded criminals were not used until later, after the games had been banned. Nor is fresh blood as a treatment for epilepsy found in other Mediterranean cultures, such as those of the ancient Greeks or Egyptians, suggesting that the blood cure was in some way related to the Etruscan origins of the gladiator games, which started around 260 BC.[29] The games were derived from an Etruscan burial ritual involving deadly sword duels. The dead warriors were human sacrifices, intended to atone for the death of a prestigious Etruscan or to accompany their commanding officer to the next world. Eating the liver of a gladiator to treat epilepsy can be traced back to the Etruscan belief that livers could be used to predict the future, as can be seen from the famous bronze Liver of Piacenza. This is as far as the Etruscan origin of the practice can help us. We do not know whether the Etruscans drank blood to combat diseases. And predicting the future is different to healing the sick. Lastly, what about the gap of three hundred years in which the blood of gladiators was not used medicinally? Older contemporaries of Celsus were unaware of this repugnant custom. We do not know why the blood cure appeared so late on the Roman medicinal market, but we do know that it did not go unnoticed. Distaste is expressed in many sources.[30] The practice left an impression and contributed to the bad reputation of blood contact. Such contact was not innocent. It offered the opportunity to approach a higher world in search of a cure or for other purposes. Anyone with the courage to ignore our deep aversion to blood could achieve things that the more reserved never would.

BLOODLUST IN ANTIQUITY

Magic was a discipline where the paths of the living and the dead crossed, and blood was the crossroads where this supernatural contact occurred. But where does bloodlust fit into this story?

For one of the best examples, we return to the arena where the gladiators are still fighting for their lives. In the fourth century AD Augustine wrote in his *Confessions* about his friend Alypius. Although Alypius had an aversion to gladiator games, his friends persuaded him to go to the amphitheatre. When he saw the blood of the dead people and animals flowing, he fell into a state of intoxication:

> As soon as he saw the blood, he at once drank in savagery and did not turn away. His eyes were riveted. He imbibed madness. Without any awareness of what was happening to him, he found delight in the murderous contest and was inebriated by bloodthirsty pleasure. He was not now the person who had come in, but just one of the crowd which he had joined, and a true member of the group which had brought him.[31]

Alypius' bloodlust was not magical, but bestial. This is clear from words and phrases like 'savagery', 'murderous' and 'one of the crowd'. Alypius had no contact with demons in the arena – it was the blood that aroused his sinful nature. The exhilarating effect was animal, not divine.

This bestial, blood-induced intoxication was well known in antiquity. Blood could turn some species of animal wild. In the *Iliad*, Homer attributed bloodlust to dogs. King Priam imagined that when he was killed his own court dogs would tear his body to pieces.[32] The anonymous author of the *Geoponica*, a tenth-century Byzantine book of agricultural folklore, drew a wise lesson from this. It advised not allowing dogs to come into contact with dead farm animals, as they would then attack living animals. Once they had tasted raw flesh it was difficult to get them to kick the habit.[33] The blood wound them up so much that they became addicted to it. Horses, too, could reputedly go wild on contact with blood. In his *Heroicus*, Philostratus, the biographer of Apollonius of Tyana whom we came across earlier, honoured the Trojan heroes, including Achilles. Achilles fought against the Amazons, killing their queen, Penthesilea, and committing necrophilia on her dead body. During the battle against the Amazons:

> The horses took on the habits of wild beasts, and as they fell upon the Amazons, who lay on the ground, the horses thrust their hooves, bristled their manes, and pricked up their ears against them, just like savage lions. They ate the naked forearms of the supine women, and after they had broken open their chests, they devoted themselves to the entrails and gulped them down. Stuffed with human flesh, they stamped around the island and raged, sated with gore.[34]

Although Achilles possessed magical powers and persuaded grazing horses to become carnivores, this imaginary form of bloodlust was a return to the comparison with wild predators. It accentuated the bestial cruelty required to defeat the Amazons.

The link between consuming blood and cruelty can also be found in antiquity, especially among barbaric peoples (after all, cruelty is not something you are likely to attribute to your own people). A number of peoples allegedly drank the blood of their dead enemies, but usually as part of initiation rituals in which novice warriors would drink blood to show their fearlessness, or magic rituals where you drank the life force of a dead person to make yourself stronger. Such ritual drinking of blood – undoubtedly as a sign of superstition and barbarism – is attributed to a long list of peoples, including the Scythians, the Thracians, the Gauls, the Chatti and the Lombards.[35] All these peoples – if we are to believe Greek and Roman sources – would drink the blood of their dead enemies. This stigma has proved difficult to eradicate. During the First World War, the Nepalese Gurkhas who fought alongside the Allies were alleged to go out at night with their knives between their teeth and cut the throats of German soldiers before drinking their blood. It was claimed that African soldiers cut off body parts and were cannibals. The *Daily Herald* wrote that 'pitch-black' colonial soldiers bit through the arteries of their victims and sucked up their blood.[36] In antiquity, too, people became exhilarated by the blood that flowed during warfare. In Greek literature, this can be found in Aeschylus' *Eumenides*, in which Athena warned that the country should be saved from division and hatred to stop the spilled blood from whipping up bloodlust among the young. Aeschylus compared the intoxicating effect of blood with that of wine, and equated the young men aroused by blood with fighting cocks addicted to spilling it.[37] In Latin history, blood lunacy was something of a cliché in the works of Ammianus Marcellinus, who documented the many sieges that the Roman Empire had to endure in the fourth century in his *Res Gestae*. He described how the Austoriani (Mauritanians) wreaked vengeance on the Roman authorities for the execution of a rebellious fellow tribesman. After tasting and smelling blood, they ran completely amok and committed all kinds of atrocities. He compared them to birds of prey.[38] When the Goths stormed Constantinople, one instance of blood lunacy made such an impression on the attackers that they lost their will to fight. The Saracens, whom the Romans used to protect the city from Goth attacks, took advantage of

> a strange event, never witnessed before. For one of their number, a man with long hair and naked except for a loin-cloth, uttering hoarse and dismal cries, with drawn dagger rushed into the thick of the Gothic army, and after killing a man applied his lips to his throat and sucked the blood that poured out. The barbarians, terrified by this strange and monstrous sight, after that did not show their usual self-confidence when they attempted any action, but advanced with hesitating steps.[39]

None of these cases of bloodlust – whether they actually happened or were fabrications – have any magical qualities and are entirely bestial. Those involved do not use blood as a means to come into contact with higher powers, but are reduced to the level of predatory animals. Cases of supernatural bloodlust or blood rush in a magical context were less common, but did happen. Contact with blood could cause such arousal that it would result in ecstasy, possession or insanity, for example when the shades of the dead or vengeful goddesses used blood contact to penalize. The fierce excitement was not a reward but a punishment. The blood caused the guilty to completely lose their minds and to kill and destroy what they loved.

This happened to Heracles, who, in a fit of madness, killed his wife Megara and their three children. While he was performing the last of his twelve labours, Lycus, the tyrant of Thebes who had murdered Heracles' father-in-law Creon, captured the hero's family and was going to kill them. Heracles' stepfather Amphitryon was too weak to change Lycus' mind, but fortunately Heracles arrived in Thebes just in time to kill Lycus himself. The blood he spilled while committing this murder, however, drove him mad – which was exactly what Hera, the wife of Zeus, had intended. She had had enough of the celebrity allure of her husband's illegitimate son. Heracles had been born after Zeus had spent three days and nights of stormy lovemaking – it had remained dark on Earth for the whole time – with Alcmene. Although a mortal, Heracles had increasingly acted as though he was a god. Such arrogance demanded that he be taught a lesson. With her handmaiden Iris and Lyssa, the goddess of madness, Hera ensured that Heracles no longer recognized his wife and children, mistook them for enemies and killed them. In Euripides' *Heracles*, a messenger comes on stage after the slaughter to explain the events to the audience: 'Meantime his stepfather caught him by his stalwart arm, and thus addressed him: "My son, what do you mean by this? What strange doings are these? Can it be that the blood of your late victims has driven you frantic?"'[40] Amphitryon suspected that his stepson's blood-thirsty madness had been caused by the blood that still clung to his hands. Through this still-fresh blood, Hera and her helpers were able to enter Heracles' consciousness and influence it, with fateful consequences. The spilled blood was the channel through which immortal beings had contact with the minds of mortals. This contact could be beneficial or tragic.

Those who practised magic communicated through blood in the opposite direction. Magicians used blood to establish contact with gods, spirits and demons. If that contact went well, prophecies and wishes would be fulfilled. But if the higher powers did not appreciate being disturbed there was a danger that they would become enraged and seek retribution. Blood magic was not for beginners. Only people with special talents and knowledge of the occult had access to the other world. That blood exhilarated them when they made contact with the higher powers was self-evident. Blood gave them power beyond the reach of normal mortals. Exhilaration, ecstasy and intoxication were all part of the drama of the seance. What the blood contact promised was so extraordinary that it was accompanied by fierce emotions and wild theatrical movements that reinforced the visions and hallucinations.

In ancient Greece, the most impressive examples of this ecstatic bloodlust were the priestesses of the temple of Pythaeus, son of Apollo, in Argos on the Peloponnese peninsula.[41] Between 1902 and 1930, on the slopes of Larisa Hill, archaeologists found a monumental sacrificial altar and the remains of a number of buildings dating from the third and fourth centuries AD. There is no consensus on exactly which of the buildings was the temple of Apollo Pythaeus. The sacrificial altar was never in the temple itself. Despite the somewhat disappointing excavations, this sacred site must have been impressive. It was built on a series of terraces hewn out of the ridge. The local people also call the site Apollo Deiradiotes, a reference to the ridge (Deiras). The buildings were imposing. Large open spaces welcomed the devoted crowds that thronged to the once extremely popular site en masse, leaving behind votive offerings. But most impressive of all was the monthly oracle of the priestesses of this Apollo cult, a practice imported from Delphi. A description by Pausanias in the second century AD shows that this strange oracle still existed at that time.[42] One night every month, a priestess sworn to chastity would drink the blood of a sacrificed ewe, after which she would fall into a rapture. She would stammer out prophecies, which male acolytes of the cult would interpret and translate for the crowd of believers. Pausanias left no doubt that, by drinking the blood, the priestess had contact with the gods, who whispered prophecies to her.

Drinking blood was not a test of chastity, as it was at other holy sites. In Aegae, a city on Achaea in the north of the Peloponnesus, priestesses at the temple of Ge drank bull's blood, not to make prophecies, but to show that they were chaste and pious enough to serve the gods. It was a dangerous act, as the blood was poisonous to those who did not fulfil the job requirements and would kill them immediately. This happened to Aeson, the father of Jason, who committed suicide by drinking bull's blood.[43] Sacrificial blood was therefore either a deadly poison or a magical potion, depending on the will of the gods. The monthly bloodlust of the chaste priestess of Apollo Pythaeus had nothing bestial about it. The blood-induced ecstasy brought her into a state of mind that transcended the human and entered the spheres of the divine. This intoxication is purely supernatural. The frenzied priestesses of Apollo Deiradiotes were the best example of magical bloodlust. They combined the supernatural power of blood with exhilaration, intoxication and ecstasy. They were bloodthirsty, but not in the predatory animal sense. They were not bestial vampires but devout blood-drinkers.

This nocturnal blood ritual was highly exceptional. The combination of sacrifice, drinking blood and ecstasy did not occur in any other Greek oracle or sacrificial ritual, with the exception of Ge. It was also almost unknown in Latin antiquity, with the exception of the spectacular *taurobolium*, the sacrifice of a bull, during which believers would be showered with blood (to which I will return later). And yet, in our imaginations, we often see sacrifice as a bloody scene with enraptured priests who touch the blood in a trance, smear it over their own bodies and drink it. Our perception of this crucial ritual from antiquity has been distorted. We now assume that pagan sacrifice always involves bloodlust, but this is historically incorrect. Sacrificial blood is much more exciting for us than it was for those who took part in the rituals. In the following chapters, I will look at exactly what the sacrifice was and how it has been corrupted by history.

SACRIFICIAL BLOOD

Anything that appeals to our imagination often gives rise to much fantasy – much more than a clear-headed description of reality permits. The ritual sacrifice of animals is one such phenomenon that stimulates our tendency to fantasize. Quite incorrectly, we see similarities between modern practices and long-gone rituals. Because animal sacrifice still fascinates us, we give it a meaning it never had in the past. Apparently, it makes us feel good to know that we have a connection with this strange ritual, even though that connection is based on what we have made of it in our imaginations rather than on historical reality. This flirtation with ritual sacrifice is to be found among some food philosophers, who cannot light a barbecue without referring back to the old ritual. For them, the summertime feast of grilled sausages dripping with fat and the herbal aroma of marinated spare-ribs is a secular continuation of the pagan meal for the gods. The American culinary philosopher Michael Pollan goes a step further in his popular book *Cooked: A Natural History of Transformation*, which – in search of the metaphysical profundity to which it aspires – takes Aristotle's theory of the four elements as its starting point. In the chapter on Fire, in which Pollan explains how to cook the ultimate barbecue, he sees animal sacrifice as the solution to the emotional and moral problems that killing animals cause us: 'The ritual lets us tell ourselves that we kill animals not for our dining pleasure but because God demands it.'[1] The sacrificial offering soothes the guilt that we feel from killing, cooking and eating animals. It makes the slaughter of the animal a divine command rather than a voluntary deed. According to Pollan, killing animals, and mammals in particular, has never been something that we take for granted. Eye to eye with the sacrificial animal, we experience reluctance, ambivalence and even moral torture. By ending a life, we become aware of how easy it is to end a human life. Those who kill become accustomed to killing. For Pollan, ritual sacrifice is a religious justification for killing animals. It is not a primitive act; on the contrary, it is the way that we now breed, torment and slaughter animals industrially that is the primitive – if not barbaric – practice. This routine process calls for abattoir workers who mindlessly kill without any moral justification, resulting in dulled senses and unfettered sadistic pleasure. Compared to the mass slaughter in industrial livestock farming, ritual sacrifice is an indication of a higher civilization, in which there was still elementary respect for the slaughtered animal. Musing over the sizzling fire of the barbecue, Pollan concludes that we have not moved on.

This perspective not only contains a great deal of fantasy about ritual sacrifice, it paints a less than flattering picture of the psychological state of mind of abattoir workers. It suggests that anyone who kills animals on a daily basis must surely have something wrong with them. On the basis of persistent myths, the modern consumer is completely alienated from the breeding and slaughter of animals, remaining at a safe distance from the cruelty of the abattoir, where the killing seems to be in the hands of psychopaths.

My favourite butcher killed a number of animals while learning his trade, but regularly refused to do so afterwards. He was afraid of becoming accustomed to it. 'I once heard,' he recalled, 'though I don't know if it is true, that butchers used to be systematically excluded from jury duty, because death and killing had become too normal to them.' That myth dates back to a story from the seventeenth and eighteenth centuries, when Enlightenment philosophers liked to believe that there were laws in England forbidding butchers and slaughterhouse workers from sitting on juries in trials for capital offences. This can be found in the works of English philosopher John Locke, and later of his colleague Bernard Mandeville, who added surgeons to the list of professions banned from jury duty. Jean-Jacques Rousseau and Immanuel Kant adopted the fallacy uncritically, mistaking wishful thinking for fact. Historians have found no evidence at all of such exclusions in English criminal law.[2] We like to believe that killing animals is not normal and not something that normal people do. Only those with a sick mind can do it day after day.

I do not wish to claim that being a slaughterhouse worker is comparable to being a computer programmer, civil servant or taxi driver. It is a physically demanding profession, which entails working with large mammals in a cold environment, surrounded by a lot of mess and all at an industrial pace. It is important to be cut out for it, prepared to do heavy work for a somewhat less bulky salary. These days it is rare to find indigenous workers in Western European slaughterhouses. Our focus on the effect of killing animals is so exaggerated that we tend to believe that it is traumatic for everyone who experiences it. If it is not, we assume there is something much worse going on. We do not realize that how we perceive this depends on time and place. It is the perspective of a modern-day Westerner, who considers the killing of animals taboo but enjoys the filleted and neatly sliced results. In times and cultures where this taboo and hypocrisy are not present, those who slaughter animals are not stigmatized.

That became clear to me when I visited a slaughterhouse in Tokyo. It has a museum area that tells schoolchildren about how meat is produced in their country and how healthy and safe it is. It is not open to tourists and, at the entrance to the enormous complex, there are no signs explaining where to find it. The staff at the porter's lodge clearly thought that I was lost and had come to ask the way to a nearby address. When I showed them a page printed from the Internet and explained that I wanted to visit the museum, one drew his hand across his throat and asked me if I was sure I'd come all the way to Japan to visit a slaughterhouse. After all, there were so many splendid temples. But once I had persuaded him that it was the museum I wanted to see, he pointed to the fifth floor of a building a short distance away and asked a colleague who spoke three words of English to escort me. I didn't understand much of the printed signs, which had many numbers and few illustrations. Nor did I learn much from the plastic replicas of cows, sheep and pigs. But what I did find fascinating was a film that the museum had made about slaughtering cows. It was clearly aimed at very young children from about six to eight years old. I didn't understand the commentary, but it was given by a comic-strip-style professor with a long white moustache and a white lab coat who appeared at the bottom of the screen with his coquettish female assistant (gender roles are still very stereotyped in Japan). The film showed every phase of the slaughtering process, from the cows leaving the truck to the vacuum-packaging of their livers or kidneys, which the Japanese love so much, preferably raw as sashimi. What is kept even from adults in the West because we find it horrifying was shown here in all its detail to young children: the tranquillizer shot that caused the cow's legs to give way; the cut in the neck through which the blood flowed out of the body; stripping the hide; removing the excess fat; cutting open the belly so that the intestines tumbled out; sawing through the ribcage and the back; sucking excrement out of the intestines; cleaning the stomach, and so on. If you were to show European schoolchildren these images during a school outing, you'd be on the news and there would be national outrage. In Japan, showing the slaughter of domesticated animals is educational, not traumatic.

Being ill at ease with the killing of animals is specific to our time and culture. Those who claim that ritual sacrifice was invented to make it easier to deal with that discomfort are projecting their own sensitivities onto those of antiquity. There are no indications that people in the distant past shared such ambivalence about killing animals, and certainly not to support claims that these qualms of conscience lay at the root of ritual sacrifice.[3] There was much criticism of the practice, but none of it took the form of moral objections to killing animals or concern about the immoral influence it might have on those who performed the slaughter. The criticisms were philosophical (how could you feed the gods?) and theological (how did you know you were feeding the right gods?), but never ethical in the sense of concern for the welfare of those performing the killing or for the dead animal. The Greeks and Romans were indifferent to the killing of an unreasoning animal. The many surviving Greek urns depicting scenes of ritual sacrifice rarely show the killing itself.[4] This is not because it was taboo – in contrast to Western slaughterhouses, it often took place in public spaces in front of temples, where everyone could see and experience it – but because it was simply not important enough to depict on an expensive urn. If they wanted a nice souvenir, the Greeks preferred a more meaningful event. There were certainly vegetarians in antiquity, including Apollonius of Tyana, the disciple of Pythagoras whom we encountered earlier. He defended himself as such when accused of sacrificing children. How could you accuse someone of eating human flesh if he did not even eat the flesh of sacrificed animals? But vegetarianism was never popular. If you did not eat meat you could not take part in some of the most important events on the social calendar and, consequently, you cut yourself off from society. Furthermore, vegetarianism was never an ethical choice, but a philosophical consideration. The followers of Pythagoras chose not to sacrifice animals or eat animal flesh not because they thought slaughtering animals was cruel, but because they believed that animals had a soul that hopped from one living being to another. Dead animals obstructed that perpetual transfer of the soul. Killing them was undesirable because it disrupted cosmic harmony.

RITUAL SACRIFICE, GRAECO-ROMAN STYLE

Besides giving us an idealized view of ritual sacrifice – they weren't primitive, we are! – our imagination allows us to interpret it in an exaggeratedly aggressive manner. While some perceptions are too soft, others are too hard, seeing the ritual as being crueller than it actually was. Since this book is about bloodlust, I am more concerned with these cruel interpretations. The central question in this chapter is how did a ritual in which blood naturally flowed – since it involved the killing of animals – ultimately, in our imaginations, become an extremely bloody ceremony? Before examining this violent interpretation in greater detail, let's look a little closer at what ritual sacrifice actually entailed.

An excellent description of Greek ritual sacrifice (known as *thysia*) is provided by Walter Burkert in *Homo Necans* (1972).[5] After bathing, the participants, for whom sexual abstinence is often required, dress in special clean clothes and put on ornaments and wreaths of flowers. They then walk in procession to the site of the sacrifice, singing. At the front is a maiden – a virgin – called the *kanephoros*, who carries a basket containing unripe grains of barley on her head. The sacrificial animal follows the procession, led along by a rope and halter, and sometimes hobbling because its hind legs have been tied together with ribbons. It wears a wreath of flowers and, if it has horns, they are covered with gold. The procession is accompanied by flute music. The destination is the sacrificial altar, a stone stained red-brown from the blood it has absorbed over the years. The older it is, the more blood it has seen, the more offerings have been made on it, and therefore the greater the reverence with which it is held. A fire burns on the altar, together with a bowl of incense, and there is a pitcher of water next to it. The participants stand in a circle around the altar, separating the secular world from the sacred. The basket of grain and the water pitcher are passed around. Those in the circle wash their hands and water is sprinkled over the animal. When the beast shakes in response, this is taken as a sign of its consent to being offered in sacrifice. The participants keep sprinkling and pouring water over the animal until it bows its head. After praying for a while, first in silence and then out loud, a handful of barley grains is taken from the basket of the *kanephoros* and thrown onto the animal, the altar and the ground. Hidden under the grain in the basket is the sacrificial knife. The priest approaches the animal, carrying the knife but keeping it concealed so that the animal cannot see it. With a rapid movement, he cuts off a few hairs from the animal's brow and throws them into the sacrificial fire. Now comes the death blow. The priest slits the animal's throat, while the women let out a loud scream that marks the emotional climax of the ritual. Great care is taken with the blood that flows out of the throat. It must not be allowed to seep away into the ground, but is captured in a bowl or pitcher (*sphageion*) and poured or sprinkled over the altar. The animal is then cut open and its intestines (*splanchna*) are removed. Tradition prescribes exactly what must be done with each organ. The heart is placed on the altar. A seer examines the liver to predict the future. In general, the rest of the edible organs are quickly roasted on the altar fire and eaten by those in the circle. The bones – and especially the thigh bones and the pelvis with the tail – are hacked into pieces and placed on the altar, sometimes with flesh still clinging to them. They are consumed by the fire in offering to the gods, as is the gall bladder, which is inedible. The remaining meat is stored, sold or cooked in the outbuildings of the sacrificial sanctum for the communal feast that will follow. The hide of the sacrificial animal is sold and the proceeds go to the sanctum, to purchase new animals or cover other expenses relating to the ritual. The skulls of bulls and rams are boiled out and hung on the walls of the sanctum, in the same way that we now display hunting trophies.

There were endless variations to this basic scenario. Though the sacrificial animals were often bulls, they could also be sheep, goats or pigs. Sometimes a number of animals would be sacrificed simultaneously, as with the Roman *suovetaurilia*, an offering comprising an ox, a sheep and a pig. These were by no means the only animals used for sacrifice. The remains of dogs, cats, pigeons and chickens, not to mention bears, wolves, vultures, lions and camels, have been found at Greek holy sites.[6] Sacrifices were made for various reasons, so that the ritual took different forms. They could be made for reconciliation, purification, celebration, supplication or as a token of gratitude. In the case of festive offerings, the gods received little and the partygoers much more; at sacrificial fire rituals, large quantities of meat were offered to the gods. At a *holokaustos* the whole animal was offered; this required special procedures, as a freshly killed ox or bull does not burn very easily. Sometimes the priest would run his knife over the back of the sacrificial animal before slitting its throat; sometimes seers would speculate on which side the animal would fall; and sometimes, instead of throwing grain over the animal, the participants would pour wine over its head.

I will not discuss the differences between and details of these rituals any further. For our purposes, the general facts are more interesting – for example, that ritual sacrifice was not universal in antiquity. The Hebrews, Phoenicians, Greeks and Romans did practise it, as did the Celts and the Germanic peoples. But there were also peoples who did not, or whose practices deviated so greatly from this basic scenario that they could not really be described as ritual sacrifice. The ancient Egyptians certainly killed animals in ritual fashion. But how they did it and their reasons for doing so were in no way similar to classical animal sacrifice.[7] The Sumerians and Babylonians never slaughtered animals in their holy places.[8] They certainly believed that their gods required food and drink, which it was their duty to provide, but the gods preferred the food itself to the smoke of fat, bone marrow and roast meat. In their temples, like the temple of Anu in Uruk, the gods were offered a daily food basket containing not only meat but vegetables, fruit, wine, milk, beer and eggs. In short, everything they needed to make themselves a decent meal; a kind of food bag that was much more varied and healthy than the burned flesh and bones of the Greek sacrificial animals. Although the *Enuma Elish*, the Babylonian creation myth, describes how man was created from a mixture of divine blood and earthly clay, no special attention was devoted to the blood in the killing and slaughtering of animals, and there was no separate ritual devoted to it.

Although not all antique cultures practised ritual sacrifice in the Graeco-Roman style, in those that did it was one of the most important religious events and had an enormous impact on daily life. Often, religion and eating meat were inseparable. In ancient Greece, the slaughter of every animal was seen as a religious event.[9] But that religious dimension could take many forms: from a simple prayer during the slaughter of an animal at home to a temple ritual with all the trappings. Ideally, every animal had to be sacrificed in the prescribed way and all animal flesh was sacred, but in reality these requirements were not strictly enforced. It was simply implausible for every animal eaten to be killed at the temple altar following the same laborious ritual procedure. It is difficult to believe that the Greeks took wild animals like lions, bears or stags to the altar while still alive and plucked a few hairs from their brows before slitting their throats; or that they did not eat dead animals that had been rejected by the temple because they were not considered suitable for some reason or another; or that they did not eat lower-status but still edible animals such as cats, rabbits, dogs or turtles because they were not usually sacrificed. During military campaigns, Greek soldiers certainly ate fresh meat, even though there were no temples in the vicinity where they could sacrifice them. Homer describes how Greek troops slaughtered an ox every day, where the religious aspect was limited to a few prayers and the offering of a little flesh and burned bones to the gods. By no means were all animals led to the sacrificial altar in a procession accompanied by flute music.[10]

There is still discussion among modern-day researchers about whether the Romans had developed a secular market for meat with no religious dimension at all in the first century BC, as Varro suggested in his *De re rustica*.[11] What is certain is that the chain from meat producer to consumer became more complex and specialized. From the sacrificial site, the meat went to the meat market, or *macellum*, where butchers (*macellarii*) with sophisticated tools stood at the ready to use the sacrificial meat that was not eaten on the spot or burned for the gods to prepare traditional delicacies for the better-off Romans to buy. Although butchers had a very low social status and were usually slaves, their various specialisms suggested a high level of craftsmanship. The *gallinarii* dealt only with poultry, the *anatiarius* specialized even further, selling only ducks, while the *pernarii* restricted themselves to ham. Roman butchers were very conscious of the difference between unprepared meat and charcuterie (*lardarii*).

Jewish ritual sacrifice was different, for practical reasons.[12] Externally it resembled that of the Greeks and Romans, though the Jews burned internal organs like the kidneys and liver in the altar fire rather than eating them. It was also more common to burn a whole sacrificial animal – the philosopher Theophrastus found the daily burnt offerings of whole sheep and bulls in Jerusalem excessive – while elsewhere it remained a rarity. As with the Greeks, sacrificial animals were slaughtered after a procession near an altar in front of the temple. Except in the case of burnt offerings, the meat was boiled and eaten communally. Purity was crucial and great care was taken with the blood of the animal, as we shall see a little later. But there was a practical reason for keeping sacrifice and slaughter separate. We do not know exactly when and how it happened, but probably sometime around 700 BC, the Jewish priest class centralized all ritual sacrifices at the temple in Jerusalem. Animals were no longer sacrificed in the tabernacle, as in the time of Moses, or in local temples, as happened much later. For several hundred years animal sacrifice took place exclusively in the temple at Jerusalem, the same one that was destroyed by the Romans in AD 70 under the leadership of Titus, following the Jewish rebellion. After the temple was destroyed, the Jews stopped sacrificing animals, with the exception of the Samaritans, who never accepted the centralization of the ritual and continued to practise it for several centuries. While waiting for a new temple and a new class of priests, the Jews, like the Christians, practised a faith without ritual sacrifice and found greater religious fulfilment in other spiritual activities, such as prayer, contemplation and Bible study. The policy of centralization also meant that not all meat that was eaten could come from sacrificed animals. Jews who did not live in Jerusalem no longer had access to meat or had to participate in pagan sacrificial rituals that were alien to them. Although all animals had to be slaughtered according to the rules of the faith, this was no longer performed only by priests in a sacrificial temple. A secular market emerged for kosher meat from animals that had not been sacrificed.

WHY RITUAL SACRIFICE?

As an important – though not universal – custom in antiquity, we know a lot about ritual sacrifice. Perhaps because it has continued to fascinate us through the generations, much research has been conducted and much has been written on the subject. Some researchers have even tested sacrificial practices in laboratory conditions, for example to discover whether a bull's tail will indeed burn in an altar fire or how long it takes to burn a complete bull. But not everything has been explained. Even elementary questions have not yet been answered satisfactorily and probably never will be. The first mystery is why animals are sacrificed. What was the original purpose and function of these slaughter rituals? No one doubts that they were intended to initiate a dialogue with the gods, in which it was hoped to get something from them by giving them a gift. The offering is grounded in the principle of reciprocity. As an insignificant mortal, I give something to the almighty gods in the hope that I receive something in return. Those who made sacrificial offerings were projecting what some of us expect from a powerful and influential individual – for example, a charismatic politician – onto the gods. Through their gifts, they hoped to please the gods and be granted all kinds of favours. They offered the gods a ritualized meal to assure themselves of a better life. But, as with politicians, the exchange had to be disguised – it should never appear as simple horse-trading. The reciprocity was socially motivated and not driven purely by economic considerations. After all, what they were after was a long-term relationship in which the exchange of favours could never really be in balance. The offering was thus much more than a quid pro quo, giving to receive.

There is little discussion about the purpose and function of ritual sacrifice. Behind every offering is a request to the gods, no matter how latent it may be. But why did it necessitate the slaughter of an animal? Why not simply offer the gods food, as in Mesopotamia? This is where the discussion begins, divided roughly into two positions. On one side are researchers who consider the slaughter unimportant.[13] Without killing animals, you have no meat, which was the most valuable food in antiquity. So you either kept the slaughter of the animals separate from the ritual or you made it a part of it, as in Greece and Rome. Other than the fact that ritualized slaughter extended the sacrificial ceremony, making it more complex and possibly more emotional (the screaming of the women), there was no need to seek a deeper meaning for it. The offering was about the ritual, religious devotion and consuming the meat while enjoying a communal meal with family and friends, and not the actual act of slaughtering the animals. On the other side are researchers who do give the slaughter of the animals a special meaning. Ritual slaughter was not an optional part of the ritual, but tapped into deeper anthropological needs. What exactly that need was varies considerably. I will restrict myself to three theories.

For Sigmund Freud, animal sacrifice symbolized the prehistoric patricide that young men committed because they desired their mothers. In their hunger, they also gobbled up their fathers after killing them. Animal sacrifice was a reminder of these shameful events, and of the feelings of guilt and the ban on incest that they gave rise to. The slaughter attracts, but also repulses. It arouses aggression and lust, but also warns against the terrible consequences of unbridled gratification of our desires. The blood excites but also inspires fear. Thanks to the sacrifice of an animal, we find a balance between our sexual desires and a social reality that does not tolerate them. As a totem for the murdered father, the animal sacrifice sublimates male lust. The number of lines I have dedicated to this Freudian interpretation of animal sacrifice already exceeds the number of people who still support it today. I mention it only because it was once very influential.

René Girard also believed that the slaughter of a sacrificial animal served a higher purpose. But this time it was intended not to keep uninhibited sex in check, but as perpetual vengeance. In societies without a central government that has a monopoly on violence and an adequate system of law and order, people took the law into their own hands. This, too, was based on the principle of reciprocity, but in a negative sense. If you take away something that is dear to me, I will do the same to you – preferably something even dearer. The consequence was a society disrupted by honour killings, as still occurs in modern-day Albania. 'Vengeance is a vicious circle whose effect on primitive societies can only be surmised,' Girard writes in *Violence and the Sacred* (1977).[14] The sacrifice relieved the pressure. First, the sacrificial animal, which could not take revenge, replaced the human victim, who could be avenged. The animal literally became a scapegoat through which human conflicts could be ended before they escalated into a spiral of violence. Second, ritual sacrifice brought human violence, as an uncontrollable force of nature, into the sphere of the sacred, where a distinction was made between 'impure' and 'pure' – or tolerated – violence. The offering could cleanse a society from impure bloodshed. All of the social functions that Girard attributed to the sacrificial offering rest on one supposition: that the slaughter of the animal was the most important moment in the ritual. Without the trio of death, violence and blood, the offering did nothing to assuage conflict. Vengeful humans wanted to see blood and death. Only the bloody slaughter of a sacrificial animal could replace real revenge.

Lastly, Walter Burkert sought the roots of animal sacrifice still deeper. Before the development of agriculture, hunters had already realized how easy it was to kill their fellow humans. People have no natural resistance to aggression. Unlike animals with large beaks, impressive claws and long, razor-sharp fangs, people are no danger to each other in their natural state. Evolution had given them no inhibition systems to keep their aggression in check when they attacked each other. The damage was usually limited to a broken jaw or concussion as the result of a few well-aimed punches. That primitive innocence disappeared with the invention of weapons. For the first time in evolutionary history, there was a species that was capable of wiping itself out. How could culture avert this danger?

Burkert saw ritual sacrifice as the answer to this aggression theory, put forward by Austrian ethologist Konrad Lorenz. It established a taboo on killing. Rather than accommodating a natural discomfort with killing, as Michael Pollan claimed, it introduced a discomfort that had not been there previously.

Killing became a problem. The screaming of the women as the throat of the sacrificial animal was slit open gave the slaughter an emotional charge it had never had before. What had once been a source of pleasure and excitement now became frightening. Ritual sacrifice replaced bloodlust with blood revulsion. Given this function, the practice did not evolve in agrarian societies, but earlier in hunting rituals. The fiction that the sacrificial animal itself wished to die and gave its consent by shaking and bowing its head was already known among Siberian nomads. They blamed other tribes for the killing of a bear, saw themselves as crows that had nothing to do with the hunt, and pretended that the animal had pity on the hungry hunter. After its death, they would use its bones and skull to reconstruct the animal in a tree or a pit, where it could live on. Greek priests reconstructed the bones of sacrificed animals on the altar in the same way, showing, according to Burkert, the continuity of this 'comedy of innocence', as well an early need to curb human aggression through taboos and rituals. Here, too, the role of the sacrifice in keeping aggression in check is unthinkable without the slaughter of the sacrificial animal being at the centre of the whole ritual.

None of these theories are considered convincing by modern-day researchers, despite the fact that, until only a few decades ago, they were widely accepted.[15] Outside the academic world, they inspired philosophers and artists. As a student, I was greatly impressed by Girard and Burkert. Freud's theory of ritual sacrifice was by then already outmoded. The weaknesses in the arguments of Girard and Burkert only came to light later. That ritual sacrifice also flourished in societies with a well-established central government and legal system in which scapegoats were unnecessary, such as the Roman Empire, is an objection that had not occurred to Girard. And that the practice was widespread in hunter-gatherer communities, as Burkert hoped, was never proven. Practically all cases of ritual sacrifice occurred in agrarian societies and almost all sacrificial animals were domesticated. The list of objections to these theories is now much longer. Yet, despite all the objections, the theories were surprisingly popular. One explanation is that they gave meaning to a practice that other researchers did not wish to give meaning to. To interested laymen in particular, this absence of meaning was strange. Unaware of their own alienation from killing animals, it was exactly this aspect of ritual sacrifice that so fascinated them. It seemed implausible that these practices had no meaning or were simply rituals, that what we find so sensational was nothing special to those who took part in it in the distant past. The theories of Freud, Girard and Burkert satisfied those frustrations. They discovered the well-kept secret that was the ultimate intention of ritual sacrifice. They presented their attractive-sounding theories in accessible books written for the public at large, no matter how inaccurate they were later considered to be.

WHY SACRIFICIAL BLOOD?

In Greek, Roman, Germanic and Jewish sacrifice, blood was a special fluid that required particular attention and treatment, and even led to specific taboos, although we do not know why. There is little disagreement that blood was important in ritual sacrifice and a broad consensus that there is no clear-cut explanation as to why that should be so. This is, of course, frustrating. Knowing that something was important without knowing why fuels speculation. Throughout the centuries, researchers have offered all kinds of explanations to better understand the importance of blood and the taboos surrounding it. But so far this has been inconclusive, raising the question once again of whether we will ever understand it better. For those who see animal sacrifice as a ritualized meal for the gods, there is no deeper reason. Blood received detailed attention and special treatment simply to emphasize the ritual nature of the sacrifice and to distinguish it from the 'normal' hunting and slaughter of animals. The ritual itself was the deeper reason. Other researchers, however, find this solution dissatisfactory. Why blood and not some other bodily fluid? Why was there a taboo on blood and not on something else?

Blood played a singular role in ritual sacrifice in ancient Greece. The blood that poured from the throat of the sacrificial animal did not flow onto the ground and dry up. It would be inaccurate to say that the participants showed no interest in the blood at all or were so revolted by blood that they wanted to be rid of it as quickly as possible. On the contrary, the blood was captured in a pot or pitcher (*sphageion*), taken to the altar and poured or sprinkled over the stone. The more blood that flowed over the altar stone, the more sacred the site of the sacrifice. The altar at Didyma was covered with layers of clotted blood, which to our eyes and – especially – our noses would have been repulsive. We do not immediately associate flies, vermin, a foul stench and danger of infection with a spiritual ritual emphasizing purity and virginity, no matter how fiercely the altar fire burned and aromatic the incense smelled. What miseries did the Greeks call down on themselves by not immediately allowing the blood to drain off into a pit in the ground, but rather exposing it to vermin and the heat of the Mediterranean sun?

Nonetheless, some scholars questioned the religious status of blood in Greek sacrifice.[16] Most certainly, not all of the blood was poured or sprinkled over the altar: some was saved for consumption as a kind of blood sausage, black pudding or a black broth soup. There was no ritual prohibition against eating blood in Hellenic culture. In Homer's *Odyssey*, the Greeks ate goat stomachs stuffed with blood and fat. Vase paintings suggest that a small quantity of the blood was dashed on the altar sides. The rest of the blood was kept, prepared and eaten.[17] If true, this culinary tradition of eating blood-based food contrasts sharply with its ritual treatment, the lavish pouring of blood over the altar, and the danger of drinking fresh blood. As we have already seen, Aeson committed suicide by drinking a bull's raw blood. Fresh sacrificial blood was certainly something you had to treat with care. How can this contradiction be explained? Did the Greeks distinguish between consuming raw blood, which was dangerous, and the safe eating of cooked or grilled blood sausages? Did they make a clear distinction between sacred sacrificial blood that must not be consumed and the secular blood of slaughtered animals that had never been close to a priest or a temple? Or did the Greeks practise different types of sacrifice, some requiring all of the animal's blood to be poured over the altar, others demanding only a few dashes on the side of the sacrificial stone? I cannot elaborate on these questions here. Though the volume of blood seems to vary, there is general agreement that some blood went onto the altar. Blood was indispensable to the ritual. This is what gave it its special status.

Much less is known about Germanic animal sacrifice before Christianization, for example precisely how animals were slaughtered.[18] From what we do know, it is clear again that blood played a very important part in the ritual. Here, too, the blood of the sacrificed animal was captured in a special urn (*hlautbollar*) and sprinkled over the altar with a brush made of twigs (*hlautteinar*). In the thirteenth-century Norse saga *Heimskringla*, Snorri Sturluson describes how, as well as the complete altar, the walls of the temple – inside and out – and the participants themselves were sprinkled with the blood of all kinds of domesticated animals, including horses. Statues of the gods and sacred trees also shared in the blood shower. Priests would stir the blood that was left in the urn to predict the future on the basis of its colour, viscosity and movement. In the meantime, participants in the ritual prepared the meat for the sacrificial meal, which was accompanied by much drinking. We do not know which parts of the animal were eaten, though the liver, heart and lungs were most probably favourites here too, because of their bloody appearance. Neither do we know whether it was permitted to drink the sacrificial blood or to eat it in the form of blood-based food.

Jews were expressly forbidden from consuming blood.[19] The Torah repeated this over and over again, though with considerable variation. Sometimes it was only blood that should not be eaten, but at others also fat (Leviticus 3:17); sometimes the blood should be allowed to drain off like water (Deuteronomy 15:23); at others, it had to be covered with earth (Leviticus 17:13). For Jews, contact with blood was taboo, but for priests officiating at sacrifices blood was an indispensable part of the ritual. During festive sacrifices, the priest would capture the blood of the animals in a bronze bowl, known as the *Mizraq*. The blood would be stirred continuously to stop it from clotting. In contrast to the Greek and Germanic rituals, the Hebrew priest would not sprinkle the blood on the altar stone, but on the four sides of the altar. He would also press decapitated pigeons directly against the altar sides. There were other, much more complicated sacrificial rituals, such as the *Hatta't* offering, during which the priest sprinkled blood seven times in the temple itself. He would use his fingertips to sprinkle the blood in front of the curtain before the shrine containing the mythical Ark of the Covenant. After that he smeared some of the blood on the horn-shaped corners of a smaller altar in the temple vestibule. Sometimes, it was permitted to enter the sanctuary and sprinkle the cover protecting the Ark with blood seven times.

It is incorrect to claim that those making an offering were indifferent to the blood that flowed during the ritual. Blood was clearly important: the main question that remains is why? What special meaning did it have for the participants? Why were Jews forbidden to eat or drink blood? These questions remain unanswered to this day. Take the Jewish ban on consuming blood. Anyone who is easily satisfied can find the answer in the Torah itself. Leviticus (17:11–14) and Deuteronomy (12:23) state expressly that humans may not consume blood or meat containing blood because it contains life and the life force. Leviticus 17:14 says: 'For the life of all flesh – its blood is its life. Therefore I say to the Israelite people: You shall not partake of the blood of any flesh, for the life of all flesh is its blood. Anyone who partakes of it shall be cut off.' This explanation certainly gives blood a meaning, and one that is not so surprising. That blood had something to do with life was clear to everyone. It was based on everyday experience. But it does not adequately explain why Jews are not permitted to eat or drink blood. Why may you not consume 'life' or the 'life force'? These fragments give no answer to this question. Saying that blood is life does not explain why you cannot eat or drink it. You could say that all blood comes from Yahweh and must therefore return to Yahweh. But, first of all, this cannot be found anywhere in the Torah and, second, it is still unsatisfactory. After all, everything was created by Yahweh and belongs to Yahweh, so why blood specifically? This is explained only in one place, in Leviticus 17:11, which says: 'For the life of the flesh is in the blood, and I have assigned it to you for making expiation for your lives upon the altar; it is the blood, as life, that affects expiation.' This explains why blood can be used in ritual sacrifice but not why it cannot be consumed in a secular context. Explaining one does not explain the other.[20]

Researchers are now generally in agreement: 'To the question whether we can give any explanation of this peculiar concern for blood, the simple answer is that we do not know' (Marc Vervenne); 'Thus, the reason for the ban on consuming blood is far from obvious' (William Gilders); 'The attempts to solve this problem are almost as numerous as the scholars who have put their minds to it' (David Biale).[21] With the Torah failing to give a conclusive answer, researchers have sought their own reasons for the strict ban on Jews consuming blood.

The same occurred in relation to the way blood was treated during Greek- and Roman-style sacrificial rituals. Here, too, the reason for the sacrificial use is not clear. What was the underlying significance of this ritual practice? There is one sober and objective-seeming answer to these questions. Anyone wishing to go further than saying 'we simply don't know' can claim that blood's association with life gave it a certain prestige that made it excellent for use during rituals. Giving blood special and complicated treatment imbued the ritual with more gravitas. And having sole responsibility for conducting these procedures was a godsend for a priest class seeking legitimation for their status. They became the VIPs of the ritual, with the exclusive privilege of dealing with the blood that flowed on their altars.

The importance of blood in ritual sacrifice and the religious ban on consuming blood and its products can thus be easily understood from a rational point of view and seen within the context of a struggle for political power and religious exclusiveness. But the gap left by the Torah can also be filled by more spectacular explanations, as we will see in the next chapter. Blood is taboo because contact with blood brings dangers that it is better to avoid. Killing and spilling blood invokes dark powers that can be held in check through careful ritual contact. If these protective instructions are not observed, terrible things will happen. There was scope for imaginative explanations in which sacrificial offerings more and more closely resembled blood-thirsty rituals. A darker, more violent and demonic interpretation of ritual sacrifice emerged. Sacrificial blood acquired something horrific, especially among those – such as the early Christians – who wanted ritual sacrifice to disappear altogether, because this pagan practice was a formidable rival to their own ritual procedures.

EVIL BLOOD

It is easy to find horrifying interpretations of the blood taboo surrounding ritual sacrifice and the slaughter of animals in antiquity. If you search the Internet for a modern Jewish explanation for the Hebrew ban on consuming blood, you will find the following: 'Eating blood is forbidden. Blood is blood, whether it comes from a human being or an animal. In prohibiting the consumption of blood, the Torah seems to be concerned that it can excite a blood-lust in human beings and may desensitize us to the suffering of human beings when their blood is spilled.'[1] The Hebrew ban on consuming blood was thus intended to prevent bloodlust and cruelty, and to stop our capacity for empathy from being numbed. Overly intense contact with blood makes people violent, because the blood excites them and brings them into a state of intoxication that makes them want more and more. That is why the blood of slaughtered animals had to be treated with the greatest care. Only priests could use it safely in sacrificial rituals; normal people were better off letting it drain straight off into the earth. In short, contact with blood is a 'channel for violence'.[2]

This explanation is not of recent origin. It can be found in old Jewish and early Christian sources, though you need to look closely. In the apocryphal *Life of Adam and Eve*, written in the first century AD, Eve tells Adam about a vision in which she saw their son Cain greedily licking the blood of his brother Abel from the palm of his hand. To Adam, this is a bad omen, and he proposes separating the two sons. They go and live in different houses and practise different professions. But nothing helps. When Cain is 130 years old, he kills his brother after all. Drinking blood and bloodlust are closely entwined here. Christian authors, too, explained the Jewish blood ban in this way. In theological works from the Middle Ages onwards it is commonplace, but the association between tasting blood and bloodlust is also to be found in the works of the early Christian apologists, such as Tertullian and Cyril of Jerusalem.[3] Tertullian immediately discovered the benefits of the association: because early Christians adopted the blood ban from the Jews – otherwise no Jew would allow themselves to be converted – the accusations of infanticide and drinking baby's blood were ridiculous. Why would Christians who did not even drink the blood of animals consume the blood of children? Among Christians, too, avoiding bloodlust was a widely given reason for banning contact with blood, even though it is not clear whether they actually believed it themselves.

Despite these early references, this can never have been the original reason for banning the consumption of blood. It is certainly not to be found in the Bible. Genesis 9:4–6 links the blood ban to the ban on murder:

> But flesh with the life thereof, which is the blood thereof, shall ye not eat. And surely your blood of your lives will I require; at the hand of every beast will I require it, and at the hand of man; at the hand of every man's brother will I require the life of man. Whoso sheddeth man's blood, by man shall his blood be shed: for in the image of God made he man.

However, it is not possible to conclude from this passage that the reason for banning the consumption of blood was to avoid bloodlust. This applies to the many passages in the Bible referring to the blood ban, making the association with bloodlust extremely exceptional. Moreover, the passage quoted above suggests no causal relationship between consuming blood and killing. It does not say that tasting blood can lead to murder, only that God demands all blood back. Consumed or shed, from animals or people, eventually all blood must flow back to God.

Linking the blood ban to bloodlust is problematic because the Bible contains overenthusiastic descriptions of blood rituals that contradict this. In Exodus 24:6–8, Moses instructs young Israelites to slaughter oxen for a bizarre ritual. Moses pours half of the oxen's blood over the sides of the altar; the other half he puts in basins and pours over the people, saying: 'Behold the blood of the covenant, which the Lord hath made with you concerning all these words [the Lord's commandments]'. Admittedly, the people do not drink the blood, but they are certainly showered with it, so that some of them would undoubtedly be covered with blood from head to toe, and it would even be dripping from their beards, mouths and lips. Later interpreters of the Scriptures were not happy with this bloody ritual. 'Pouring' became 'sprinkling' and 'over the people' was changed to 'before the people'. All of these modifications completely disregarded the original. Moses poured basins of blood over his people, while it was strictly forbidden for Jews to taste even the smallest morsel of blood sausage. If blood contact was dangerous because it aroused bloodlust, why did Moses pour bowls of animal blood over people, which would excite them and make them violent?

Apparently Moses had another explanation in mind for the biblical ban on consuming blood. Besides the bestial explanation, there was a demonic one. You avoided contact with blood because something in blood made you bloodthirsty, but in addition consuming blood was a magical practice that invoked evil spirits. According to twelfth-century Jewish theologian Moses Maimonides, the historical reason Jews prohibited anything to do with blood was because of the pagan practice of drinking blood in order to come into contact with demons.[4] Maimonides cited the example of the Sabians, a group about which we know very little, but who probably adhered to a Hermetic philosophy.

The Sabians drank fresh blood to learn more about their future from fortune-telling demons known as djinns. Those who shuddered at the thought of this repulsive drink would feed the demons with a dish of fresh blood, which the djinns greedily licked up. If, as a Jew, you wanted to avoid such a demonic meal, you were better advised to let the blood flow directly away into the earth. Maimonides believed that the Jewish ban on blood had its origins in the Hebrew ban on magic, where blood was used as a medium for contact with spirits and demons. In the monotheistic faith of the Jews, such supernatural contact was an obstacle to the exclusive attention for Yahweh. Consuming blood was tantamount to idolatry.

Modern researchers further substantiated Maimonides's explanation and were of the opinion that the Jewish ban on consuming blood was a response to Greek blood magic.[5] Although this explanation cannot be dismissed, it is based on somewhat unsound assumptions. First of all, there are no indications that the Greek religion had any impact in ancient Israel. Second, the extent to which blood was drunk in ancient Greece for magical reasons must have been exaggerated in Israel since, as we have seen, it was not commonplace. Greek magic books show that blood was used as a magical agent, but fresh blood was rarely drunk: in the *haimakouria*, the dead 'drank' fresh sacrificial blood, but the living did not. The drinking of blood by epileptics was a Roman, not a Greek, practice, and I have already said how exceptional the blood rush of the priestesses of Apollo Deiradiotes and Ge were. Of course back then, too, imagination could have been stronger than reality, but we can only surmise whether this was indeed the case. Finally, few Jewish sources refer to the demonic explanation. Maimonides, in the twelfth century, was the first. If it is the real historical reason for the Jewish blood ban, why do we not find earlier references to it?

Who knows, perhaps Maimonides took it over from Christians living in his home town, the Islamic city of Cordoba. Christians used the demonic explanation not so much to justify the Jewish ban on consuming blood but more to condemn pagan animal sacrifice as a whole. In their view, it was not only drinking or eating sacrificial blood that invoked evil spirits – the blood that flowed during sacrificial rituals had the same effect. Pagans would have found this ridiculous, but Christians believed that spilling blood for any reason in religious rituals was dangerous. It was better to avoid ritual sacrifice completely and, ultimately, to forbid it. Slaughtering animals and eating meat thus had to become a purely secular practice. How Christians came to ban all ritual sacrifice is a remarkable history full of contradictions, but it is indispensable to a better understanding of why blood acquired its darker side. Without the Christian ban on pagan offerings and especially the way in which it was enforced, bloodlust would have had a much less powerful impact on our imaginations. If we see ritual sacrifice as an ecstatic, wild, frenzied event in which the spilling of blood intoxicated the priests and other participants and incited them to horrific acts, it is because of the way Christians portrayed this pagan ritual. They turned it into a cruel and sensational piece of theatre in which blood, killing and violence played major roles. A pagan Greek or Roman would not have recognized their form of ritual sacrifice in the Christian interpretation and would have left the theatre aghast.

CHRISTIANS AND RITUAL SACRIFICE

And yet Christ himself had nothing against ritual sacrifice, even taking part himself.[6] On the first day of the feast of unleavened bread, the day on which Jews slaughtered a lamb for Passover in the temple, he sent his disciples to fetch sacrificial meat and prepare it for the Passover supper (Matthew 26:17–20; Mark 14:12–17). The meat that Jesus ate together with his twelve apostles at the Last Supper was sacrificial meat. No one had a problem with that. All Gospels relate how Jesus cleansed the temple, throwing out the merchants, including those who sold pigeons for sacrifice. That angered the priests. Despite centuries of analysing the Scriptures, the deeper reasons for Jesus' anger are still unknown. There is nothing to suggest that he had anything against ritual sacrifice as such. If so, why would he ask his disciples to buy sacrificial meat only a few days later? Most likely, he was angered at the vulgar trade in sacrificial meat in the temple. He was opposed to this commercial exploitation of the ritual, but not against the practice itself.

Paul, too, had nothing against ritual sacrifice as such. At least not when it came to Jewish sacrifice in the temple, in which – unlike the evangelists – he had taken part. He also had no objection to eating meat sacrificed in pagan temples. He allowed the Christians of Corinth to buy and eat anything that was available on the meat market. A Christian who was invited to dinner by a pagan was permitted to eat everything the host had to offer. That was logical: if Christians were permitted to eat meat, these were the only ways for them to do it, as there were as yet no Christian butchers. They were only advised not to eat meat that their hosts expressly described as having been sacrificed in the temple – not because it would lie heavily on their consciences but because to eat it would disrupt the ritual of those of other faiths, who wished to share their meat with fellow believers. Paul did not wish Jews or pagans to be upset at the behaviour of early Christians, who were still a small sect. Nevertheless, he condemned the pagan culture of ritual sacrifice in the strongest of terms. He expected no Christian to take part in pagan sacrificial rituals. He justified this with the same reasons given by Maimonides: 'But I say, that the things which the Gentiles sacrifice, they sacrifice to devils, and not to God: and I would not that ye should have fellowship with devils. Ye cannot drink the cup of the Lord, and the cup of devils: ye cannot be partakers of the Lord's table, and of the table of devils' (1 Corinthians 10:20–21). What, for Maimonides, was the historical reason not to eat or drink animal's blood was for Paul the religious reason to condemn pagan blood sacrifice: every pagan temple was a place where sacrifices were made to evil spirits and demons.

After the destruction in AD 70 of the only monotheistic temple of offering – the one in Jerusalem where blood sacrifices were made to Yahweh – all temples of offering were suddenly seen as houses of demons. Neither Jews nor Christians had their own places of sacrifice where ritual blood flowed. This gave Christians the opportunity to condemn all sacrificial blood as food for demons – a wild generalization that was unthinkable before the destruction of the temple in Jerusalem. Why would Jewish sacrificial blood not attract demons while that in pagan temples did? Consequently, this generalization cannot be found in the stories of Jesus (in the Gospels) or Paul, who never condemned Jewish ritual sacrifice. It was also ridiculous to Jews, who dreamed of a new temple of offering after the destruction of the old one. Sooner or later, sacrificial blood would once again flow in a third temple in Jerusalem, but those who believed this would happen by no means wished for the blood to be consumed by demons. Seeing all sacrificial blood as food for demons was especially popular among Christians who did not want to see the Jewish temple rebuilt and who saw all pagan sacrificial cults as religious rivals. Only those who wished to put an end to animal sacrifice could claim that sacrificial blood was demonic.

From the second century AD, demonic sacrificial blood became a weapon with which Christian apologists condemned animal sacrifice. The most fervent of these were Tertullian and Origen. Tertullian saw demons as extremely fine, wispy beings that fed on the blood and the blood vapour of ritual offerings. They entered the bodies of humans on their breath and nestled in their minds, bringing them to ruin. In his *Apology*, he wrote:

> By a contagion similar in its obscurity the breath of demons and angels achieves the corruption of the mind

in foul bursts of fury and insanity, or in savage lusts, along with every kind of delusion; and of all delusions that is the greatest which they use to recommend those gods to the captive and outwitted minds of men – and it also serves to secure for themselves their peculiar diet of smell and blood, offered to their likenesses and images.[7]

'Insanity', 'possession' and 'frenzy' were the fate of those 'who by sniffing at altars' inhale a demonic power together with the vapours of the sacrificial offerings.[8] Demons were of course by no means a Christian invention. What was completely new was that, for Christian theologians, they only performed pernicious acts.[9] There were no longer good demons, as Plato still believed. People only came into contact with evil demons, who were all under the control of Satan. Origen explained how this had come about:

Moreover, if it is believed not only among Christians and Jews, but also by many others among the Greeks and Barbarians, that the human soul lives and subsists after its separation from the body; and if reason supports the idea that pure souls which are not weighed down with sin as with a weight of lead ascend on high to the region of purer and more ethereal bodies, leaving here below their grosser bodies along with their impurities; whereas souls that are polluted and dragged down to the earth by their sins, so that they are unable even to breathe upwards, wander hither and there, at some times about sepulchres, where they appear as the apparitions of shadowy spirits . . . It is moreover evident that this is their character, when we add that they delight in the blood of victims, and in the smoke odour of sacrifices, and that they feed their bodies on these, and that they take pleasure in such haunts as these, as though they sought in them the sustenance of their lives; in this resembling those depraved men who despise the purity of a life apart from the senses, and who have no inclination except for the pleasures of the body, and for that earthly and bodily life in which these pleasures are found.[10]

Through the blood spilled during ritual sacrifice, the sin reproduced itself. Every diabolical demon – itself once the soul of a depraved human who had indulged in lechery, lasciviousness, earthly pleasures and superstition and was so heavy with sin that its soul remained close to the surface of the earth – kidnapped the mind of an equally depraved soul-mate, whom it artfully tempted to engage in revelry more frequently and lavishly. In that way, it survived to do its devilish work, thanks to the sacrificial blood it had licked up, and so demand new victims. At the centre of this vicious circle of evil stood the pitcher of sacrificial blood on which the hungry demons had set their sights, leering like predators from behind the red-brown altar stones.

For Christians, spilling sacrificial blood was not cruel in the bestial sense. They never criticized ritual sacrifice because contact with blood led to violent bloodlust. Such criticism would have been absurd. Those performing the sacrifice did everything they could to avoid violence. The sacrificial animal died 'voluntarily' and the blood was treated with great care. There was nothing violent about the sacrifice: on the contrary, the whole procedure was extremely serene and ritualized. Accusations of cruelty convinced no one. For that reason, the notion that Christ's crucifixion was actually a form of ritual sacrifice – 'the Lamb of God taking away the sins of the world' – was completely incomprehensible to both Jews and pagans. The violent execution of a human being by nailing them to a cross could never be seen as a sacrificial offering. But, to Christians, the ritual was cruel in a supernatural sense. It was not the blood but the blood-drinking demons that made those involved in the sacrifice wild, immoral and bloodthirsty. Although the great majority of Roman pagans found this criticism extremely exaggerated, based as it was on two generalizations – all demons are bad and all sacrificial blood invokes demons – they were able to understand it to a certain extent. Such criticisms of ritual sacrifice were not completely unprecedented.

THE THIN LINE BETWEEN ANIMAL
AND HUMAN SACRIFICE

Roman pagans knew that blood was a magical medium for establishing contact with the supernatural world. As we saw in an earlier chapter, practitioners of magic established contact with supernatural beings, whether they were demons, spirits or gods, through contact with blood. The Romans knew, however, that magical sacrificial blood came not from animals but from people, preferably spilled through ritual murder, particularly of children, or during a gladiator fight or execution. It was the vapour rising from the blood of a human victim, not of a sacrificed animal, that seduced spirits and demons to grant favours and make predictions. Because real magical blood was human, all black magic was strictly forbidden. Roman pagans had a fascination for human offerings and ritual sacrifice which, if we are to believe Pliny the Elder, the Senate expressly banned in 97 BC.[11] A century earlier, Rome had banned human sacrifice among the Lusitanians and the Bletonesii, who lived on the Iberian peninsula. This was followed later by a ban, under Emperor Augustus, on taking part in the rites of Celtic druids and a general ban on druids under Emperor Claudius.[12] The Romans shuddered at wild tales of horrific practices from the territories they had conquered. Caesar, Strabo and Diodorus of Sicily give accounts of human sacrifice in Celtic Gaul, where dozens of people were burned, together with domesticated and wild animals, in gigantic wooden effigies.[13] Tacitus speaks of human offerings among the Germanic Cimbri and Teutons, who hung captured enemy soldiers in trees or nailed their skulls to tree trunks or temple walls.[14] Plutarch, Tertullian and Diodorus of Sicily tell of new-born children sacrificed to the gods Baal-Hamon and Tanit – later Saturn and Caelestis – and their remains preserved in urns, though these horror stories had long been in circulation.[15] Archaeological research has shown that these rumours were not entirely unfounded. Urns have been found to contain more remains of children than can be explained by natural deaths alone.[16] And few researchers dispute that Germanic and Celtic tribes sacrificed humans.[17]

The horror of human sacrifice appealed to the Romans.[18] They easily believed rumours that it was practised by foreign peoples, not to mention Christians, Jews and all kinds of gnostic sects. Whether they saw human sacrifice as an extreme variation of the animal sacrifice they themselves practised is not clear.[19] The Romans generally saw animal sacrifice as an excuse to eat meat and enjoy a meal together with friends; sacrificial offerings were the start of a feast. The victims of human sacrifice were not usually eaten, though there were exceptions. Christians and Jews were alleged to hold cannibalistic feasts. The utter repugnance of human sacrifice was a strong argument against equating it with ritual sacrifice. No pagan god could be so degenerate as to wish to feed on the meat of slaughtered and burnt humans. The Romans saw human sacrifice as an act of desperation by super-stitious people driven to such heinous deeds either by need or by religious delusion. And yet it must have taken little for a Roman to imagine the throat being slit during a sacrificial offering as a human, rather than an animal, one. Writers and poets flirted with the idea, and political assassinations and war were portrayed as forms of human sacrifice.[20] If exchanging animals for humans as sacrificial offerings was, in rational terms, a horrific misconcep-tion, in the Roman imagination the distinction between the two was much more fluid.

A glimpse of this imaginary view of human sacrifice can be found in various versions of the conspiracy led by Lucius Sergius Catiline to overthrow the Roman Senate.[21] In the earliest version, by Sallust, Catiline and his fellow conspirators swore an oath by drinking a mixture of wine and human blood. It is unclear where the blood came from. Sallust does not specify whether it came from a victim of murder, or even of human sacrifice. But Plutarch apparently knew more about this secret meeting. He reports that the conspirators certainly did sacrifice a human, then divided up the flesh and ate it. The wine and blood cocktail they consumed to seal their conspiracy was a sacrificial offering. Lastly, Cassius Dio – who made describing horrific acts his literary speciality – took the comparison with animal sacrifice to the extreme. Not only did Catiline sacrifice a young man, but the conspirators took the oath to commit their coup over his bloody entrails (*splanchna*) and then ate them. As with animal sacrifice, the entrails were the most important body parts of all during Catiline's oath sacrifice.

When the Christians announced that all sacrificial blood invoked demons and evil forces, Roman pagans, although they thought this was a wild exaggeration, could certainly see something in it. What they themselves alleged about human sacrifice was simply being extended to include animal sacrifice. In rational terms, it was ridiculous and offensive, but for people with a lively imagination or a sensitive stomach, it was not entirely beyond the realms of belief. Nor were Christians the first to take this exaggerated view. Demonizing all forms of sacrifice can be traced back to philosophical movements like Pythagoreanism, Orphism and Neoplatonism, the proponents of which propagated vegetarianism. They substantiated their plea to refrain from eating meat with the argument that animal sacrifice was a veiled form of human sacrifice (Theophrastus) or that sacrificial blood pleased not the gods, but demons (Porphyry).[22] A Greek writer and eclectic philosopher like Plutarch, who did not devote a single word to the emerging Christians, said that the wild sacrificial rituals in mystery cults 'are not performed for any god, but are soothing and appeasing rites for the averting of evil spirits'.[23] Christian criticisms of ritual sacrifice may therefore have been radical, but they were not new.

The Christian apologists and church fathers persistently emphasized the thin line between human and animal sacrifice. In the fourth century AD, Athanasius of Alexandria left his readers in no doubt at all:

> But some have been led by this time to such a pitch of irreligion and folly as to slay and to offer in sacrifice to their false gods even actual men, whose figures and forms the gods are. Nor do they see, wretched men, that the victims they are slaying are the patterns of the gods they make and worship, and to whom they are offering the men.[24]

This demonic equation of animal and human sacrifice can also be found in the writings of Clement of Alexandria, Marcus Minucius Felix and Tertullian – at a time when they themselves were accused of practising human sacrifice. How better to repudiate such accusations than to claim that it was not those who complied with the Jewish ban on consuming blood and refused to make sacrificial offerings who would be open to temptation, but the Roman pagans, who were so attached to their bloody animal sacrifices? If anyone was vulnerable to the dangers of the slippery slope leading from animal to human blood, it was the Romans, not the Christians.

The Christian critique of ritual sacrifice was like a three-stage rocket: first, all sacrificial blood is demonic; second, all demons are evil; and third, all animal offerings eventually lead to human offerings. The more popular Christendom became, the more damage the explosions of this rocket caused. The anti-sacrifice campaign became increasingly effective. What started as ridiculous stigmatization of a centuries-old religious institution that embraced so many positive experiences for normal people – including piety, friendship and the pleasure of eating meat – was now portrayed negatively as a horrific practice full of cruelty and madness. The moral disqualification disguised an underlying political ambition to destroy religious rivals. Temples that offered their followers meat had a significant competitive advantage. Unlike now, meat was a costly and highly coveted commodity that was eaten only very rarely. For many people, visiting the temple was the only affordable way to eat meat from time to time. Official temples received subsidies to organize meat feasts. But sacrificial meat was the trademark of pagan religions. Christians were permitted to buy expensive meat on the market or to eat it at the home of a pagan host, but visiting a temple to get a cheap meat meal was taboo. For pious Christians, the aroma of roast or boiled meat was tempting, but the poorer among them were forced to forego it. The demons were very tangible seducers. The scent of meat acquired something irresistible, and it required courage and resolve not to give in to it. The fight between good and evil, sin and salvation, was fought out on the taste buds and in the nostrils of baptized Christians, or pagans who were considering baptism. Pagan offerings were not a thorn in the side but balsam to the nose and mouth, and consequently more delicious and appealing than high-flown speeches about redemption and resurrection. For the first Christians, the fight against bodily and sensual desires was part of every walk through the city, past smouldering altars and temples full of singing participants in ritual sacrifices. For a religion with ambitions to become a world faith, it was a masterstroke to eradicate ritual sacrifice completely. It immediately destroyed the greatest appeal of the pagan religions. No pagan considering conversion to Christianity would now be tempted by the delights of cheap temple meat.

TOWARDS A BAN ON RITUAL SACRIFICE

The sacrificial fires did not immediately go out when Emperor Constantine converted to Christianity in 312. Nor was there a clear-cut line of increasing restriction and intolerance up to 391–2, when Emperor Theodosius issued three edicts banning ritual sacrifice in public and private temples.[25] And the cultic fires flared up again more fiercely than ever during the eighteen-month reign of Julian the Apostate (361–3), who also adopted the plan to rebuild the Jewish temple in Jerusalem and to open it up for ritual sacrifice.[26] That Theodosius' successors – Arcadius (r. 395–408), Theodosius II (r. 408–50) and Marcian (r. 450–57), all emperors of the Eastern Roman Empire (Byzantium) – had to re-enact the ban on ritual sacrifice over and over again suggests that animal sacrifice was still common in the fifth century (Theodosius II demanded that the temple be destroyed and cleansed through a Christian sign and Marcian imposed the death penalty).[27] The last sacrificial offerings disappeared with the final vestiges of religious freedom when Emperor Justinian (r. 527–65) introduced enforced conversion to Christianity. This was sweet revenge for the obligation to participate in ritual sacrifice and consume blood sausage during Diocletian's persecution of Christians two centuries earlier.[28]

The edicts of Theodosius I had already left no doubt at all that the Christian rulers of the empire wished to curb the sacrifice of animals, publicly and privately. In November 392 a law was imposed on the people of Constantinople that went even further. Anyone who made offerings with incense or wine or by hanging wreaths of flowers in trees risked the confiscation of their property. It is not inconceivable that this sharp tightening of the legislation was inspired by rumours of a strange sacrificial ritual. Throughout the fourth century, all kinds of 'oriental' mystery cultures were popular among the Roman elite, such as the Mithras cult, which was popular among soldiers, the Isis cult from Egypt, the Dionysus mysteries with their roots in ancient Greece, and the Magna Mater cult, whose adherents worshipped the Phrygian goddess Cybele. The term 'oriental' is misleading – an exoticism of a phenomenon that was simply part of the cult culture and had nothing to do with its supposed roots in the East. Many of these religions had either long been practised in Rome or had emerged there entirely. Members of the Magna Mater cult underwent an exceptional ritual at least once and sometimes twice in their lives – the second time after being members for twenty years. The ritual involved the sacrifice of a bull (*taurobolium*) in a Phrygianum, a shrine to Cybele (a number of which have been found in Rome). Epigraphic remains of this cult, which existed in Italy from as early as the first century BC, show that the *taurobolium* was not an especially uncommon form of animal sacrifice. The bull was slaughtered and its blood and testicles (*vires*) were placed in an urn. The blood was then probably poured or sprinkled over the altar, and the testicles ritually buried at the foot of the altar stone.

This was nothing out of the ordinary – with the possible exception of the testicles – until the Christians, who were of course not permitted to attend this clandestine ceremony, turned it into a sensational ritual that was as horrific as it was ludicrous. According to Roman Christian poet Prudentius, the high priest wore an extravagant headband and a silk robe closed by a Gabine girdle. He stood in a trench (*fossa*) over which planks with holes in them had been laid with spaces between them to form a kind of grating. The bull, decorated with garlands of flowers, was then led onto the wooden grating and killed by a consecrated hunting spear through its chest. Blood spurted in great gushes from the wound and poured through the holes in the floor, showering the priest below. He ensured that every drop of blood landed on his face, head and body. He turned his head so that the blood could run into his ears and nose, 'not even keeping his mouth from it but wetting his tongue, until the whole of him drinks in the dark gore'.[29] Prudentius added that the members of the cult saw this repugnant blood shower as a form of virtuous purification and that sometimes a hundred bulls would be slaughtered so that the initiates could swim in a river of blood.

Since no other source confirmed this abhorrent version of the *taurobolium*, and also because it was packed with such improbable details, some researchers consider it a Christian fiction intended to show how animal sacrifice led to extremes of behaviour.[30] How long would it be before blood-drinking pagans were no longer satisfied with a hundred bulls and wanted to sacrifice humans? Or before blood-slurping demons persuaded the members of 'oriental' cults to replace animals with people on the altar stone? If such wild extremes were to be averted, a stricter and more radical ban on ritual sacrifice was crucial. The *taurobolium* proved that every pagan animal offering contained the seeds of bloodthirsty insanity. Moral and religious progress would not be possible until this institution had been wiped out and replaced by a serene baptism with consecrated water.

As Christianity victoriously spread through northern and eastern Europe, it sustained its virulent opposition to animal sacrifice, though it sometimes had to turn a blind eye. Pope Gregory the Great permitted the Angles of Britain to sacrifice animals, but requested them to restrict it to Christian feast days or the dedication of a church.[31] This tolerance was understandable. Missionary priests encountered people with the strangest of customs, some of which made the *taurobolium* look tame. The European forests were home to some notoriously barbaric tribes. The Lombards were alleged to dress as dogs and drink the blood of their enemies, while the Huns ate raw flesh which they had tenderized by laying it between their saddles and the backs of their horses.[32] But the most spectacular tales were told about the Vikings.[33] Every nine years, the Danes would engage in mass human sacrifice at Lejre in Sjaelland. The Swedes sacrificed large numbers of animals and humans together in Uppsala, where 'the incantations which they are accustomed to sing at this kind of sacrificial rite are manifold and disgraceful, and therefore it is better to be silent about them'.[34] During their pillaging raids, the Vikings were supported by elite warriors called Berserkers, who looked like wolves, bears, lions or dogs and who protected themselves from fire and iron weapons by drinking blood and eating raw flesh.[35] Once Christian missionaries had sufficient standing to do so, they forbade these practices. Penitentials, books containing guidelines for penance, prescribed a variety of punishments for consuming blood and raw flesh, including fasting, pilgrimages and monetary fines.[36] But such religious atrocities also occurred closer to home. The Frisians were alleged to sacrifice newborn babies and those guilty of violating the temple to the gods by casting them into the sea, the latter after being relieved of their genitals and ears.[37] These were by no means all Christian fantasies. The tenth-century report by Arab merchant Ibn Fadlan of the Rus' or Varangian people – Vikings who lived on the mouth of the River Volga – was disconcerting. The funeral of a rich Viking was invariably the scene of the brutal gang rape and ritual slaughter of slave girls.[38]

Christianity did not fabricate all of these stories, but it did evoke the idea that such atrocities were something typically pagan. All human cruelty was seen to come from the blood spilled by the sacrificial knife – not so much because blood itself contained the potential for immorality, but because it attracted demons, who seduced those attending the sacrifice to further immorality. These bloodthirsty demons were to be found anywhere associated with sacrifice, primarily in temples, but also in forests, caves and deserts. Only a hermitage, chapel, church or monastery could purge these wild places full of demons. A chapel in the woods could deconsecrate Germanic holy trees sprinkled with sacrificial blood.[39]

If you are exhilarated by blood, as I was in the cellar, you cannot escape the Christian demonization of animal sacrifice.

Blood certainly had a special significance before the advent of Christianity. It was a magical fluid through which contact with the supernatural world was established. The fact that fresh blood gave off vapour only stimulated the imagination further. That is why participants in ritual sacrifice took great care with it. But we have the Christian crusade against animal sacrifice to thank for the notion that sacrificial blood was a dangerous liquid that summoned demons. It no longer needed to be consumed, and it did not have to come from humans. Seeing blood flow during a religious ritual was enough to wake the demons. Although it is true that some Neoplatonic philosophers like Porphyry shared this opinion, most of their followers were quick to disagree with it. Iamblichus, like Porphyry a Neoplatonist, inspired Julian the Apostate to restore the Roman and Jewish cult of sacrifice to its former glory and found the idea that every sacrificial altar concealed demons licking their lips at the prospect of tasting blood completely ridiculous.[40] But Christians were in universal agreement: sacrificial blood was evil blood that invoked criminal behaviour, desire and superstition. The solemn trance of the prophetic priestesses of Apollo Deiradiotes was a thing of the past. In Christian propaganda, classical ritual sacrifice became a diabolical blood ritual. The blood that flowed enslaved people to their own desires. Sacrificing animals made you not a better person but a wild predator.

RED URINE

I received my confirmation on the same afternoon that the Turk Mehmet Ali Ağca shot Pope John Paul II: Wednesday 13 May 1981. The pope survived and granted his assailant forgiveness, but he lost a lot of blood. He later donated a fragment of his bloodstained robe to a church in the remote mountain village of San Pietro della Ienca, in the Abruzzo region to the east of Rome, where he often went walking. In the spring of 2014, just before the popular Polish pope was to be canonized, the relic was stolen. The theft caused a lot of commotion, and there were immediate rumours that a satanic sect had taken the robe for the blood it contained. The belief that blood – and especially papal blood – was food for demons led by Satan was still alive and well in the twenty-first century. The relic was found a few days later in a box in a garage. Drug addicts from the village had taken it to sell and use the proceeds to invoke – or perhaps drive off – their own demons.

John Paul's blood was used to create three relics. One, containing the still-fluid papal blood, is a golden monstrance bejewelled with twelve gems. It is kept in a shrine in Washington, DC, but regularly tours the world. In its PR material for the tour, to avoid misunderstandings and false expectations, the Vatican emphasizes that the blood remains liquid by the addition of an anti-coagulant.

It is one of those strange and tortuous quirks of history that a religion that so fervently condemned the bloody pagan practice of ritual sacrifice later came to revere blood so obsessively. There was nothing at first to suggest that this would happen.

Crucifixion is not a bloody death, as the victim dies of asphyxiation. Only the gospel of St John records Christ's side being pierced by a spear, causing blood and water to flow from the wound (John 19:34). It is highly unlikely that Christ died from loss of blood. In the other three gospels, Jesus' blood was 'spilled' only once, on the Mount of Olives the evening before his death, when he sweated so much from fear that his sweat fell to the ground as 'drops of blood' (Luke 22:44). During the Last Supper, he may have asked his disciples to eat his body and drink his blood, but that was intended purely symbolically. After Christ's resurrection, the disciples only broke bread; there is no further mention of wine or blood (Luke 24:35; Acts 2:42). It was initially unthinkable that Jesus saw himself as a sacrificial lamb offered to forgive us all our sins. Sacrificial offerings were not violent executions and only very exceptionally involved drinking blood. Moreover, they were not a one-off event but a recurring ritual. It was also completely unclear how the victim of a sacrificial offering could rise again and enjoy eternal life. For the first Christians, who, for the record, had nothing against the Jewish practice of ritual sacrifice, interpreting Christ's crucifixion as a form of offering was insulting. Despite Tertullian's famous statement that 'the blood of the martyrs is the seed of the Christian church', the Acts of the Martyrs avoid bloody descriptions of their suffering and deaths. Torture, execution and other atrocities originally failed in miraculous ways. Milk, rather than blood, flowed from their decapitated bodies.

Despite its initial aversion to blood and sacrifice, from the early Middle Ages Christianity evolved into a religion with an unprecedented devotion to blood.[1] Jesus' crucifixion, including the prelude to it with bloody drops of sweat, flogging and the crown of thorns – in short the whole story of the Passion – gradually became increasingly bloody. In medieval iconography Christ literally dripped blood; he was riddled with gaping wounds and veritable fountains of blood spouted from his hands, feet and side, showering his sinful followers with the purifying liquid. While meditating and praying, pious believers counted the whiplashes he endured and the drops of blood that fell with every torment, envisaged the *Arma Christi*, the Instruments of the Passion, which the Roman soldiers used to wound Jesus, or experienced visions in which they licked his blood or passionately kissed his wounds. When the Church canonized at the Fourth Lateran Council of 1215 that the bread and wine administered during the Eucharist not only symbolized the body and blood of Christ, but actually transubstantiated itself into his Real Presence, the wine became blood, even though it still looked like wine. This devotion turned into a true blood craze. On occasions the Eucharistic host (that is, the sacramental bread) would bleed to prove this doctrinal truth, sometimes because unbelieving Jews had pricked holes in it, or would emerge bleeding from a fire that had not harmed it. Sacramental wine would seethe and boil in the chalice. Relics appeared everywhere with the blood of Christ or the saints. In northern Europe in particular, there were mass pilgrimages to the sites of such blood miracles or where relics were kept. The more popular sites would receive tens of thousands of pilgrims a year hoping for a miraculous cure or other wonders. Theologians wracked their momentous brains trying to answer questions that would today seem absurd – as absurd as the use of a special Eucharistic reed (calamus) through which priests would suck the blood of Christ so as not to spill any of the sacred fluid: how could Christ's blood have remained here on Earth if he sat, *totus et integer*, on the right hand of God? How could his body be both in heaven and in a host? If Christ's blood had remained behind on Earth, how could believers hope for the complete resurrection of his body at the end of days? And my personal favourite: during the *triduum mortis*, the three days from Good Friday to Easter Sunday, was the blood of Christ that of a decomposing human or of an eternally vital divinity? This last question was of practical importance to artists wishing to depict the Descent from the Cross as authentically as possible, in theological terms. Did the blood of the dead Christ decompose, in which case would it appear as a dark-brown crust around the wound? Or did it retain its fresh red hue and continue to flow freely until the day of his resurrection? If Christ was a man, his body would begin to rot. But if he was divine, he would transcend decomposition and decay.

Although many relics did not survive the Reformation, holy blood remained a medium through which Christians could make contact with God. This contact was possible during the Eucharist, pilgrimages or processions like that on the Feast of Corpus Christi, when the sacred host is carried around the parish. In that sense, medieval Christians simply took over the Greek practice of blood magic, adapting it to their monotheistic faith. The holy blood was limited to only one supernatural recipient. There was, nevertheless, one fundamental difference. The Christian obsession with holy blood meant that the blood of normal people and animals was no longer sacred. All that mattered was the blood of Christ, or that of martyrs and saints. The blood of normal Christians and, especially that of animals, had no significance. Animal blood became a profane liquid that could eventually be consumed freely.[2] The Church's last ratification of the Jewish ban on consuming blood was by Pope Calixtus II during the Concordat of Worms in 1122. After that, the Church abandoned this taboo and Christians were permitted to eat food containing blood. The more important holy blood became in theology and the liturgy, the less significant profane blood became. The wild days of pagan blood offerings, to which Christians objected so vociferously, were long gone, as was the Christian hope that the ban on consuming blood would encourage Jews to convert to Christianity. The Church became increasingly and more openly anti-Semitic. Rumours of Jews desecrating holy blood frequently led to deadly pogroms.[3]

HIPPOCRATES AND ARISTOTLE

The Christian faith in effect gave full freedom to the science of blood. Only holy blood was magical; that of normal mortals and animals was just physical matter. The path was now clear for scientists and physicians to break the chemical code of blood. But it was not that simple. The philosophical authority that underpinned Christian theology, the Greek thinker Aristotle, had very clear views on the origins and function of blood.[4] He had introduced a new kind of blood magic that was no longer theological, but purely philosophical. Anyone who rejected Aristotelian philosophy also immediately jettisoned the whole scholastic edifice that gave Christian thought its intellectual legitimacy.

Aristotle took from his predecessor Empedocles the idea that all matter comprised four basic elements: fire, water, air and earth. The more developed living beings were, the warmer they felt and the more fire they contained. From a certain level of development, that life heat was to be found in the blood, resulting in a division in the animal kingdom between animals with blood and those without. This was roughly equal to the distinction between vertebrates and invertebrates. Of all blooded animals, the male human was the warmest and therefore the most developed. For that reason, men also had the largest brains, as this organ cooled them down when they became overheated (this worked less efficiently with bald men). If the male animal became hot with desire, his warm blood would boil to become sperm, causing his female partner to bear children. Women never got as hot. Excess blood was expelled during menstruation or, when they became pregnant, turned into a different, very useful liquid – mother's milk. With all blooded animals, blood was produced by food being burned up in the heart, which fed all organs and tissue through the circulation system. The blood also carried conscious thoughts, mental representations and inner reflections around the body.

The blood contained not only natural, vital and animal spirits that made movement, observation and thought possible, but a higher spirit (*pneuma*) that connected us to the spiritual world of the fifth element, ether. In Aristotelian biology, therefore, blood was certainly not a purely material liquid. It contained an immaterial element that provided access to the spiritual world. Blood, not the brain – as Plato claimed – was the seat of the soul. Aristotle gave Homer's blood vapour, which linked mortals to the supernatural world, a philosophical basis.

If you looked at blood through Aristotle's eyes, it was still a magical fluid. But what was it actually made of? The fifth-century Hippocratic text *On the Nature of Man*, now attributed with great certainty to Hippocrates' pupil and son-in-law Polybus, contains the first reference to the idea that 'the body of man has in itself blood, phlegm, yellow bile and black bile; these make up the nature of his body, and through these he feels pain or enjoys health.'[5] This text linked the four fluids to the seasons in which they were dominant (for blood that was springtime) and to four elementary qualities (for blood these were warm and damp). Only much later, under the influence of the Roman doctor Galen of Pergamon, were the four fluids associated with four temperaments or humours – for blood the humour was sanguine.

This was not the only theory of fluids in antiquity. There were alternative hypotheses, with water in place of bile, or comprising ten fluids (none of which were blood), proposed for example by Praxagoras. Where the Hippocratic school got the four-fluid theory from and how it came to be the standard model is still a mystery. An attractive hypothesis is that it is based on observation.[6] If you drain half a litre of blood from your veins and leave it to stand for a few hours in a test tube, you will see that it separates into different layers, like a perfectly made Irish coffee. On top floats a light-yellow liquid known as serum or plasma, which consists mainly of water and proteins like albumin. At the very bottom there is a dark-red or even purple-black sediment in which fibres have formed. This is the fibrin that Aristotle also knew of – and which he thought to be absent in the blood of deer, roes and hares – which causes the sediment to coagulate and form a solid cake. The clotted sediment was known in Latin as *cruor*, or as *caillot* in French. Above this is a layer of primarily red blood cells which have not yet clotted. The colour and fluidity of this layer resembles fresh blood for the longest. It is tempting to see the plasma as yellow bile, the sediment as black bile and the as yet unclotted blood as blood. Of course, that only comes to three layers and three fluids. There is also a fourth layer, now known as the buffy coat, which is transparent and contains primarily white blood cells and blood platelets. This layer, which you can compare with the white of an egg or – why not? – phlegm, floats on top of the red layer and below the yellowy serum. Was this the layer that Hippocrates also called phlegm? It is unlikely. It is usually possible to see this layer only after blood has been centrifuged. Normal human blood separates into serum and sediment with the still unclotted blood in between. But there are exceptions. The red blood cells of people with a high fever and of pregnant women sink a lot faster, so that the buffy coat forms of its own accord. Is this exceptional blood what Hippocrates and his followers had in mind when they devised the four-fluid theory? Tempting as it may be, this simple explanation is not convincing. Not a single author in antiquity makes a link between the fluids and the layers in blood.

That was to change in the Middle Ages. Until deep into the nineteenth century, blood was seen as both a mirror of, and the key to, health and sickness. A person's health depended on the right balance between the four fluids in the blood.[7] Bloodletting was the accepted treatment to combat a disrupted balance, and blood testing – after bloodletting – was the way to determine the nature of the imbalance. This *haematoscopy* was, however, something completely different to what we now understand by blood testing.[8] Medieval physicians tested the colour, smell, texture and taste of the blood they had taken from the patient. They stirred it with their fingers, held it up to the light, smelled it and tasted it to detect all kinds of disorders. Every self-respecting doctor would possess a catalogue with descriptions and illustrations of all the sensual properties of the blood of sick patients. They would also compare the colour, smell and perhaps even the taste of the blood with that of the patient's urine and saliva. They would check the temperature of the blood, its viscosity and fluidity, the speed with which it clotted, and the aromas it gave off as it did so. Anyone who stuck their fingers, their noses and even their tongues into the blood of sick patients on a daily basis clearly saw a link between the four fluids and the four layers of clotting blood.

The link was, however, far from consistent. It was easy to identify the black bile at the bottom and the blood above it, but the layers of yellow bile and phlegm varied widely. Sometimes, the phlegm referred to the frothy spume (*spuma*) on the surface of the blood rather than to a layer within the clotting blood. We must not forget that Hippocratic medicine – as we would call it today – was holistically orientated. It was not interested in separate layers, material and objects with spatially defined limits and which differed fundamentally from each other. Differences were gradual and proportionate, qualitative rather than quantitative. It was not a demonstrable difference in a specific part of a blood sample that was key to medical diagnosis, but the general impression created by the sample as a whole.

As to what blood actually was and what constituent parts it was made up of – a Hippocratic doctor would not understand the question. Like everything else, blood was a mixture of air, water, earth and – in this case – a lot of fire. In addition, it was moist and warm. Aristotelian science had no interest in its deeper structure. Since all its properties were observable, what was the point in delving deeper into the nature of the material? From an

Aristotelian perspective, a microscope was the least useful of all instruments for acquiring knowledge. You could understand the whole world with your reason and senses. Everything took place within the spectrum of our senses and there was no reason at all to look beyond it.

MICROSCOPES AND CHEMISTRY

From the sixteenth and seventeenth centuries, cracks started to appear in that cosy, self-contained view of the world.[9] Alchemists like Paracelsus and Jan Baptist van Helmont discovered that certain substances enabled the transition between the four elements. Chemicals like salt, sulphur and mercury caused a transition from solid (earth), liquid (water), flammable (fire) and gaseous (air) and were more fundamental than the four basic elements. In bubbling distillation flasks, the alchemists tried to determine the chemical composition of all kinds of materials. Blood, too, was heated up in cellars and back rooms.

But Aristotle's influence proved too strong. There were repeated and insistent claims that blood was not as banal as urine or saliva. In his *Ortus medicinae* (1648), Van Helmont stated that blood contained a higher spirit, or *archeus*. Alchemists used blood as a mysterious medium in their occult efforts to turn mercury into silver or gold.[10] In England, William Harvey (who discovered the body's circulation system) and Robert Boyle (whose *Memoirs for the Natural History of Human Blood* (1684) was the first chemical treatise on blood), refused to believe that blood was nothing more than an amalgam of chemical components. Boyle sent Marcello Malpighi, the Italian founder of microscopy, a flask containing the 'the spirit of human blood'. Malpighi asked this spirit to help an employer, an Italian count who suffered from a wide range of ailments. The count had undergone several bloodlettings but to no avail. Unfortunately the flask was damaged in Italy and the magical gift was lost.[11]

Around 1660, Malpighi himself discovered something that Aristotelian philosophy considered impossible: blood contained red particles that you could see only through a microscope. Biologist and microscopist Jan Swammerdam may have made the historical discovery of red blood cells (erythrocytes) a few years earlier. He saw oval particles swimming in the serum of frogs. The descriptions of Antonie van Leeuwenhoek some years later were certainly more detailed and more consistent. Malpighi was not sure whether the particles were genuinely part of the blood and whether they were present in all kinds of blood. Van Leeuwenhoek removed that uncertainty completely. This was the start of a new trend: blood was no longer studied with the naked eye, but with increasingly advanced microscopes and chemical analysis. The new scientific method produced unprecedented results. Blood was an uncommonly complex fluid that did not yield its secrets easily, and it was decades rather than years before the patience of researchers eventually paid off. In 1773 William Hewson discovered the existence of white blood cells (leukocytes), followed in 1818 by Everard Home's discovery of blood platelets (thrombocytes).[12] The latter were not described in detail until 1842, by Alfred Donné. Vincenzo Menghini discovered in 1746 that blood contained iron. In 1753 J. J. Rhades suspected that it was this metal that gave blood its red colour. In the meantime, it had been discovered that the red colour became lighter or darker depending on how much 'air' there was in the blood. When Antoine Lavoisier's theory of oxygen (1777) replaced the previous phlogiston theory of combustion, it became clear that Aristotle's element 'air' was actually oxygen. In the first decades of the nineteenth century, researchers from France (Lecanu, Denis and Fourcroy) and Germany (Engelhard and Hünefeld) discovered a ferrous molecule that retained oxygen in the blood. They initially called the chemical globulin and hematosine, but it was eventually to be called haemoglobin.[13]

The new science of blood benefited from all kinds of parallel inventions and discoveries. Better microscopes and more refined colouring methods enabled scientists to determine how blood cells are created. In 1868 Ernst Neumann and Giulio Bizzozero simultaneously discovered that blood cells are produced not by the heart or liver, but by bone marrow. Blood research also drew on new theories like cell theory, which considered cells the atoms of living material, and germ theory, which no longer sought the cause of disease in intangible miasma but in micro-organisms like bacteria, fungi and viruses. Sickness and health were thus no longer a matter of the correct balance between bodily fluids but had everything to do with the presence or absence of certain cellular structures that could be observed through a microscope and defined spatial dimensions.[14] Towards the end of the nineteenth century, thanks to these theories, bacteriologists developed effective medicines against diseases like diphtheria, rabies, tetanus, smallpox and cholera. The new ideas did, however, sometimes cause emotions to run unnecessarily high. When Russian immunologist Élie Metchnikoff, a top researcher at the Institut Pasteur in Paris, discovered in the 1880s a type of white blood cell known as the phagocyte, which resisted the anthrax bacillus, he laid the basis for a new form of immunology that closely followed cell theory. Antibodies – the term created by Paul Ehrlich – are cellular bodies that you can multiply to combat pathogens. In 1890 the German physiologist Emil von Behring and Japanese physician Shibasaburō Kitasato showed that cells were not necessary to fight diphtheria or tetanus, and that the same result could be achieved with immune serum. The French research community responded with incredulity. The German high chief of cellular theory Rudolf Virchow protested against this obscure discovery. At that time, serum was considered a cell-less – and therefore lifeless – fluid with no effect. There were fears of a return to Hippocratic fluid theory and the Aristotelian idea of qualitative relationships between liquids. With their discovery of serum immunity, Behring and Kitasato trod on the toes of all those who adhered dogmatically to cellular theory. And they clearly took pleasure in doing so, as they ironically closed their blasphemous article with Goethe's famous words 'Blut ist ein ganz besonderer Saft' (blood is a very special fluid).[15]

But there was no radical return to Hippocrates and Aristotle. On the contrary: all the ideas of both thinkers on blood were eventually discredited, one by one. The microscope made it clear that sperm was not blood but contained spermatozoids, that the female ovum – rather than menstrual blood – was required for procreation, that invertebrates like snails and prawns also had blood (which was blue rather than red), that the red liquid that ran out of fresh meat was not blood but myoglobin, and that the notion of blood relations had no biological foundation as not a drop of mother's blood flowed into the foetus growing in the placenta. What doctors had believed for centuries to be black or yellow bile, or phlegm, looked completely different under a microscope. It became embarrassing that intelligent people had believed all this for so long. Parmentier and Déyeux were right when they had written in their *Mémoire sur le sang* (1791), 'If we wish to deprive blood of its imaginary marvellous properties [*ce merveillieux imaginaire*], we have to penetrate into the composition of this fluid through experimentation.'[16] Half a century later, French professor of histology Charles Robin expressed his irritation at Romantic colleagues who continued to call blood 'liquid flesh' (*la chair coulante*), as the same epithet could be applied to urine.[17] The demystification of blood could be measured by the extent to which scientists equated it with urine. Being compared to pee was the ultimate humiliation for a bodily fluid under the delusion that it was better than all the others. The German biologist Karl Vogt became famous for his provocation that thoughts were to the brain what urine was to the kidneys.[18] Blood now experienced the same downfall. It was this demystification, unacceptable to so many, that led to the emergence of a new philosophical form of blood magic which retained the mystery that mechanistic science had destroyed, and once again caused exhilaration, blood rush and philosophical happiness.

MALAISE WITH MODERNITY

What did Goethe actually mean when he said that blood is a very special fluid? The words were spoken by Mephistopheles in his famous warning to medieval alchemist Faust, who wanted to sell his soul to the devil in a contract signed with blood. As Goethe no longer believed in blood-licking demons, he could not have been referring to that form of blood magic. He also knew that Christianity attributed magical properties only to holy blood. In that sense, the blood that dripped from Faust's finger was very trivial. Why did Mephistopheles consider blood so special? Was it perhaps just a literary device? Not at all: Goethe found inspiration from his own doctor, Christoph Wilhelm Hufeland, for whom blood was still very magical. 'Yes, I believe what the holy writ says: "The life of man is in his blood",' was how Hufeland summed up 25 years of practising medicine in his *Enchiridion medicum* (1834).[19] He remained convinced that bloodletting was the best therapy to promote the health and state of mind of his patients. He had his own blood-balsam theory, which involved removing the life force from the blood to achieve a soothing effect.[20] Hufeland was at home in many fields, especially pseudo-scientific disciplines. He is considered a founder of macrobiotics, aimed at prolonging life for as long as possible, he was obsessed by cases of apparent death and he had an excellent relationship with Samuel Hahnemann, founder of homeopathy. Hufeland had problems with the mechanistic view of the human body, that much was clear. During his student years in Göttingen there was no pupil more estranged from his tutor Albrecht von Haller, who had written the entry on blood in the *Encyclopédie* of Diderot and d'Alembert in 1777. The article, which contained only physical and chemical data, settled accounts with the Aristotelian view of blood. In Hufeland's eyes, it was soulless report on a substance that clearly had a soul.

Belief in a distinct life force fuelled this discontentment and gave renewed hope that the universe was more than a conglomeration of particles held together by physical and chemical laws. In 1795 Hufeland wrote his confession of faith to vitalism.[21] Twenty years before this publication, German physician Friedrich Casimir Medicus introduced the term *Lebenskraft*, life force, explicitly claiming that organic or animal chemistry could not be derived from inorganic chemistry.[22] A special force ruled the higher chemical processes in operation in living beings. That life force could not be reduced to, or derived from, the known forces of physics. Because of this *vis vitalis*, living beings acted differently to lifeless matter. Towards the end of the eighteenth century, we also see this vitalism in the work of Reil (who later renounced it), Metzger, Burdach, Trevinarius and Hufeland. Just as many physiologists were opposed to it, while some were favourably inclined to the underlying idea of irreducibility but found the existence of a separate life force implausible. Philosophers Immanuel Kant and Friedrich Schelling did not believe in it, though they did suspect that life could never be reduced to physics or chemistry. Hufeland, however, was convinced of the existence of this additional natural force that only occurred in living beings and which, in humans, was of course to be found in the blood. It was the life force that made blood special and magic. Admittedly, no one had ever observed this force but, unlike Aristotle's *pneuma* and Van Helmont's *archeus*, it was something material – like electricity or gravity – and observable. In anticipation of its discovery, 'life force' was a hypothetical notion that was used as a trump card in debates on questions to which the exact answer was unknown.

One of those questions was why blood clots. The best medical encyclopaedia of the nineteenth century, Dechambre's 78-volume *Dictionnaire encyclopédique des sciences médicales*, admitted as late as 1878 that the coagulation of blood was still an unexplained phenomenon.[23] The question was not answered satisfactorily (more or less) until 1905, when Paul Morawitz proposed a theory with four factors that adequately described the cascade of coagulation processes in normal blood.[24] During the twentieth century, this theory was continually added to and refined with a large number of new factors so that now we understand most – though not yet all – of the variations in the coagulation process. Given the extreme complexity of biochemical reality, the first explanations were childishly naive – but of course you have to begin somewhere. Around 1820 the Dutch anatomist Jacobus Schroeder van der Kolk summed up (in Latin) the arguments in favour of and against the four most important theories: that blood clotting was caused by loss of heat, lack of movement, exposure to light, or the life force. Proponents of the latter theory were Metzger, Hufeland, Burdach and Sprengel in Germany, Dumas, Milne-Edwards and Denis in France, and Hunter, Thackrah and Corrie in England. The life-force theory suffered from the handicap that it had been interpreted in contradictory ways from the beginning. While Charles Thackrah, for example, saw coagulation as the result of loss of the life force, John Hunter argued that it was the expression of that force. Hunter – after whom the Hunterian Museum was named – compared the clotting of blood to the contraction of muscles with the onset of death. For some vitalists, therefore, coagulation was the final spasm of a departing life force, while for others it occurred precisely because that force was no longer there. Either way, there was good reason to continue testing the hypothesis that the life force had something to do with blood coagulation. The other potential explanations were also far from problem free. Blood did not clot in fish that swam in extremely cold water and, as the priests of antiquity were aware, movement could delay clotting but not stop it entirely. Blood was consequently diluted with adder poison or deep frozen to see how the clotting process was affected. Adder poison caused coagulation to stop immediately. This was a point in favour of the life-force theory. Unfortunately, it did not eliminate the possibility of a purely chemical explanation. The poison may have killed all forces in the blood, not only the life force. More unfortunate was the discovery that, after frozen blood had thawed out, it would still clot, which meant one of two things: either the life force protected itself very effectively against the cold, or coagulation had nothing to do with the life force. By the end of the 1820s the theory had lost most of its supporters, though Henri Milne-Edwards obstinately continued to believe in it until the middle of the century.

Supporters like James Corrie admitted that the hypothesis was more philosophical than scientific.[25] He did not exclude the possibility that the vital power would never be identified, although he continued to hope that it was to be found in the serum. But what exactly was concealed in that serum, one might ask? Even if it were possible to observe the life force in blood under a microscope, it would not mark the end of the explanation but the beginning of a whole new batch of questions. Science is not satisfied with observable forces, but wants to know exactly what they consist of. Billions of euros are spent today trying to determine exactly what gravity is. Does the Higgs boson really exist or not? The life force was mysterious not only because no one could observe it and anyone who believed in it simply took it for granted, but – especially – because it could not be traced back to more elementary components combining to produce it. If it were possible to reduce it in this way, then it would be no different from any other physical force, while vitalism envisaged a force that could not be purely physical. The life force appeared only at a certain point in Creation, when life was created; before that point, it was completely absent. It suddenly appeared from nothing, just as it would suddenly return to nothing when a living being died. That is what gave the life force its philosophical magic. While other forces could be created out of fresh ingredients, like a delicious meal, it was impossible to construct the life force from its constituent parts. The life force was not made up of ingredients, but was a dish in itself that came out of the vitalist oven, ready to go.

Corrie was right. As a hypothesis, the life force was more philosophical than scientific. That is why German philosopher Immanuel Kant rejected it.[26] Although Kant believed that we would never understand life as a purely physical-chemical process, that lack of comprehension could never be attributed an observable force. It was caused by a gap in our knowledge, not by a gap in reality. Kant was the first philosopher to understand with unusual clarity that science – our most reliable form of knowledge – forced us to think in reductionist and causal terms. There was no escaping it. Anyone who believed that there were things that were not caused or were not reducible to something else placed themselves outside the bounds of science. God, the beginning and end of the universe, free will and life: these were all incomprehensible phenomena to anyone who restricted themselves to science. As far as 'life' was concerned, Kant ultimately proved to be overly pessimistic. We now understand life as a physical-chemical process. But, in essence, he had been right. Either you were a serious scientist who looked at the world through causal and reductionist spectacles, or you were a dreamer who held on tightly to special phenomena that fell beyond the realms of science. There was no middle way. Not that you were not permitted to have philosophical dreams – Kant remained an idealist – but you had to be aware that they were only dreams. Or even better, that there was no reliable way of knowing whether your dreams were real or fantasy.

That was a difficult conclusion to swallow. In the two centuries that followed, philosophers responded in various ways, some accepting Kant's verdict and others finding it impossible to live with and seeking ways around it. Among the latter group was Goethe, who dreamed of a romantic alternative to mechanistic science, which threatened to reduce everything special to microprocesses and chains of cause and effect. Vitalism was only one of the alternatives that Goethe envisaged. Holism, intuition and introspection were other hopeful concepts that the anti-modern movement embraced to preserve the magic in the world.[27] Whatever the most fruitful solution, Goethe believed that no poet-scientist could live in an aimless cosmos in which atoms danced to the laws of nature like marionettes. That disenchanted cosmos was an ugly, meaningless and immoral hell. In that respect, Mephistopheles' diabolical warning that blood was a special fluid was a breath of fresh air. No doom was more dismal than the idea that nothing was sacred. The devil brought divine news.

Blood fought hard to resist demystification, despite its ultimate inevitability. The many discoveries of the nineteenth century, to which German scientists in particular made such great contributions, confirmed Kant's prediction. It came as no surprise when chemist Justus von Liebig described blood in terms of a soulless chemical formula.[28] But this desecration actually prevented quite a lot of misery. At the end of the century, not a month went by without a new serum being discovered or a new vaccine being tested on humans and animals. Disease after disease was eradicated thanks to immunized, vaccinated or antibacterial blood revealing its secrets. Modernity may have sold its soul, but the body benefited from it. Religious and philosophical demystification was compensated for by the magic of scientific and technological knowledge.

In November 1917 the German sociologist Max Weber succinctly summed up the ambiguity of the spirit of modern times in a lecture at the University of Munich.[29] In front of an audience of revolutionary students and nostalgic teachers, both of whom doubted the value of liberal democracy for Germany's future, Weber admitted that science ate away at all mystery and mystique, ultimate meaning and purposiveness, ethical value and deeper emotional colour like a corrosive acid, leaving us at the mercy of a soulless, cold causal mechanism. He was aware that this was a severe blow for many of his listeners. But, he concluded, that was just the way it was. You can't have one without accepting the other. Like Kant, you have to understand that there is no possibility of a compromise. For anyone who adhered to a scientific view of the world, all beauty was fleeting, every ethical value relative and every truth – including those of science – always subject to revision. In a philosophical sense nothing was special.

Not everyone accepted this stoical, 'sad-but-true' attitude. Again, all kinds of escape attempts were launched. Vitalism, holism, intuition and introspection once again fuelled dreams of a non-reductionist and acausal science. Some constructed a new science that ultimately had nothing more scientific about it. In his anthroposophy, which influenced the post-war artist Joseph Beuys, Rudolf Steiner attributed blood a special place in his richly imaginative thinking.[30] In October 1906 Steiner gave a lecture in Berlin with – of course – Goethe's famous statement as its title.[31] In contrast with Goethe's subtle vitalism, there are no traces of real science to be found in Steiner's thought. For him, blood is once again a supernatural liquid that permits contact with the immaterial world, a medium that connects our physical bodies with our astral bodies. And, again, he locates our mental representations in the blood, so that the latter carries not only oxygen and disease, but a whole cultural legacy of passed-on memories. Although we will encounter this idea later in a completely different context, it is clear that Steiner was a dreamer who distanced himself completely from scientific thought. He was one of the many intellectuals in the first half of the twentieth century who felt that modern science, with its nihilistic perspective, threatened the beauty of great ideas and deep feelings. It was time for a new myth and a new philosophy that reunited meaningful contradictions and dichotomies that had been rent apart: past and present, body and soul, individual and community. For anyone who felt lonely in an aimless universe, in a chaotic metropolis, and who found the successes of modern science and technology unbearably one-sided, blood retained its anti-modern appeal. This life-giving fluid offered stubborn resistance to the modernist machine that pulverized all mystery.

WHOLE-BLOOD TRANSFUSION

In a recent book, Swiss historian Myriam Spörri provides a little known example of this resistance.[32] By contrast, the background to her example – the history of blood transfusion – has been much more widely documented.[33] It is a history full of astounding episodes in which belief in the magical power of blood is a recurring theme. As most of the episodes take place in very different times, it is surprising that Spörri's magical story about blood transfusion dates back only to the last century. Moreover, the myth was popular in one of the most modern countries in the world, and not among 'normal' people but in the elite medical corps of surgeons of the German Weimar Republic.

Blood transfusions as we now know them date back to the final years of the First World War. People suffering severe blood loss had never before been injected with blood from human donors to help restore their strength. But blood transfusions for other purposes were much older. Under the influence of Aristotle's idea that blood was the seat of the soul, doctors in the seventeenth century tried to imbue people with specific characteristics by administering transfusions.[34] When Robert Boyle wondered whether it would be possible to transfer retrieving skills from a trained to an untrained dog via blood, Richard Lower and Francis Potter in England and Jean-Baptiste Denis in France started conducting experiments. After all, blood was where consciousness, character traits and memories were stored. The experiments came to an abrupt end when Denis – one of Louis xiv's personal physicians – applied the treatment to human patients, with fatal consequences. Denis wanted to cure the untreatable, mentally ill Antoine Mauroy by injecting him with the blood of a docile lamb. The unfortunate patient did not survive the second dose. Denis was tried but acquitted, and the therapy was banned in France and by Rome. A century and a half later, the English obstetrician James Blundell experimented with human-to-human blood transfusions to save patients with severe blood loss caused, for example, by complications in childbirth, or by accidents and injuries.[35] In the early nineteenth century, he developed instruments that circumvented the need to connect the donor's artery directly to that of the patient – which was not only uncomfortable but also dangerous because it was impossible to tell how much blood the latter was receiving and the blood pumping out of the donor's artery could cause excess pressure in the patient's heart. Blundell devised a 'gravitator', in which a visible quantity of the donor's blood was captured in a copper bowl, which then dripped into the patient's vein through a vertical tube. As the intravenous drips used in today's hospitals still prove, gravity is enough to ensure that the donor's blood flows into the patient's veins.

And yet Blundell did not force a breakthrough. He did not believe in the nutritious effect of blood. For him, it was not the quantity of blood that would save the patient, but the administration of blood as the essential elixir of life. With one foot still in the Hippocratic tradition, he believed that blood contained some form of life-saving property, no matter how much of it was administered. The idea that it was the quantity, rather than the quality, of pressure, oxygen and nutrition spreading through the body that was beneficial did not take hold until the beginning of the last century. Most 'transfusions' during the second half of the nineteenth century were actually not blood transfusions at all, but injections of saline (salt) solutions, sometimes mixed with blood, alcohol or even milk – in the belief that the white globules of milk would turn into red blood cells. In 1894 *The Lancet* wrote an enthusiastic comment on saline transfusions: 'There can be little doubt that the injection of salt solution . . . is certainly a great step in advance . . . [over the] established . . . injection with actual blood.'[36] Saline solutions, alcohol and milk all had the advantage that they did not coagulate, a problem that continued to plague Blundell's gravitator: after half an hour, the blood in the gravitator would clot, bringing the transfusion to a halt.

By the end of the First World War, after a series of break-throughs, wounded soldiers were systematically being given blood transfusions. After that, transfusion became a regular form of treatment at hospitals. In the first decade of the twentieth century, the American surgeons Alexis Carrel and George Washington Crile discovered that saline injections were not effective in patients who had lost a lot of blood. Blood pressure would fall sharply following sudden blood loss, and only blood could restore it. Because saline solutions were no use in treating these shock patients, Crile and Carrel returned to administering transfusions using whole blood. By doing so, they were faced with the familiar dilemma of choosing between a direct trans-fusion with the fast-flowing blood from the donor's arteries – which was uncomfortable and, more importantly, dangerous – or an indirect transfusion with venal blood from the donor, which was safer and less unpleasant but brought with it the risk of the blood clotting and blocking the instruments, halting the transfusion prematurely .

A simple solution to this dilemma was found in the early years of the First World War. Almost simultaneously, doctors in America (Lewisohn and Weil), Belgium (Hustin), Argentina (d'Agote) and Russia (Yourevitch and Rosenberg) discovered that citrate, a derivative of citric acid, could prevent clotting. Citrate blocks the working of calcium, one of the four basic elements in the coagulation cascade. Adding a small quantity of citrate – a concentrate of 0.2 per cent is perfect – to blood would keep it in fluid form and usable for transfusions for days or even weeks. The chemical additive is harmless; in such small quantities, it is not toxic and is quickly broken down by the liver. Its practical advantages as an anti-coagulation agent seemed irresistible. When American and Canadian troops started their offensive in the First World War, they carried 10-litre bottles of citrate blood along with them in the holds of their ships. The blood, which would remain usable for four weeks, saved the lives of many wounded soldiers. No one at the time concerned themselves with incompatible combinations of blood groups that caused agglutination. Few understood the importance of the discovery of blood groups by Viennese pathologist Karl Landsteiner at the very beginning of the century – that awareness only developed later. And the loss of human life in the war was so high that those who died as a result of blood agglutination were very unlucky indeed.

The benefits of citrate blood cannot be overemphasized. Because the blood could be stored, it was no longer necessary for the donor to lie next to a sick or injured patient. Up until then donating blood had involved lying arm to arm, face to face, with the patient and feeling your blood flowing into their body. With their groaning breath in your face, you silently hoped that a technical fault would not cause the blood to flow in the wrong direction, or that it would not flow so strongly after the arm clamp was released that the patient would die from the excess pressure. With small taps and valves, these risks were eventually reduced but, for many donors, direct contact with delirious, drivelling, infectious and dying patients remained a horrific experience.[37] And you always had to be at the ready. Hospitals employed special 'summoners' who would politely but urgently request donors, often at ungodly hours of the night, to get dressed and hurry to the emergency department. For that reason, donors usually restricted themselves to their own family members, or nurses and other hospital staff were asked repeatedly to donate blood themselves. Nevertheless, volunteers were also called upon to help and it was not unthinkable that, during a hospital visit, you might find yourself on a donor's stretcher. Although some hospitals did at least place a screen between the heads of the donor and the patient, citrate blood unquestionably had immense advantages over whole blood. Donors could decide for themselves when they gave blood, and did so in a room where they had no contact at all with the recipient. After the addition of a few drops of citrate, the blood was stored in a refrigerator and administered when necessary. You could hardly imagine a more elegant method.

In Germany, however, the story was very different. Until the Second World War, German medicine – a world leader – continued to swear by direct transfusions with whole or fresh blood. There were exceptions: small children, and babies especially, were not subjected to complex direct transfusions; nor were women in childbirth, for whom sudden and heavy bleeding could be fatal. They were given citrate blood. But for planned operations, German surgeons in the interwar period preferred whole-blood transfusions. They undoubtedly knew about the citrate method, about which German émigré Richard Lewisohn had written with such praise in German-language journals, and of its many practical benefits. Foreign proponents of the citrate method made every effort to debunk all the misunderstandings about it and Lewisohn considered the stubbornness of the German surgeons criminal. Nevertheless, across ideological and political borders, they persisted in their obstinate belief that adding citrate caused substantial harm. There could be no doubt about it: the alien chemical additive must have an effect on pure blood. The effect may not have been immediately visible, but the German dissenters were convinced that time would prove them right. To make the contact between donor and recipient a little more comfortable, experiments were conducted in Germany whereby venal donor blood was captured in glass flasks and then injected into the patient's body through a system of pumps, taps and tubes. To postpone coagulation, so that donor and recipient did not have to lie next to each other, the insides of these instruments were smeared with paraffin wax. But the wax did not always stop the blood from clotting and created the risk of an embolism if it found its way into the tapped-off blood.

Citrate blood was much simpler, but the German surgeons resisted its use for more than two decades. According to Spörri, there were cultural reasons behind this stubborn refusal. Scientifically, it was accepted that the whole-blood method had its disadvantages and was in that respect inferior, but it was culturally unacceptable that fresh, pure blood be mixed with an artificial chemical and industrial product. Citrate blood demystified the whole romantic ideal of pure blood to which German doctors were so sentimentally attached. Whole blood represented everything that Germany stood for in the crisis of modernity it was suffering in that period. It symbolized the importance that German culture attributed to everything that was natural, pure and irreplaceable. That authentic, 'natural' culture that believed in the soul was not ready to accept products of an 'artificial' Americanism that considered the soul as deriving from crude material. The fact that citrate blood opened the door to the capitalist sale of tapped-off, stored blood only intensified the German aversion. The psychological advantage of using citrate blood – the distance between the donor and the recipient – was interpreted within a cultural historical context of alienation between people who, like individual atoms, were no longer joined by ties of family and society. Whole-blood transfusions were seen as bringing them back together.

Germany was not comfortable with the *tabula rasa* that modernity had made of traditional beliefs. Capitalist America – and Communist Russia – promoted a new way of looking at the individual, society and the cosmos that the Germans were not yet ready to embrace. That they chose nostalgia for magical forces above scientific efficiency was surprising enough, considering the enormous contributions that German researchers and companies had made to science and technology but, at the same time, showed just how deeply and broadly that desire for enchantment was felt. And blood played a special role in that crisis. Hope focused on whole blood, and citrate blood was viewed with repugnance. Meddling with this magical fluid was seen as a taboo. This can be compared with the way in which many people today resist genetically modified crops and swear by what they consider to be natural, organic food, even when it is more harmful to the environment and less profitable. Humankind cannot deviate from the primal state of nature with impunity. Intervention destroys a hidden unity, harmony or even salvation. Nature has an inherent goal that allows ultimate understanding and meaning, and it cannot be debased to the level of a morally indifferent mechanism. The traditional belief in a deeper purpose in nature and the cosmos clashed here with the modernist ideal that life and society can be (re)constructed artificially.

MENOTOXINS

Stubborn adherence to blood magic was also to be found in another area of scientific research. Again, it was primarily German scientists who most fiercely resisted demystified modernity. If normal blood was magical, then menstrual blood was many times more so. No other bodily fluid was the subject of more fantasies.[38] Top of the list of menstruation-related myths is undoubtedly the belief that menstrual blood is poisonous, an early reference to which can be found in Pliny the Elder's *Natural History*:

> But nothing could easily be found that is more remarkable than the monthly flux of women. Contact with it

turns new wine sour, crops touched by it become barren, grafts die, seeds in gardens are dried up, the fruit of trees falls off, the bright surface of mirrors in which it is merely reflected is dimmed, the edge of steel and the gleam of ivory are dulled, hives of bees die, even bronze and iron are at once seized by rust, and a horrible smell fills the air; to taste it drives dogs mad and infects their bites with an incurable poison.[39]

Such stories adapted themselves admirably to modern times. People continued to believe menstruation-related tales until well into the twentieth century. When menstruating women were in the vicinity, not only would ham fail to cure, beer to brew, dough to rise and flowers and plants to grow, but photographs would not develop and even vegetables in sterile cans would go off.[40] Such superstitions are now less common, yet all the knowledge required to debunk them was available much earlier. A century ago, there was already no reason to believe such stories uncritically. Medical encyclopaedias confirmed time and again that uterine blood has the same composition as the blood that flows through our veins.[41] By about 1925, gynaecologists had an extremely accurate description of the course, function and hormone-driven nature of the menstrual cycle. One phenomenon, however, continued to fire the imagination – menstrual blood does not clot. No one knew why, and that made it something special.

How could scientists have known that menstrual blood was not toxic? Strange as it may seem, they still don't know it now. There are no studies – at least, to my knowledge – that definitively debunk the superstition that mayonnaise made by menstruating women is more likely to fail.[42] And that is understandable: showing that something does not have a toxic effect is difficult, since a lack of evidence is not proof of a lack of causal effect. A negative result can be attributed to all kinds of factors that researchers may not have noticed. There has never been a crucial experiment that proves conclusively that menstrual blood is not toxic. That is not how science works. Nevertheless, scepticism remains the most rational option. After all, the question of whether menstrual blood is toxic has been addressed in literally dozens of scientific studies, mainly in Germany, Austria and Switzerland, but also in the u.s. and, to a lesser extent, Israel and France. This wave of publications peaked between 1920 and 1935 with at least thirty, mostly in German, but some also in English. After 1935, the flow as good as stopped, with only the occasional article still appearing on the subject. There was a revival of interest between 1974 and 1977, with four articles in *The Lancet*, which did not completely exclude the possibility of so-called menotoxins. The discussion was not settled one way or another, but simply died out due to lack of renewed interest and stimulating hypotheses and, of course, inconclusive results. As late as 1975, after a critical and frustrating discussion on all kinds of chemicals – including arsenic, iodine, choline and necrosin – that could in theory explain the alleged toxic effect of menstrual blood but failed to do so in tests, one researcher at least remained extremely optimistic, saying, 'The possibility that menstruating women can in certain cases have a harmful effect on living organisms cannot be excluded.'[43] He ultimately suggested another toxic substance – trimethylene – as the most likely culprit.

It continues to surprise me that such a wild idea with such dubious roots – in blood magic – could have preoccupied so many serious scientists. They certainly could not be accused of not having tested it thoroughly. It is remarkable that, to date, no one has devoted a separate study to menotoxins.[44] It was not for lack of curiosity: samples of sweat, saliva, menstrual and venal blood, urine, even tears, were taken from female volunteers – often nurses or patients – using sanitary pads, sponges, mini-balloons, glass tubes and tubular vaginal specula. The samples were taken from women of different ages and at different stages of their menstrual cycle. Some laboratories also tested the menstrual blood of apes, one of the few other animal species with a menstrual cycle.[45] Researchers tested the effect of menstrual blood, and control substances, on the growth of plants, rising dough and the fermentation of beer, and injected it into rats and mice to see how they would react. The number of species of flowers and plants fed with menstrual blood between 1920 and 1940 is beyond counting.

Why did scientists test this superstition so obsessively? It all started with the pioneering work of Viennese paediatrician Béla Schick in 1920.[46] Schick was the first to test the existence of menotoxins experimentally and to give them their name. He was apparently a much-loved doctor who regularly received flowers from his patients. One day, he was given a bunch of dark-red roses. Although his maid told him she was menstruating, she put the roses in a vase. The following morning, they were limp and turning brown, the leaves were dropping off and they looked generally wilted. This aroused Schick's curiosity. During her following menstrual periods, he would ask his maid to arrange flowers or knead dough – sometimes with and sometimes without gloves, and always with a non-menstruating woman as a control subject. Schick was astounded. When the maid arranged the flowers with her bare hands, the flowers would wilt within ten minutes. Although this research was largely anecdotal, such positive results of course called for a response. In the following decade and a half, researchers published dozens of studies – both of experiments and field research – with varying results. Opponents suggested a contaminating effect due to insufficient hygiene, but proponents continued to observe effects, including in experiments involving very fresh menstrual blood and antibiotics. In 1934 one proponent of the menotoxin theory summed up the debate with the following decisive words: 'There can be no more serious doubt about the factual reality of menstrual toxin.'[47]

What did the supporters of the theory find so attractive about the existence of menotoxins? Why did they so much want menstrual blood to be harmful? Between the dry, technical accounts of the experiments, there was a palpable sense of relief that superstition did not have to be completely without scientific basis. The experiments showed that age-old beliefs did have some basis in truth. Those arrogant medical scientists who mocked menotoxins as old wives' tales could finally be taken down a peg or two. This desire for unity between tradition and modern science is to be found very clearly in Schick's pioneering article, which he ends with a reference to a famous passage from Shakespeare:

> We should be delighted that this belief has not been eradicated and we should be thankful to the people for preserving facts that have been passed down through word of mouth. Science often only confirms their truth much later. There are many more things between heaven and earth than are dreamt of in our school books.[48]

The most comprehensive study of menotoxins, by Americans David Macht and Dorothy Lubin in 1924, started and ended with an ode to popular belief and superstition and a sneer at the arrogance of science:

> Of course such ideas are classed by modern intellectuals as 'superstitions', figments of imagination and products of benighted minds; but the fact remains that these beliefs persist today and that references to such a menstrual contagion or poison are found in all classical writers of ancient and medieval times and have also crept into modern literature.[49]

Their positive findings are

another illustration of the truth of many empirical observations made by the laity . . . [as] such folklore when
surviving many ages is very apt to be the consequence of
sound perception and accurate observation . . . [giving it]
some basis of truth, not to be ridiculed without further
critical inquiry.[50]

Supporters were pleased that scientific research had shown the
truth of superstition and the falseness of scientific prejudice.

Anyone who had a problem with modernist demystification was happy to believe in menotoxins. Science showing that
menstrual blood was toxic offered solace in two ways. First, it
forged a bond between folklore and science. Modernity was
not diametrically opposed to tradition – the two could form
a unity. Anyone who dreamed of a deeper truth underlying
both superstition and science – and, who knows, perhaps also
behind mysticism, intuition and introspection – found a shining example in the discovery of menotoxins. Menstrual poison
restored the unity between all kinds of knowledge, a unity that
had been destroyed by the advent and success of the scientific
method. Undemocratic as it is, science does not tolerate unreliable knowledge in any form. The discovery of menotoxins – itself
the work of scientists – punished science for its arrogance and
lack of tolerance. Second, it also gave menstrual blood the special quality back that science had taken from it. Even though
no one had yet put their finger on the actual toxin responsible,
menstrual blood was after all not normal blood, but contained
magic, no matter how harmful it could be. Menstrual blood did
not give life; it took it. Either way, it had a strange quality that
had been known for centuries. That it was impossible to identify the substance that made it toxic only confirmed its magical
peculiarity. Menotoxins did not easily give up their secrets, but
no one could claim any longer that menstrual blood was entirely
harmless.

The debate continued during and after the Second World War, with varying test results. In 1953 Jerusalem doctor Bernhard Zondek concluded that 'the existence of a specific toxin in menstrual blood has not yet been conclusively demonstrated'.[51] Zondek was critical of earlier positive findings which he considered to have been based on tests using insufficient bacteria-free blood. In the 1970s, scientists published an appeal in *The Lancet* for more research, from the naive assumption that all the stories must have some core of truth. The final study of menotoxins in 1977 produced the surprising outcome that, far from obstructing it, menstrual blood stimulated the growth of plants.[52]

Although Béla Schick continued to defend his discovery until his death in 1967, and called on young scientists to conduct more and better research, the post-war generation showed little interest in the subject. There were various reasons for this. There had been experiments enough and they had produced nothing. What young scientist was willing to risk conducting research that offered so few prospects of positive results? The philosophical and cultural incentive to continue to stubbornly seek and find menotoxins also disappeared. The post-war generation were much less susceptible to malaise with modernity. They had reconciled themselves to the modern way of life. They had seen the horror that too much enthusiasm for anti-modern irrationalism could lead to. For that generation, 'Americanism' was no longer synonymous with artificiality, alienation and dislocation, but with jazz, Pop art, youth culture, sexual freedom and individual pleasure. In a world that was recovering from the mass destruction that malaise with modernity had unleashed, intellectual flirtation with blood magic was suspect. If blood was a special fluid that could release intense feelings and bring us to a state of exhilaration, it was not because it contained magical properties. Blood was not a medium that brought us into contact with a supernatural world or which demons could use to drive us to insanity, nor did it transcend mechanical reality. It was simply red urine. And it was time that modern men and women accepted that banal conclusion.

BLOOD 2.0

'Do you see those red pearls?' she asked me. 'That is the blood we are cultivating here.' Through the eyepiece of the microscope I could indeed see a large number of shining red globules floating neatly alongside each other in a sea of transparent fluid. It was difficult to distinguish any further details. I could see a few small black dots, like minute eyes looking at me, but that was about all the magnification could offer. This microscopic image of cultivated blood cells in a Petri dish was the visual high point of my visit to the Sanquin Research Centre. Sanquin is a unique Dutch organization that provides a range of blood services on a not-for-profit basis. It was created at the end of the 1990s after a merger between Dutch blood banks and the Central Laboratory of the Netherlands Red Cross. Sanquin Research, located in Amsterdam, is a real 'blood university', with professors, departments, a library and dozens of PhD students, who are learning to be researchers and write groundbreaking theses and papers. My appointment there was with Marieke von Lindern, whom I had met at a very lighthearted but nonetheless completely scientifically sound event, the Halloween Science Late Night Show in Leiden. We had both been invited to say something about blood, as long as we were dressed up as Dracula, Frankenstein or some other horror monster. In a bloodstained lab coat, she gave a flamboyant presentation on the state of the art in blood cultivation research. She is the head of the Haematopoiesis department, which is conducting the research. She hopes to hold the first clinical trials of artificial blood within two years.

Blood – or the buffy coat, to be more precise – contains a small fraction of stem cells that later grow to be red or white blood cells or blood platelets.[53] These stem cells can be artificially matured to form embryonic and then juvenile red blood cells, with a normal haemoglobin content but not yet the concave form of adult red blood cells. Lastly, ingenious molecular processes allow the young cells to evolve into mature red blood cells. Von Lindern's team wants to understand all the factors involved in the development of red blood cells, so that all stages of that development can be replicated more quickly outside the human body in large vats or tanks. The maturing and growing process currently takes place in an immersion bath full of erythropoietin (EPO), stem cell factor and hormones (glucocorticoids), which is a very expensive medium, but Von Lindern hopes that improved insights will lead to cheaper alternatives where the ratio of medium to cells is less disproportional. At the moment, she needs 700 litres of medium to produce 1 litre of blood.

This is only one possible recipe for cultivating artificial blood. An alternative to working with blood stem cells is to use embryonic stem cells, which can still develop in all directions. Or adult specialized cells can be reprogrammed back to stem cells. In 2007 Japanese pioneer Shinya Yamanaka was awarded the Nobel Prize in Physiology or Medicine for showing that it was possible to make a versatile stem cell from an adult skin cell. A Scottish team is now applying this principle to produce red blood cells from skin cells. But there is no reason why reprogramming cells should be the final station for scientific and technological research. Scientists have now succeeded in producing bacteria and viruses artificially. The first synthetic antibiotics are expected to be available within a few years. Recently, researchers produced a complete chromosome, chromosome 3 of the sixteen chromosomes contained in yeast. They synthetically produced the 273,871 DNA building blocks it contains and, in the process, introduced 50,000 'improvements' that had no effect at all on the working of the yeast. They hope to be able to replicate the other fifteen chromosomes within four years, so that 'yeast 2.0' will be a fait accompli.

When will blood 2.0 follow? Von Lindern does not know, of course, but is delighted with this development. She becomes enthusiastic when she thinks of the many benefits. We are now sitting in the guest room, where we are joined by her colleague Dirk de Korte. De Korte heads the Blood Cell Research Department's laboratory for transfusion technology. He knows all about the complexities of blood cells. Von Lindern sums up the many benefits, such as tailor-made blood transfusions for patients with a wide variety of blood disorders. Take, for example, the millions of people who suffer from sickle cell anaemia. As the result of a genetic defect, their red blood cells are malformed and transport less haemoglobin. The patients often need blood transfusions, but these are not much help as recipients cannot adapt to the haemoglobin-rich blood. Modified blood can also help people who are suffering from anaemia, painful bones and a wide diversity of infections. Another example is the danger of infection posed by transfusions, which can never be completely excluded – either the risk diagnosis is exorbitantly expensive or you have to discriminate against certain groups. Artificial blood poses no health risks.

De Korte nods. Artificial blood will save lives, though this high-tech product will not replace classic donor blood. But he has his doubts about the synthetic replication of blood cells. He has great admiration for the semi-permeable membrane that surrounds cells. He does not immediately see how we can ever imitate this ingenious achievement of nature. It is something very special. Nor is blood simply a soup of red blood cells; it is much more than that. White blood cells and blood platelets are not yet being cultivated artificially, as they are not yet so interesting commercially. De Korte says it is clear that the deeper you penetrate into the material before building it up again, the more complex the problems become. And those problems are piling up. Every solution generates side effects, so that you can end up a long way from where you started. 'Some things', he says, 'simply refuse to be tied down to the laws of nature.' This is a remarkable statement in a remarkable setting. In the Valhalla of futuristic medicine, philosophical blood magic has not been completely extinguished.

On the train back from Amsterdam, my story about super-natural bloodlust comes to an end. I say my final farewells to the idea that blood has magical properties that can bring us into contact with a different world, and with beings and forces that do not belong to material reality. Blood is not a magical sub-stance but a chemical product that you can replicate without losing any of its properties. You may even be able to add some new ones. Artificial blood is the death blow for blood magic. That fantasy started in ancient Greece. Of course, blood had something to do with life and death, but the vapour rising from bleeding bodies gave rise to the belief that blood was a medium between humankind and the gods. Centuries later, Christians banned all animal sacrifice because animal blood allegedly only fed demons. Contact with blood acquired something diabolical; only the blood of the saints retained its miraculous properties. Under the influence of Aristotle and Hippocrates, blood magic continued to exist, but took on a more philosophical form. Blood was no longer special in religious terms, but remained so philo-sophically. There was something in blood that prevented it from being derived completely from banal physical/chemical reality. This philosophical variant excited intellectuals who were not content with demystified modernity. Christian blood devotion was something for the superstitious masses, while the elite found solace in the knowledge that blood was philosophically special. That exhilaration was certainly not as exuberant as the elevated trance of Apollo Deiradiotes, who drank ewe's blood, or the *taurobolium* experienced by the followers of the Magna Mater cult, or the visions of the Christians who licked the blood of Christ or kissed his wounds, but it did have something that united them. All of these experiences connected believers with a higher reality. Furthermore, the spiritual experience released powerful feelings that varied from emotion at the mystery of the philosophical blood magic to intoxication, inebriation, ecstasy and even orgasm, in the case of religious blood magic. Despite this difference in intensity, all of these variants of supernatural blood shared a sacred belief in the immaterial dimension, which gave meaning to life and the cosmos. Without that spiritual dimension, all enchantment disappeared. Although the medical progress we acquired to replace it was a glittering gift, the world also lost something of mystery and beauty. On the train home, I put that behind me for ever.

PART
TWO
BLOOD
THIRST

HAEMOTHYMIA

We begin again with the murder of a baby. And again, the horrific act is fictitious. This time, however, everyone was aware of that immediately – rather than after a century and a half of discussion, as with the Christian orgies. In Thomas Mann's masterpiece *The Magic Mountain* (1924), the leading character, engineer Hans Castorp, finds himself tossed back and forth between the anti-modern Leo Naphta, son of a Jewish butcher who has converted to Catholicism, and Enlightenment philosopher Lodovico Settembrini. During a snowstorm, Castorp seeks refuge in a barn. Exhausted from ploughing through the snow, he falls asleep and has his famous dream in which he sees the sacrifice of a young child:

> The bronze door of the sanctuary stood open, and the poor soul's knees all but gave way beneath him at the sight within. Two grey old women, witchlike, with hanging breasts and dugs of finger-length, were busy there, between flaming braziers, most horribly. They were dismembering a child. In dreadful silence they tore it apart with their bare hands – Hans Castorp saw the bright hair blood-smeared – and cracked the tender bones between their jaws, their dreadful lips dripped blood.[1]

We are already familiar with much of this horrific ritual. The old women were witches like Horace's Canidia or Lucan's Erichtho, who mixed the flesh of babies – raw, boiled or roasted to ash – in magic potions and ointments. In wild trances, they used the blood of children to make predictions, curry the favour of demons or cause evil to befall their victims. We know by now why they thought that blood had magical properties. And witches had a predilection for dead babies – preferably unbaptized – although it is not clear whether they had killed the child themselves or stolen the young corpse. The hanging breasts and finger-length nipples – a medieval detail – suggest that the old women nursed the unfortunate child for a while before killing it.[2]

Half-naked witches performing spells with dead babies was an old tale that Mann was certainly familiar with, but he added something to the cliché. The horror was not perpetrated in a dark cellar or in the woods at night, but in a sunny Mediterranean temple – the sacred site of the Graeco-Roman cult of ritual sacrifice. He replaced the pagan priests, who slaughtered their animal offerings without violence and were very careful with the blood they spilled, with cannibalistic witches who ripped babies apart with their bare hands and consumed their raw flesh and tender bones. This witches' meal turned the classical sacrificial supper on its head. Everything that gave the offering its religious integrity was replaced by its perverse opposite: priests became witches, the sacrificial animal became a human victim, the meat was not boiled or roasted but eaten raw, the complex ritual was replaced by bestial gluttony. This horrific image would certainly have appealed to Christians crusading against pagan animal sacrifice. Such a reversal perfectly suited their demonization of the ritual. They were in no doubt at all that shedding blood for religious purposes would lead to sadism. What had once started with the peaceful sacrifice of an animal in front of a magnificent temple would end up in brutal infanticide behind closed metal doors. That, too, was a stereotypical image.

Mann added something extra. By portraying the witches as wild animals who ripped babies apart and ate their raw flesh, while flickering fires heated up pans in which they would cook the small children in true witch tradition, he linked these horrific practices to the Hellenic tradition around Dionysus (Bacchus).[3] According to myth, the female priestesses of this god of wine and poetry, known as maenads or bacchantes, loved to indulge in *sparagmos* (ripping animals or people apart) and *omophagia* (eating raw flesh). Besides oxen, goat and sheep, these mad-women – who wore fawn skins and used a long stalk of thyrsus (giant fennel) with a twig of ivy on the tip to lean on – sacrificed children. Even Pentheus, King of Thebes, fell victim to *sparagmos*, being torn to pieces by his own mother, who mistook him for a lion. This myth was a favourite theme in ancient Greece. Euripides' play *The Bacchantes* is still performed, but at least six other writers had dramatized the story before him – Aeschylus twice. With the exception of that of Euripides, however, they have all been lost, though many allusions to the story have been preserved.

The real cult of Dionysus appealed to the imagination even more than the myth.[4] Inscriptions in Magnesia, Miletus and Physkos – though none have been found in Attica – and eye-witness reports by Diodorus of Sicily, Plutarch and Pausanias, provide conclusive proof that there was a real Dionysus cult in Greece until the third century AD. Women would dress as maenads – with fawn skins and Bacchus staffs – and go into the mountains on cold winter nights to perform a strange ritual. In the wildest accounts, the maenads would hunt goats and tear them apart with their hands and teeth. They would throw the pieces into the crowd who, ecstatic from the blood, would sink their teeth into the raw flesh and devour it. This would be fol-lowed by an orgy of gluttony, drink and wild sex. Even in the more civilized versions, such as that of Diodorus of Sicily, which was probably closer to the historical truth, animal blood clung to the hands, arms and robes of the dancing women, but they cut the dead animal up with a knife and then put the pieces in a basket as an offering to Dionysus. There was no more mention of *sparagmos* and *omophagia*. The maenads no longer had raw flesh between their teeth and blood dripping from the corners of their mouths. The emphasis in the Dionysian ritual lay on dance, poetry and music. The bacchanal became a festival rather than a wild hunting party. The goat's meat was not boiled or roasted, as with a normal sacrificial meal, but was offered to the god raw. In that sense, this sacrificial offering remained different.

It is no longer possible to say where *sparagmos* and *omophagia* came from. It may have had something to do with the god Dionysus being born twice: first as the incestuous child of Zeus and his daughter Persephone and the second time – after the Titans had torn him to pieces and devoured him (with the exception of his heart) – as the child of Zeus and the mortal Semele.[5] The maenads were undoubtedly honouring the rebirth of their god by imitating his cannibalistic death. But it was not this imitation of death and rebirth that gave this maenadic ritual its appeal. It was sensational because it was the complete opposite of classical pagan sacrifice.[6] It was led by women, who played a negligible role in Greek religion. It took place in uninhabited natural surroundings and not in an urban temple. The sacrificial meal consisted of raw flesh from an animal that had been torn apart while still alive, rather than the boiled or roasted flesh of an animal that had been slaughtered and cut up with a knife. The ritual was accompanied by sexual promiscuity, while ritual sacrifice required sexual abstinence. It took place at night in the winter, while classical offerings were made during the day and preferably in the sunlight. Maenadic sacrifice was actually an anti-offering, where the participants were not seeking supernatural contact with gods as much as debasing themselves to the level of wild animals hunting prey, which they then tore to pieces. It was a crazed feast rather than a restrained ceremony. Although it is an exaggeration to see maenadism as 'a survival from the early times of Neolithic or even Palaeolithic hunters', or to believe that the cult of Dionysus 'preserved the memory of ancient tribal savagery',[7] the cult was undoubtedly founded on the wild, animal and uncivilized side of human nature. This cult of sacrifice did not elevate its participants to the level of pious, civilized, order-loving and god-fearing beings, but lowered them to the level of cruel, bloodthirsty, chaotic and primitive animals. The blood that flowed during the ritual made the believers blood-thirsty in a bestial, rather than a spiritual, sense. The blood did not invoke religious rapture through its magical properties, but spoke to our animal instincts. Although no surviving texts or artefacts depicting maenadic rituals refer directly to the intoxi-cating nature of the blood contact, blood was an integral part of the Dionysian orgy of violence and most certainly played its part in creating the atmosphere of elation. This passage from Euripides' *The Bacchantes* depicts the association between *sparagmos*, exhilarating violence and the spilling of blood:

> Thereat we fled, to escape being torn in pieces by the Bacchantes; but they, with hands that bore no weapon of steel, attacked our cattle as they browsed. Then wouldst thou have seen Agave mastering some sleek lowing calf, while others rent the heifers limb from limb. Before thy eyes there would have been hurling of ribs and hoofs this way and that; and strips of flesh, all blood-bedabbled, dripped as they hung from the pine-branches. Wild bulls, that glared but now with rage along their horns, found themselves tripped up, dragged down to earth by countless maidens' hands. The flesh upon their limbs was stripped therefrom quicker than thou couldst have closed thy royal eye-lids.[8]

I have already given a number of examples in the first part of this book showing how the Greeks and Romans were familiar with the bestial exhilaration caused by blood. Humans and animals were believed to be driven wild by blood. The maenadic cult was well aware that blood had this effect. Because blood-induced

exhilaration was considered unacceptable in classic animal sacrifice – the animal power of blood was repressed rather than
emphasized – such wild abandon fitted perfectly in Dionysian
'anti-sacrifice'.

MAENADIC CROWDS

The maenadic fantasy survived the Graeco-Roman world.
Thomas Mann was not the only writer to refer to it; blood
remained an unmodern fluid in modern literature. Although it
was no longer special in religious or philosophical terms, blood
could do something that other bodily fluids could not: it could
drive people into a frenzy and make them act like animals. Blood
may not bring us into contact with a higher world, but it does
remind us of a lower reality from which we are separated by
only a wafer-thin layer of civilization. Modernity was intolerant
of confrontations with our animal nature. The more modern a
person felt, the more distanced they were from the animals they
despised. Dionysian bloodlust rejected this arrogance. Authors
who wanted to give their readers this shocking message told
stories of women driven to distraction by blood.

Jules Barbey d'Aurevilly and Émile Zola replaced the religious offering with social and political protest and the old
maenads with howling mobs who hunted the enemies of the
people. The most well-known example is the horrific scene from
Zola's *Germinal* (1885), in which striking miners, led by infuriated
women, hunt Maigrat, a shopkeeper who allowed his poor and
exploited female customers to buy goods in exchange for sexual
favours. The vengeful crowd hate him even more than they hate
the mine-owners, who live from their investments. When he
takes flight from the striking maenads like a modern Pentheus,
Maigrat clambers up onto the roof of his besieged shop in blind
panic. The loud screams from below – 'After the cat! Do for him!'
– make Maigrat tremble with fear, causing him to lose his grip

and roll off the roof. He falls to the ground, breaking his neck and splitting his skull open:

> They were stupefied at first . . . and forgot the shop, with their eyes fixed on the wall along which a thin red streak was slowly flowing down. And the cries ceased, and silence spread over the growing darkness. All at once the hooting began again. It was the women, who rushed forward overcome by the drunkenness of blood. 'Then there is a good God, after all! Ah, the bloody beast, he's done for!' They surrounded the still warm body. They insulted it with laughter, abusing his shattered head, the dirty-chops, vociferating in the face of death the long-stored rancour of their starved lives.[9]

In his *Bewitched* (1852), Barbey d'Aurevilly also knew 'that the blood had, as usual, its cruel fascination. In the place of calming the mob, it intoxicated it, adding thirst to drunkenness.'[10] Yet it was Zola who took the comparison with maenadic violence the furthest. The women stuff Maigrat's dead mouth with earth – 'the bread he had refused to give' – and move around the body 'smelling him like she-wolves'. They have yet another reason for wreaking revenge on Maigrat.[11] The *sparagmos* becomes a castration. They do not stick the head of Pentheus on their thyrsus staffs, but the penis of the unfortunate shopkeeper. The women carry 'the pitiful flesh [which] hung like a waste piece of meat on a butcher's stall' like a trophy on their protest march.[12] Onlookers who watch the barbarous events from a distance think it is a piece of pork or a rabbit skin. Here, Zola was referring indirectly to the maenadic practice of *omophagia*; real cannibalism would have made the horrific scene less credible.

Zola did not see the intoxicating effect of blood as a myth. It fits in perfectly with the naturalist philosophy underpinning all his writings: some people still have a predatory nature which, thanks to the right genes and in the right circumstances, pierce the veneer of civilization. Zola was by no means the only one in nineteenth-century France to attribute importance to the intoxicating power of blood. Influential historian Hippolyte Taine knew that blood had had an exhilarating effect during the September murders of 1792, when a hysterical mob killed hundreds of opponents of the Revolution.[13] Georges Clemenceau, later premier of France, saw the Dionysian power of blood during the Paris Commune in 1871. As mayor of Montmartre, he witnessed the mutilation of generals Lecomte and Thomas by revolutionaries.[14]

French and Italian intellectuals who were concerned about the increasing mass protests demanding greater social justice and democratic power-sharing were quick to pick up on such anecdotes.[15] Frightened by riotous demonstrations and tenacious strikes that would sometimes get out of hand, they presented themselves as researchers of the masses and formulated imaginative theories about the evocative power, the infectious influence or the semi-conscious violence that emanated from protesting crowds. How could normal adult citizens turn into befuddled and brainless animals that unquestioningly followed their most primitive instincts? How could a crowd achieve such a hypnotic effect, changing individuals into submissive, pugnacious or self-sacrificing cells of a malignant organism? In an age obsessed with loss of control, whether during a spiritualist seance, a hypnosis show or a street protest, and with the overthrow of traditional, hierarchical roles – the plebs seizing power or women taking positions usually filled by men – these intellectual fantasts found a broad readership.

A good example was *La folla delinquente* (1891) by Scipio Sighele, a disciple of the better-known Cesare Lombroso, which was quickly translated into French and English. A year later, Henry Fournial published his dissertation on the same theme and Gabriel Tarde wrote a summary article for the notorious *Archives d'anthropologie criminelle*, but these publications did not reach a wide public. The same year, 1892, saw the publication of the French translation of Lombroso's two-volume work (co-written with his colleague Rodolfo Laschi) on political crime and revolutions. A few years later, in 1895, the anti-Semite and popularizer of science Gustave Le Bon produced what may be the best synthesis on the hysteria of crowds and mobs in his *La psychologie des foules*, published in English as *The Crowd: A Study of the Popular Mind*. This was followed later, in 1907, by a study by unknown doctor Henry Chantala with the explicit title *Les folie de la foule* (The Madness of Crowds). Although the opinions expressed in these publications varied widely, the authors were convinced that contact with blood had an exhilarating effect. They all spoke of *ivresse de sang* (the intoxication of blood) that drove mobs wild. Sighele added that bloodlust was often accompanied by sexual lust. One perversion aroused the other, and the doubled pleasure spurred the cruelty and violence even further. This state of arousal was particularly dangerous for women. While men knew no equal in individual cruelty, women surpassed them in collective sadism. In Sighele's words: 'If a woman becomes dizzy from the blood [*vertige de sang*] she becomes a hyena that knows no limits or inhibitions.'[16]

Chantala was aware that this bestial bloodlust initially came up against our normal aversion to blood: 'When the mob sheds blood, they first experience revulsion, but if they do not stop, and overcome their initial disgust, they taste it full of passion and fall upon their prey like an alcoholic on his victim and tremble with sensual pleasure.'[17] Everyone agreed that blood drove mobs into a frenzy.[18] On the bloodbath of the September murders of 1792, Lombroso and Laschi concluded that

> The witnesses of the bloodbaths of 1792 confirmed that, by the third day, the throat-slitters [*égorgeurs*] could no longer stop. It was the sight of blood [*vue de sang*] that

urged them to carry on. The killing instinct is like a fire that slumbers below the ashes, but awakes at the first breath of air.[19]

Blood was like oil on the revolutionary fire.

HAEMOTHYMIA

The maenadic fantasy was revived in the crowd. That was remarkable. Until the nineteenth century, no one knew that blood could send mobs into a frenzy. Not that crowds had never got wildly out of hand before that. The Belgian historian Vincent Vandenberg has collected examples of cannibalistic mania but found no allusions to the inflammatory effect of blood on crowds before the modern period.[20] The only group driven crazy by blood, as in Ammianus Marcellinus' description of the Austoriani, was that of soldiers or warriors who turned into beasts at the sight, smell or taste of blood. In exceptional cases, the transformation was more positive. When the Moors laid siege to the Spanish city of Daroca in the thirteenth century, a Communion cloth hanging over the chasuble of a priest, and on which the stains of six bleeding hosts could be seen, gave the Christian soldiers so much energy that they repelled the attack, launched a counterattack and forced the Moors to retreat. In what is certainly not the official version of events, holy crusader St John of Capistrano tells how the blood of Christ incited the soldiers to violence 'as blood excites elephants'.[21] In the nineteenth century, too, some authors knew that intense blood contact turned men into beasts, though they abandoned the comparison with elephants. Other animals were more suitable. In boys' adventure books on the life of wild animals, the frenzied actions of soldiers intoxicated by blood who could not stop killing were compared with the bloodthirsty behaviour of tigers and wolves. In *L'homme et les animaux* (Man and Animals, 1877), Marquis Bourbon del Monte compared the inexhaustible attacking power of tigers with 'a soldier who, at the end of a battle, wades up to his knees through corpses and continues to kill everything that moves, drunken at the sight of blood'.[22]

The notion that crowds became bloodthirsty, especially if there were women among them, was thus new. Another new phenomenon was nineteenth-century doctors encountering patients in their practices, hospitals and institutions who became sexually aroused by blood; people for whom, in Lombroso's words, 'blood gave a special stimulation to indulge in carnal love'.[23] This psychiatric disorder would be given the name *haemothymia*, though others called it *mania sanguinis* or *folie sanguinaire*. Doctors' waiting rooms were full of varied groups of patients: a five-year-old boy who would get an erection if a schoolmate had a nosebleed; an adolescent who masturbated in the bath while fantasizing about blood flowing in the bathtub; a French surgeon who became aroused when he opened a woman's abdomen during an operation, clearly a case of *sadisme chirurgal*. More common were the *piqueurs de filles*, who liked to prick young women with a knife in the street in the hope of getting excited at the sight of flowing female blood. Around 1820, when attacks by *piqueurs* in Paris reached epidemic proportions, these erotomaniacs were classified more specifically, depending on their favourite part of the body. The *piqueurs de fesses* preferred the buttocks, *de doigts* the fingers and *de jambes* the legs.[24] There were women in the waiting rooms, too. Although they were more likely to experience bloodlust during collective violence, some would have an orgasm during dog fights or while leafing through illustrated books on Christian martyrs. One woman would cut her husband's buttocks with a knife during their nocturnal lovemaking. The resulting flow of blood would turn her into a lascivious wildcat. Her doctor attributed this exceptional form of female bloodlust to the irregular menstrual cycle of the *piqueuse*.[25]

These were largely innocent deviations from normal behaviour. But how many murderers safely behind bars had not been driven to kill by bloodlust? This was the question posed by psychiatrist Thomas Claye Shaw in 1909 in an address to the Medico-Legal Society in London. It was Claye Shaw who coined the term *haemothymia* to describe the subject of his lecture. So as not to appear overly keen to create a sensation, he had given his address the neutral title 'On a Prominent Motive in Murder'. 'Lust for blood' would certainly have made the society's censors a little more nervous.[26] Claye Shaw's less sensational title showed that he wished to rectify something. Research into the motives for murder neglected the role played by blood. He admitted that blood did not have the same effect on everyone. Some people would feel ill at the smell of blood, while it could calm others. But there could be no doubt at all that, in certain circumstances, it could have an arousing effect. The court doctors nodded in agreement. In a discussion that followed the lecture, one of Claye Shaw's colleagues expressed doubts that bloodlust was a prominent motive for murder but 'agreed that the smell and sight of blood tended to exercise a certain effect in many cases and did not doubt that the bloody scenes of the guillotine had assisted in inflaming the passions of the mob during the Terror in Paris.'[27]

Haemothymia was not something to be proud of. Sweet ladies full of compassion would become violent and ruthless. At the sight of blood 'the face of even a beautiful woman is transformed, with injected eyes, gnashing teeth, and convulsive tremors'.[28] Healthy men would become pathologically perverse. Bloodlust was a relapse into barbarity. When combined with sex, it became a psychiatric disorder for which it was possible to be committed to an asylum or sent to prison. Bestial bloodlust was repugnant. No one liked to be compared to a cruel beast. And yet, in apposite doses and in the hands of experienced men, bloodlust was an impulse that was not pathological but completely normal. When hunting or fighting, or in times of war, it was considered tough and manly to show your animal nature. In circumstances that called for aggression, it was appropriate to feel and to enjoy bloodlust.

There was always something of the animal and the barbarian in a real man. Nothing was worse than a lack of bloodlust.

BLOODHOUNDS

The duke contentedly looked through the lowered window of the first-class carriage. He could hear the barking of his hounds and the thumping of horses' hoofs against the sides of the rear wagons that he had especially reserved for the animals. Within a few minutes, they would be able to leave the train. After four days of travelling, they had reached the station at Poitiers. Instead of the steam and smoke that the locomotive blew across the platform, they would soon be breathing in the fresh country air again. The doubt that had been gnawing at him for the whole journey disappeared: what had possessed him to leave his cherished hunting grounds around Badminton House to come to the depths of France to hunt an animal that no one had seen in the forests of his homeland since the seventeenth century? It had all started with a letter from Monsieur Auguis, head of wolf hunting in the department of Vienne, who had asked the 8th Duke of Beaufort to sell him a number of his hounds. The eccentric English aristocrat replied that his hounds were not for sale, but that he would be pleased to present Monsieur Auguis with a pair as a gift, on condition that he visited his country house in Gloucestershire to select them himself. Both were sportsmen and passionate about hunting with hounds. The first volume of the prestigious sports encyclopaedia the *Badminton Library of Sports and Pastimes*, which the duke initiated in 1885, was devoted entirely to hunting and had been edited by the duke himself. Some months later, on the gravel drive in front of his country house, the duke said farewell to Auguis and two of his best hounds. He assured the Frenchman once again that he would go to Poitiers the following spring to hunt wolves for the first time in his life, and would do so with his own pack of hounds and his thoroughbred horses. Despite Auguis' insistence that the duke accept his invitation in exchange for the magnificent hounds, as the coach containing the Frenchman and his two barking acquisitions disappeared in a cloud of dust, the duke realized that it was not a good idea.[29]

He was not concerned about the hunt itself. He knew that wolves, especially the old males, had enormous stamina and that a hunting party could easily last for several days. Sometimes, you would be 50 kilometres (30 mi.) from your starting point before you cornered the exhausted beast. The almost forty-year-old aristocrat was in excellent physical condition and had no problem at all with the idea of sitting in the saddle in rough weather from 9 a.m. until midnight, spurring on his tired hunting horse. To spread the burden of all that galloping, he had loaded eighteen horses onto the ferry at Folkestone, and would share them with the three friends who had accompanied him and his son, the young Lord Worcester, who was only too happy to take more than a month off from Eton College. Nor was the duke overly worried about the much-feared animal that attacked cattle and children in the French countryside, killing them or infecting them with rabies. While he knew that a few of his sixty hounds would not be making the return trip to England, to limit the damage he ensured that collars were made for each hound, with sharp spikes to discourage the wolf's jaws. Auguis also permitted the use of a pistol or hammer to put the wolf out of its misery, if necessary. There was no need for it to fight to the bitter end. Yet the best way to spare your hounds was, as always, to make sure that they themselves were in a frenzy. The less bloodthirsty your hounds were, the greater was the chance that they, rather than the wolf, would become the prey. And that was what the duke was concerned about.

Of course, the hounds had to learn how to follow a wolf's trail, hunt it down and kill it. No animal does that of its own accord. Turning a dog into a hunter was a long process of training and learning from older, more experienced hounds. Dogs have, by nature, a sharp nose and a predator's instinct, so that they are willing to follow their prey for a long time and to kill it so as to enjoy a meal of fresh raw meat. But training them to know just which prey they should smell, kill and tear apart was the work of the *piqueur* in charge of the pack. How could you teach English hounds to hunt wolves instead of foxes in only a few days? The duke didn't need to worry about the characteristics of his reddish black bloodhounds, however. They were descended from the legendary hounds kept at the abbey at Saint-Hubert, in modern-day Belgium. These hounds, which weighed around 50 kilograms (110 lb), were used by the English to hunt jackals in India and by American plantation owners to pursue runaway slaves. They were normally well-behaved family dogs, but if you fed them meat they would turn into monsters that would obey only the cracking of a whip. The duke's thoroughbred hounds were the source of great envy in France, where, like many of their owners, they had not survived the Revolution. All credit was due to Auguis for not giving in to this jealousy and instead asking Beaufort to sell him a few of his dogs so that he could crossbreed them with his own *Persac* and *Griffon fauve de Bretagne* hounds. He urgently needed fresh blood to avoid problems caused by inbreeding.

The greatest obstacle was that dogs are not keen on wolves.[30] Whether the smaller foxhounds, whose job was to follow the trail, the faster greyhounds that chased after the prey and kept it at bay until the rest of the pack arrived, or the bloodhounds that finished the job, none liked the taste of wolf's meat. Dogs are, on the other hand, easily tempted by hare's flesh and blood. The French writer Alexandre Dumas was of the opinion that the pope should excommunicate Neapolitan chefs because they could not prepare *civet de lièvre*. There were plenty of recipes, but the liver and the blood of hares went to Italian hunting dogs and not to French tourists, which Dumas considered unforgivable.[31]

Nor is it difficult to arouse bloodlust among dogs for deer, but it is much more work to get them interested in foxes or wild boar, and certainly in wolves. You have to literally force dogs to eat wolf's meat. You would only know that you had overcome this natural aversion after the hunt, if the hounds devoured the *curée du loup* with sufficient gusto.

The *curée* is the traditional conclusion of the hunt when the hungry pack, their tongues lolling out of their panting jaws, wait for the signal from the horn before falling upon the dead prey and tearing it to pieces.[32] This ritual takes place either at the spot where the prey has been killed (*curée chaude*), or somewhere more practical (*curée froide*), for example where the hunters are spending the night or where they gather at the start of the hunt. Sometimes the hounds are given the whole animal, but often only certain parts that are not suitable for human consumption. Hunting handbooks contain recipes with meat and blood as basic ingredients, complemented by cheese and milk. Every *curée* serves a double purpose. Rewarding the dogs means they become accustomed to the smell and taste of the animals being hunted. In this way, the *curée* satisfies and refines their hunting instinct. The problem was, dogs turned up their noses at the *curée de loup*. After the horn sounded, they stood their ground, wagging their tails, and turned their backs on the wolf or sniffed a little at its pelt. Their bloodlust was gone. Several explanations have been put forward for this. Perhaps wolves have a strong scent, like martens and weasels, which secrete a strong, unpleasant smell from their anal glands. Do dogs – like people – not like to eat the flesh of other carnivores because it may contain more pathogens? Or do wolves have a surplus of *salvajum* or *ferum*, the mythical odour and taste of the wild woods and the uncivilized world?[33] No one knew the exact reason, but when the Grand Wolfcatcher, Breton Baron Halna du Fretay – whose father had held the same position before him and who had been born into a prominent family whose love of horses and dogs was as hereditary as its aristocratic titles – told everyone how difficult it had been to get his *Griffon fauve de Bretagne* to enjoy a *curée de loup*, it was a bad omen. The baron added that this resistance, almost impossible to overcome, only disappeared in hounds whose forebears had always hunted wolves.[34] The duke had been warned. The humiliation he most feared during his journey to France was not too much desire to hunt among his hounds, but too little.

His misgivings dissipated briefly when he arrived at the station in Poitiers on 1 April 1863. The spring sun was shining brightly. The hounds and horses were unloaded without difficulty and the Comte de Chabot, one of Augius' aristocratic hunting friends, gave the duke a charming welcome. He offered the Englishman – whom he immediately recognized on the platform in his long green corduroy jacket, his brown leather trousers and his impeccable tall riding boots, which were turned down just below the knee – the hospitality of his hunting lodge in Nieuil-l'Espoir. There the duke and his English entourage could rest for a few days to recover from the journey, together with his French friend Auguis, while waiting for the two coaches and the luggage wagon that still had to cross the Channel. And it allowed them time to think of how to give the English hounds an appetite for wolf meat.

The first encounter with French wolves was a failure. In the forest near Cartes, the French *piqueurs* got the two best tracker dogs in the region, including the famous Clairon, to hunt down a young wolf. The dogs virtually drove their prey right under the duke's nose, but his hounds hardly noticed it. There had been rumours that, to arouse his hounds' appetite for the *curée du loup*, the duke had bought a wolf from a zoo and had his pack tear it to pieces. Whether this was true or not, the duke's hounds did not acquire a taste for wolf's meat. After a few weeks they followed their French counterparts better, but came running back barking once the wolf had disappeared into the thick undergrowth of the first wood. They chased the wolf away, but did not go after it. After a second failed attempt in the woods near Persac, Émile de La Besge, another friend of Auguis', invited the duke to his chateau for a light lunch washed down with copious quantities of claret. As the atmosphere became more cheerful, La Besge enticed the duke with a glass of cognac to take a look at his kennel of several dozen Persac hounds, a breed famed for hunting wolves. He made the duke an offer, which the latter accepted gracefully: 'Milord, if it pleases you, you may make use of my hounds. They are excellent at hunting wolves and I can assure you that they will be able to train your dogs.'[35] A few days later, full of renewed energy, the British dogs went hunting through the forest of Verrière, accompanied by Ténébro, the most famous Persac hound with a formidable service record. But again it ended in fiasco. The first time, Ténébro was forced to hunt the wolf down on his own and grab it by the throat. His owner found him just in time to tie the wolf up with his whip in its jaws and saddle straps around its head and legs. After sounding the call on the horn, the lost foxhounds and Persac dogs came running from all over the woods to tuck into the *curée*, now with a little more enthusiasm.

The duke was severely saddened by the fact that the English hounds not only made a mess of the hunt, but they confused their French counterparts. During the final hunt, however, after a wolf's head had been spotted sticking up out of the bushes, the fox- and greyhounds followed the Persacs closely as they chased it across the open fields and sank their teeth firmly into its legs and buttocks. The duke was almost happy when he saw his own bloodhounds following suit about 100 metres (330 ft) away. That only made his disillusionment even worse when he galloped into a small wood and saw that all his dogs were no longer following the wolf but two deer that had taken flight at the sound of the barking pack.

The Duke of Beaufort should have followed his intuition. When he went to Paris at the end of April to relax after the fiasco of his hunting trip, he found himself a laughing stock in both France and England. French hunters sung humiliating songs about his haughtiness. The English magazine *Punch* depicted the moribund duke on foot, his pack of hounds milling around him, while an aged wolf peed against his impeccable riding boots with their turned-down tops. Despite all the mockery, the French could appreciate the daring, the eccentricity and the obsession of this English aristocrat who lived completely for his sport. Although his famed bloodhounds did not have the same obsession for tracking wolves down and biting them to death – in that respect, he had to admit the superiority of the French breeds – the duke epitomized the ideal of barbaric masculinity that had a great following among a European elite with sufficient time to indulge in sports and pastimes. The duke may have lost out to the French wolves, but a certain way of life, in which bloodlust was not disapproved of but valued highly, did gain in popularity. In opposition to the effeminate intellectualism of the enlightened citizen who expected so much from modernity, the English aristocracy revered the nostalgic pleasures of physical effort, the smell of horse sweat and steaming manure, the exhilarating yelping of the hounds and the beauty of the greenwood and the countryside. Happiness lay not in the future but in the past. It was sought not by leaving our animal origins behind but by returning to them. Leaping over a stream in the saddle of a galloping horse, flanked by swimming hounds, on the trail of a wild and dangerous beast, made ancient instincts rise to the surface, together with feelings of unprecedented joy. Following the scent of a wolf, the hunter became himself a predator who revelled in flying spatters of blood, the tearing of raw flesh and the wildness of violence.

BLOOD SPORTS

Hunting – and certainly with bloodhounds – fitted in perfectly with that ideal of barbaric masculinity. And as hunting was largely a privilege enjoyed by the nobility, the ideal remained sufficiently refined. It was never barbaric in the sense that wild savages were. The bestiality of the hunt was not based on a lack of civilization or a need to survive, but was a self-chosen diversion. By contrast to bourgeois intellectualism, this ideal accentuated the importance of physical and animal pleasure, which found its zenith in the controlled cruelty of the hunting party. Hunting was bloodlust that was not perverse or threatening, a primitivism that the aristocracy took seriously, a form of maenadism that was tolerated because it was controlled by men and performed by dogs. Because women were kept away from this mix of violence and lust, the bloodlust could not get out of hand. The bestial revelry was in safe hands.

Hunting is full of blood rituals that immerse its participants in an atmosphere of wild barbarism. The blood emphasizes the fact that we are in a primitive external world, with its own laws – or lack of them. English hunters underwent a rite of passage called 'blooding', whereby their fellow hunters would smear a novice's face with the blood of his first kill.[36] Belgian hunters still push the faces of new comrades into the open abdomen of a deer or boar so that the red-black blood clings to their nose, chin and cheeks. For a few seconds, they inhale the scent of the game and taste the blood, while the other hunters, laughing and singing, hit them on the buttocks with a broomstick. Traditions vary from country to country.[37] In Hungary, after an exceptionally good hunt, a glass of deer's blood would be poured over the head of the best hunter. In Poland, the sign of the cross would be made in blood on his forehead. In France and Germany, tradition prescribed that the hunt end with a *brisée du gibier*, or *Bruch* in German. This ritual – the disappearance of which is much lamented by modern-day hunters – entailed laying a fir twig on the left flank of the dead animal, with the top end of the twig pointing to the head if it was a male, and another in its mouth. The master of the hunt would then gently push a third twig into the blood of the wound and lay it on the skinning knife or hat of the hunter who had made the kill. This closing ritual was repeated for every kill, although the animals varied from region to region. Sometimes, female animals were excluded. All these blood rituals emphasize that hunting, no matter how elitist, will always be controlled barbarism. There is no such thing as a clean and non-violent hunt. But this ritualized contact with blood does not incite blood rush among the hunters. On the contrary, they tend to feel an overpowering disgust for the blood, the entrails, the excrement and shattered bones. It is a fixed rule of hunting in every region that every hunter guts his own kill.[38] It is an unpleasant task that must not be left to someone else.

And yet the blood of dead game can bring hunters into a state of exhilaration. An often-cited example is that of Spanish philosopher José Ortega y Gasset who, in his *Meditations on Hunting* (1942), described this double-edged experience as follows: 'Blood, the liquid that carries and symbolizes life, is meant to flow secretly, through the interior of the body. When it is spilled . . . a reaction of disgust and terror is produced.' This response, which precedes all ethical reflection, is 'the frightening mystery of blood'. But that is only a first impression: 'If the blood insists on presenting itself, if it flows abundantly, it ends by producing the opposite effect: it intoxicates, excites, maddens both man and beast.' According to Ortega, who himself hardly hunted but who devoured books on it (he wrote his *Meditations* for friend and hunter Count de Yebes), blood possessed an 'unequalled orgiastic power'.[39] It was because of this power that spectators at bullfights or Roman gladiator fights could become addicted to this 'stupefying drug'.

The American food philosopher Michael Pollan showed in an article for the *New York Times Magazine* in 2006 that blood rush can also affect modern hunters. Pollan begins the article with a few scornful remarks about the 'hunter porn' of Ernest Hemingway and Ortega, who sit on the cadavers of freshly killed elephants and spout drivel about hunting as an authentic experience that releases primitive instincts. But then he shoots a wild boar himself and discovers the truth behind the cliché. A photograph of the hunt arrives in his inbox the following evening, and he freely admits that the bloodlust is unmistakable. In the picture, Pollan is kneeling next to the boar he has killed. Blood is pouring from the animal's head and spreading 'like a river delta' towards the bottom of the picture. In one hand Pollan is holding his gun and, with the other, he is leaning on the dead boar's flank. What he had found obscene and laughable about the hunter porn of Hemingway and Ortega he now recognizes in himself. He is sitting next to the dead animal, full of pride, sporting a maniacal grin. He did not exclude the possibility that the flowing blood had befuddled his mind, saying, 'If I didn't know better, I would have said that the man in the picture was drunk. And perhaps he was, seized in the throes of some sort of Dionysian intoxication, the bloodlust that Ortega says will sometimes overtake the successful hunter.'[40] What appeared from the outside to be nothing more than a worn cliché of barbaric masculinity was for those involved an unforgettable experience. Anyone who loved hunting cherished the experience of bloodlust because it assured them of a deeper connection with an uncivilized world of savagery and violence. Anyone who experiences that connection will realize that every civilization has been nothing more than an artificial island floating on a sea of uncontrollable natural forces. Bloodlust brought us into contact with an elementary understanding that our primitive ancestors still possessed. Those who condemned hunting did not doubt the intoxicating effect of blood. For them, however, this bestial bloodlust served a completely different purpose. It proved that hunting brought out the worst in people, and did not occur in such a controlled and civilized way as was often claimed.[41] Hunting was not an ode to moral virtues like courage, self-control and patience, but an immoral debasement to our animal selves. No matter how diametrically opposed their views were, both sides saw bloodlust as a real phenomenon.

This ideal of barbaric masculinity was by no means restricted to those who could afford to hunt for sport. In the eighteenth and nineteenth centuries, it spread to more democratic blood sports. Dogs now not only chased wild animals and tore them to pieces in the open countryside or thick forests, but fought them or other bloodhounds, or ran after rats at exuberant village fairs or in back alleys and squares in the grim suburbs of big cities. In France, until the start of the twentieth century, you could bet on how quickly *chiens ratiers* – usually fox terriers – would bite rats to death in a wooden 'arena' called a *ratodrome*. In parts of the Dutch and Belgian countryside, around the same time, dogs would be set upon chained-up badgers. The first dogs would be no match for the badger but after some hours it would be exhausted and no longer able to fight them off. In England, dogs were baited to attack chained-up bulls and bite them in the rump. This was officially to tenderize the meat since it was believed that stress improved the quality. Unofficially, it was because the spectators enjoyed the combination of bestial violence and human omnipotence, which the bull-baiters found so masculine.[42]

It was not only animals that fell victim to all this masculine aggression: men did not spare themselves either. German students hacked away at each other with daggers in smoky student halls during the *Mensur*. English public schoolboys boxed with bare fists in school playgrounds. Frenchmen crossed rapiers or shot at each other with pistols from a safe distance during dawn duels in the Bois de Boulogne. Georges Clemenceau proved his honour in more than twenty duels.[43] Across all social classes, physical violence has always been the preferred way to protect or restore masculine identity. The more enthusiastic you were about blood sports, the more you believed religiously in core male values like honour, patriotism, perseverance and respect for superior leadership. Here, too, the notion that blood could incite the emotions served both the proponents and opponents of blood sports. For the former, bloodlust was the deeper emotional reason for organizing or participating in these activities. Blood brought a real man back into contact with his deeper nature, while civilization and moral progress distanced him from that primal masculine nature and forced him into an effeminate intellectualist corset. For a small but growing group of opponents of blood sports, who made mincemeat of every rational justification for them, the bloodlust of hunters was no different to the perverse, sadistic, dangerous variant that scientists encountered in large mobs and among psychopaths and crazed women. For these activist opponents, there was no such thing as morally acceptable bloodlust. All bloodlust was *haemothymia*, and thus pathological.

As happens ever more frequently in Western history, the activists won out. The civilization offensive defeated the civilization defence. Blood sports were banned and gradually replaced by bloodless competitions. The age of barbaric masculinity passed and the ideal of athletic heroism ignited a non-violent Olympic flame. Declining numbers of upper-class students were leaving top English universities with 'no degree but a pedigree of dogs' as the illustrious result of their expensive studies.[44] Football fields and lawn tennis courts replaced the hunting grounds through which bloodhounds had run free, searching for the tracks of wolves and foxes. At the end of the nineteenth century, the famed Badminton Library concluded its series of sports encyclopaedias with cricket, football and athletics. The series had started fifteen years previously with hunting, fishing and shooting. Not that the non-violent alternatives to blood sports were any less patriotic or militaristic; good athletes were still good soldiers willing to sacrifice themselves for their countries, but the new athletic ideal of masculinity offered a balance between brains and brawn that was better suited to modernity. Fair play, the new moral code that originated in England, did not allow wild, unruly behaviour to cross the chalk lines that marked out the playing fields of civilization.[45]

WILD ORIGINS

A weak winter sun entered the hall through the left eye of the red deer. The pale light was just strong enough for the visitors to see the row of stained-glass windows, while the guide asked us to follow her along the carpeted floor between the ribbons marking out the route. The carpet wound its way through the hunting lodge, like a footpath through an old Japanese garden. Our eyes were not fixed on our obedient feet but on the wild hunting scenes depicted in brightly coloured windowpanes designed by the German Expressionist artist Arthur Hennig. Anton Kröller and his wife Helene Kröller-Müller had commissioned Hennig to portray the legend of St Hubert, the patron saint of hunters, in stained glass for the hunting lodge in their country estate in the Netherlands, De Hoge Veluwe. Famed architect Hendrik Berlage had designed the lodge in the shape of a stag's head. The first series of windows were considered too dark and classical for this *Gesamtkunstwerk* and were replaced a year later, in 1923, by a design with more movement and emotion. The original scene, which had been rather respectable and static, became an explosive and turbulent painting. On the extreme left is the wild world of the hunt, with deer fleeing from the pack hounds. The hounds bite a rearing stag in the neck and bring another crashing to the ground. In the middle is St Hubert, kneeling by a stag with a shining cross in its antlers. While hunting on Good Friday, he is admonished by the stag and pledges to give up worldly pleasures and lead a monastic life of prayer and spiritual purity. In the window on the right, which is a complete contrast to the one on the left, the forest is at peace. Wild animals no longer have to flee, but stroll lovingly along woodland paths or lie down for a while to take a rest from doing nothing. At the bottom we see a fawn drinking at his mother's breast while she herself calmly drinks from a stream. The hell of the hunt has turned into a leisurely, green paradise.[1]

In a hunting lodge, a stained-glass portrayal of the eternal struggle between good and evil – wild violence versus peace-loving tranquillity – seems ambiguous to say the least. On the paving stones in front of the entrance, where the stag's antlers are depicted architecturally, there was never a shining cross to be seen, only the dead animals that Anton Kröller and his friends had shot while hunting in the Veluwe park and laid out in rows, species by species. Part of the architectural antlers consisted of kennels for the hounds. The dogs no longer chased the game to rip it to pieces – Anton hunted in the modern way, killing with guns rather than dogs – but did stir the animals up so that the hunters could shoot them. Either way, the wild animals were certainly not left in peace to drink from a forest stream.

Despite the abundance of philosophical works in the library of Anton's smoking room, the evening conversation around the stove was more likely to be about hunting than about Nietzsche and Bergson. Although José Ortega y Gasset described philoso-phers as alert hunters of the inner world, who would descend into the perilous jungle of ideas,[2] no thought, no matter how profound, could equal the smell of skinned game, the sensation of physical exhaustion, the image of a stumbling stag or the taste of a woodcock. The wild world of the hunt was a sinful one, but without the sin there was simply no hunt. That world may have been repugnant to pious believers, but it exercised a great attrac-tion, not only for depraved minds but for wealthy Christians with a passion for hunting. Compared to the peace and purity of the religious life, that sinful existence was a lot more exciting. If Anton had to choose between the two panes of stained glass, left or right, he would in all honesty prefer the life before St Hubert's conversion.

Anyone who loved hunting would do better not to live in the biblical Paradise. There was nothing of interest to a hunter there. The Garden of Eden was a bloodless world with no pain, suffering, fear or violence. If there was fire, you could not burn yourself with it. Nor could you drown in the babbling waters of the forest streams. Pine needles did not prick, like those on artificial Christmas trees. The most remarkable feature of Paradise was that no one ate meat, making hunting completely futile. 'The wolf and the lamb shall feed together, and the lion shall eat straw like the bullock: and dust shall be the serpent's meat. They shall not hurt nor destroy in all my holy mountain, saith the Lord', wrote Isaiah (65:25) about paradise. Genesis 1:30 makes it clear that this vegetarianism applied not only to predatory animals but to people: 'And to every beast of the earth, and to every fowl of the air, and to every thing that creepeth upon the earth, wherein there is life, I have given every green herb for meat: and it was so.' Since Adam and Eve walked around naked, they had no need to hunt animals for their skins. Hunters should be grateful to Eve for eating the apple, after which Yahweh expelled her and Adam from paradise. Admittedly, life did become a little less comfortable after that. You could now burn yourself on fire and it was a good idea to take swimming lessons if you didn't want to drown in a deep lake. The Earth, too, became wilder. Thistles and thorns now grew alongside the harmless plants, flowers and fruit. If you pricked yourself on a pine needle it would hurt. The ground became rockier and less fertile and you had to work hard to grow food. Fleas, mosquitoes and other irritating pests appeared. For women, bearing children became a painful ordeal. Contractions and the menstrual cycle reminded them of the original sin, to such an extent that some over-imaginative theologians thought that menstrual blood was fermented apple juice.[3] The most spectacular development was that animals threw off their yokes and became wild. They turned on each other. Lions and wolves were no longer satisfied with the taste of hay and grass. They sunk their fangs and open claws into the bones of fleeing deer. And if their regular prey was not available, they would attack people. That put paid to peace and harmony. The world was divided into violent predators and their frightened prey. Even pets now had to be forced into obedience. If people wanted to survive, they needed to be aggressive to keep everything under control, they needed meat to give them the strength to fulfil that arduous task and animal skins to conceal their ridiculously pale bodies. The good news was that now they could hunt.

Western cultural history is full of extremes – dreams and nightmares, utopias and dystopias, civilization and savagery – and forced contrasts about which we have ambiguous feelings that go deeper than self-evident moral standpoints. While we know all too well which world we would prefer morally, that wild alternative often holds a greater fascination and, as we muse about the ideal civilization, we fear that it would be tedious and dull. The anti-world harbours a life that is taboo or which violates our most elementary rules of civilization, but it makes us curious or offers us pleasures that are difficult to find in civilized society. It is a world without morals, which we have eagerly depicted in all kinds of myths, of which the biblical Fall of Man is but one. According to the poet Hesiod, in his time the Greeks believed themselves to be surrounded in time and space by the 'silver generation'. This generation was preceded by an idyllic 'golden generation', from which it could not have differed more greatly. The silver generation was violent by nature, lived short lives, endured endless suffering and knew no religion. It was so godless that it made no sacrificial animal offerings to the gods.[4] On the borders of Greek civilization lived cannibalistic monsters, like the giant Polyphemus, from whom Odysseus succeeded in escaping, man-eating tribes like the Massagetae, related to the Scythians, who drank the blood of their dead enemies from skulls, and the Issedones, who lived in the far north and ate their own dead. Roman authors added the remote Irish to the list.[5] For the Greeks and Romans, too, uninhibited sex, violent cruelty and taboo-free eating habits were excesses that you could expect to encounter in remote areas and primitive ages. And yet, such barbarity was, in theory, present in all humans.

In *The Republic*, Plato admits that:

> Our fierce bestial nature, full of food and drink, rouses itself and has its fling and tries to secure its own kind of satisfaction. As you know, there's nothing too bad for it and it's completely lost to all sense and shame. It doesn't shrink from attempting intercourse . . . with a mother or anyone else, man, beast or god, or from murder or eating forbidden food. There is, in fact, no folly nor shamelessness it will not commit.[6]

Fortunately, when awake, it was possible to keep that dormant desire under control. But these inhibitions decreased with time and distance. At the historical origin and the geographical end of civilization, the dividing line between sleep and wakefulness disappeared. And then we humans became a real nightmare. Ebstorf's thirteenth-century *Mappa Mundi*, which was lost during the Second World War, depicted the known world in medieval times around Christ on the cross. His hands and feet protruded through the map, making it obvious how it should be interpreted. Around the edges of the civilized world, just before everything sank below the waves of the eternal sea, lived all kinds of cannibalistic peoples. Christian encyclopaedists added Thracians, Mongols, Tartars and Turks to the list of cruel peoples surrounding civilization. Anyone who was different and lived far away, and was conspicuous by their strange customs and especially their military ambitions, was portrayed as a terrifying barbarian. It was safe only at the centre of the world, close to

Athens, Rome or Jerusalem. If you left the centre and ventured into the big, dark forest, you would find yourself in a wild and godless world; a world full of primitive people as savage as the wolves that stole through the forest.

Although the arms and legs of the cartographical Christ figure became longer and longer as trade, war and colonization added new lands to the world map, the stereotypical division between the civilized centre and a primitive periphery remained intact, as did the contrast between a primitive past and a better present basking in welcome progress. To support his secular variant of the Fall of Man, influential English philosopher Thomas Hobbes referred to the primitive nature of life in pre-colonial America. In an illustration in the first edition of his *De Cive* (On the Citizen, 1642), a political tract in Latin that preceded his much more renowned *Leviathan* (1651), he contrasted the American *Libertas* with the European *Imperium*, in the same way that Hennig juxtaposed savage wilderness and meditative peace.[7] On the right of the frontispiece to *De Cive* stands a half-naked man with a skirt of leaves around his loins, barefoot, with a bow across his chest and spear in his hand. In the background, in the wild natural landscape, it becomes clear why he needs weapons – to kill animals and people. On the left is Lady Justice, clothed, wearing shoes and holding a balance – and a sword. Behind her is an agrarian landscape that brings not only abundant harvests, but law and order, cities full of stone buildings and moments of rest and pleasure for those who work hard on the land. Compared to the constitutional state, which was only possible with a strong central authority – a Leviathan – that restricted your freedoms, the pure state of nature was a primitive hell. The New World was, above all, an unpleasant surprise for Europeans.

The discovery of America presented Christian theologians with a puzzle. Until the end of the Renaissance the world consisted of three continents, Europe, Asia and Africa, as symbolized by the three tiers of the papal tiara. Who were the people that

Columbus and Vespucci discovered? If they were children of Adam, then they had to descend from Noah, but from which of his three children? The people of Asia descended from Shem, those of Europe from Japheth and of Africa from Ham. Had there been a fourth son or a second Adam which the Bible – the Book of Truth – had forgotten? Or were the primitive native Americans, who took scalps and worked gold from Asia, originally Scythians from Eurasia who, according to Herodotus, combined highly developed metallurgical skills with military cruelty? Or were they simply not children of Adam but something between animals and humans that would never be able to understand the mysteries of the Christian faith, as believed by Dominican missionary Domingo de Betanzos (though he retracted this opinion on his deathbed)? Anyone who knew the answer to this question had imagination in abundance to work out why God permitted such primitive godlessness.[8]

How much more elegant was Hobbes's secular anthropology, in which every human community underwent a process of evolution, from wild freedom to controlled civilization? Natural causes like climate, food, conflicts or geography determined why one society was higher up the evolutionary ladder than another. No one doubted that these differences were sometimes grotesque. The list of deficiencies that made Betanzos doubt whether the Spanish or Portuguese colonists were dealing with real people included absence of reasonable notions such as property rights; the eating of unclean food such as raw meat or half-raw fish, and eating without utensils, with dirty hands and at irregular hours; not covering their private parts (even to the extent that missionaries ordered them – not always successfully – to wear clothing when performing forced labour in the gold mines); living in places offering natural shelter, such as under trees, in tents or in damp tents that could not withstand strong winds; the lack of laws, inheritance rights or any form of central authority; the absence of a written language, money-based economy, elementary hygiene, sexual restraint, psychological stability and self-control, and so on.[9] Hobbes saw all of these primitive characteristics in the native inhabitants of Virginia and Bermuda, as portrayed on the frontispiece of *De Cive*, despite being fully aware of the complex nature of the political authority that ruled these territories before colonization. These societies were not willing to surrender their property to foreigners from across the sea without putting up a fight.[10]

On the basis of this colonial fiction, Hobbes built up his anthropological hypothesis that there had never been a paradise or a great exodus from a stranded ark, but that all humanity had once lived in a world in which violence, cruelty, fear and pain reigned. From this amoral primal soup in which man preyed on man like wolves on sheep, civilized humanity had evolved by trial and error, and had developed to such a degree in Europe that it had even become fascinated by those who had not progressed further than the lower levels. In the luxuriant leather armchairs of the colonial empire, he found pleasure in comparing the two extremes on the balance of civilization and felt intense suspense when he visited the dens of his less fortunate fellow humans, not only in remote hamlets and tropical regions but in the dangerous slums of his own capital city.[11] Although he mistrusted religion as an immature form of knowledge, his viewpoint was just as biblical in its dichotomous interpretation of the world. The whole of human history still swung like a pendulum between Hennig's two stained-glass panes.

PREDATORY NATURE

Between 1800 and 1914, three British thinkers saddled us with a pitch-black interpretation of that moral zero. It looked like a prehistoric version of the *ratodrome*, with fox terriers hunting fleeing rats. It was indeed difficult to believe that any god would have devised such a cruel game. For Hobbes, due to the absence of a protective Leviathan, the earliest human history was a deadly struggle of all against all. For Thomas Malthus humans reproduced excessively like rats, creating famine which would bring out the worst in them. For Charles Darwin, the most influential of them all, only the animals that adapted best could survive in a world of scarcity ruled by a ruthless process of selection. Combat, competition, aggression and cruelty honed the scythe of natural selection. The noble savage of French philosopher Jean-Jacques Rousseau could do little to resist all that British violence. In *Prehistoric Times* (1865), the most popular nineteenth-century book on human prehistory, John Lubbock was ruthless in his treatment of such romantic exaltation. In the conclusion, he wrote that:

> There are, indeed, many who doubt whether happiness is increased by civilization, and who talk of the free and noble savage. But the true savage is neither free nor noble; he is a slave to his own wants, his own passions; imperfectly protected from the weather, he suffers from the cold by night and the heat of the sun by day; ignorant of agriculture, living by the chase, and improvident in success, hunger always stares him in the face, and often drives him to the dreadful alternative of cannibalism or death.[12]

For Lubbock's generation, it was crystal clear. Prehistoric man – then limited to *Homo sapiens* and the Neanderthals – only had a greater chance of surviving all that primal misery by becoming a better hunter or a better fox terrier. It was only by perfecting his predatory nature that he could catch more nutritious prey to still his chronic hunger. The other option was not considered: why did he not become a better rat rather than a better dog? We now know that there were many other hominids than *Homo sapiens* and the Neanderthals, but they were smaller and therefore more vulnerable. They made little impression as predators. There are good reasons to believe that those early hominids were likely to have been the prey of packs of hunting hyenas, the extinct sabre-toothed tiger and other big cats, and deadly animals like pythons, crocodiles and large birds of prey that could pluck human children from the ground. Though the hominids ate meat, it would most probably have been the leftover prey of these more imposing predators. In this dangerous world, prehistoric man had better flight and concealment techniques. Defence was more important than attack.[13]

But back then there was no support for the idea of 'man the hunted'. Prehistoric men were seen as hunters who needed high-calorie meat, and that meat came from animals with impressive qualities: crushingly gigantic mammoths, powerful bears, woolly rhinoceroses, and fleet-footed deer, hares and wild horses. If people wanted to kill and eat these animals without coming off worst, then a little skill, cooperation and perseverance was necessary. If the hunt was successful, the rewards were enormous. The fresh, bloody meat tasted good and was nourishing; the skins protected from the cold; better weapons could be made from the bones and tents built from mammoth tusks to protect from the midday sun. And, in their tents, the best hunters had the best sex. In short, life was starting to look good – at least, if their hungry neighbours weren't waiting outside the tent to run off with their meat and their women. So defence against human predators was a must too. Here, again, biting dogs proved more effective than fleeing rats. Developing a predatory nature was rewarding for two reasons: it led to more prey and fewer competitors.

The image of man as a predatory animal dominated the biology and psychology of the second half of the nineteenth century.[14] And the cliché survived into the twentieth century in the work of Raymond Dart, Sherwood Washburn, Robert Ardrey and Richard Wrangham, to name but a few.[15] They continued to believe that hunting and killing was necessary not only for the survival of *Homo sapiens* and the Neanderthals who roamed the cold plateaus of glacial Europe in search of animal protein, but for the australopiths that lived on the African savannah or in the tropical rainforests. The further you went back into the past, the more our expressions of rage resembled those of roaring lions or growling dogs, and the sharper our fangs and finger-nails became. These eventually disappeared as we became more skilled in making weapons. Weapons became our permanent claws and beaks, and because we were not born with them, we had no natural inhibitions about using them against members of our own species. Prehistoric men were fighting, killing, hunting apes who survived by means of unbridled bloodshed. Like a pack of hunting dogs, they ate their fill of mauled carcasses of dead animals until they were satiated.

So much inherited aggression had to leave its traces. The American Darwinist psychologist William James told his audi-ence at the World Peace Congress in Boston in 1904 that 'man, biologically considered . . . is simply the most formidable of all beasts of prey, and, indeed, the only one that preys systematically on its own species.' A few years later he warned that, although it is not senseless, pacifism is certainly very utopian: 'the earlier men were hunting men, and to hunt a neighboring tribe, kill the males, loot the village and possess the females, was the most profitable, as well as the most exciting, way of living . . . War is the *strong* life; it is life *in extremis*.'[16] As late as 1953, the Australian palaeontologist and discoverer of *Australopithecus africanus* (the Taung Child) Raymond Dart surmised that all bloodshed has its roots in that hunger for animal or human flesh that distinguished us from other hominids and primates:

> The blood-bespattered, slaughter-gutted archives of human history from the earliest Egyptian and Sumerian records to the most recent atrocities of the Second World War accord with early universal cannibalism, with animal

and human sacrificial practices of their substitutes in formalized religions and with the world-wide scalping, head-hunting, body-mutilating and necrophilic practices of mankind in proclaiming this common bloodlust differentiator, this predaceous habit, this mark of Cain that separates man dietetically from his anthropoidal relatives and allies him rather with the deadliest of Carnivora.[17]

All human cruelty appeared to be the consequence of our predatory prehistoric nature. Unlike Dart, who simply lumped everything together, Darwin was the perfect example of nuanced distinction and cautious statement. He never said anything about man being carnivorous by nature, he found social feelings as important as lethal weapons, and was sceptical of the assumption that prehistoric behaviour was stored in the genetic material of modern humans. Although his theories encouraged this simplistic, one-sided view of man's predatory nature, he himself rejected it. Nevertheless, in his younger years, Darwin also had his weaker moments. In his *Beagle* diary of 1836, he noted that 'love of the chase is an inherent delight in man, a relic of an *instinctive passion*'.[18] His personal love of hunting undoubtedly fuelled such over-enthusiasm. In his autobiography, the great naturalist, who for a long time was more interested in hunting than studying, confessed: 'The autumns were devoted to shooting, chiefly at Mr. Owen's Woodhouse, and at my Uncle Jos's, at Maer. My zeal was so great that I used to place my shooting boots open by my bed-side when I went to bed, so as not to lose half-a-minute in putting them on in the morning.'[19]

From the end of the nineteenth century, stories full of prehistoric misery in which predatory humans hunted each other or wild animals were also to be found in science-fiction novels such as *La Guerre du feu* (The Quest for Fire, 1909) by the Belgian author J.-H. Rosny. They had great impact because the reader could identify with the characters – scratch a gentleman and you

get a savage. The fact that the two *Homines sapientes* were separated by hundreds of centuries was not a hindrance. Civilized
modern man was linked to his prehistoric bestial ancestors by
heredity. Beneath every Dr Jekyll lurked a Mr Hyde. 'We inherit
the warlike type,' William James assured us: 'Dead men tell no
tales, and if there were any tribes of other type than this they
have left no survivors. Our ancestors have bred pugnacity into
our bone and marrow, and thousands of years of peace won't
breed it out of us.'[20] Our ancestors gave us an instinct to hunt,
fight and attack – New York psychologist Edward Thorndike
distinguished no less than seven such instincts – so that we were
always ready to do battle and enjoy the bloodshed that accompanied it. William James was the most emphatic. Anyone who
thought that human cruelty was a pathological disorder or a
cultural invention was mistaken, because:

> If evolution and the survival of the fittest be true at all,
> the destruction of prey and of human rivals *must* have
> been among the most important of man's primitive func-
> tions, the fighting and the chasing instincts *must* have
> become ingrained. Certain perceptions *must* immedi-
> ately, and without the intervention of inferences and
> ideas, have prompted emotions and motor discharges;
> and both the latter must, from the nature of the case,
> have been very violent, and therefore, when unchecked,
> of an intensely pleasurable kind. It is just because human
> bloodthirstiness is such a primitive part of us that it is
> so hard to eradicate, especially where a fight or a hunt is
> promised as part of the fun.[21]

In a footnote to this passage, James added that blood is 'a very
special object' and is 'the stimulus for a very special interest
and excitement'.[22] Although people would sometimes faint or
panic at the sight of blood, just as cows sometimes respond

with fury to contact with it, bloodlust was an adaptive element of our predatory nature. Once this violent instinct had been given a name, it could be used to explain a lot of phenomena. In 1916, a colleague of James, the philosopher Howard Moore, gave a series of lectures to American students with a title that left little to the imagination: *Savage Survivals*. In the lectures, he explained that we love to read sensational stories about murder and killing 'because our ancestors were beasts of prey. The thirst for blood is very old – one of the oldest and most deeply seated cravings of our nature – and this is why it is so slow in passing away'.[23]

For this hunting instinct to remain, it had to be practised and kept up to scratch. Too much tender loving care would weaken it and it would disappear in later generations. Hunting clubs like the elite Shikar Club in London, whose members would hunt big game in the colonies, were proud that they kept the male hunting instinct alive. The club was a 'community of blood' united by a passion for 'sporting blood-lust' and an antidote for the feminizing effect of the growing interest in non-blood sports like athletics and lawn tennis.[24] A remarkable British tactic to arouse man's predatory nature was applied in the early years of the Second World War. English recruits had to attack carcasses with bayonets in slaughterhouses, or run through an obstacle course carrying full packs and fully armed, after which, exhausted, they were sprayed with sheep's blood, again with the intention of making them bloodthirsty. Megaphones shouted out slogans like 'Kill that Hun! Kill that Hun!'[25] Military manuals recommended this 'slaughterhouse method'. Civilized people had to feel once again the desire to kill for killing's sake. War veterans believed in the stimulating effect of bloody fighting. The American surgeon George Washington Crile described a bayonet fight in very sensual terms as 'an orgy of lustful satisfying killing . . . when the grunted breath of the enemy is heard, and his blood flows warm on the hand'. He, too, saw the bloodlust as a remnant from prehistoric times: 'This is a fling back in phylogeny to the period when man had not controlled fire, had not fashioned weapons; when in mad embrace he tore the flesh with his angry teeth and felt the warm blood flow over his thirsty face.' This was the kind of bestial frenzy that military commanders hoped to incite by showering their recruits with sheep's blood. 'In the hand-to-hand fight,' says Crile, 'the soldier sees neither to the right nor to the left. His eyes are fastened on one man – his man. In this lust-satisfying encounter injuries are not felt, all is exhilaration.'[26] The effect of this blood training was disastrous. Rather than aggressive and ruthless, the military *taurobolium* made the recruits despondent and wary. The revulsion that made them faint or vomit deprived them of the will to fight. The gruesome training method was scrapped after the BBC reported on it in April 1942 and members of parliament asked whether it was Christian and British. It was not considered decent to arouse the predatory nature of British soldiers in so abrupt a fashion.

REMNANTS OF A WILD PAST

Was the British gentleman losing more of his predatory nature than was to the Shikar Club's liking? Not according to the German enemy. Exaggerating the hunting instincts of your opponents was good war propaganda. It explained their excessive cruelty much better than your own lust for war. On the English side you could read this in the writing of renowned neurosurgeon Wilfred Trotter. Trotter feared that English soldiers who survived the trenches would find it difficult to adapt to the tedium of civilian life after the war as they had, as it were, tasted blood.[27] Trotter devised the concept of the herd instinct, which he saw as taking three forms. The aggressive form of herd instinct found among hunting wolves offered the best explanation for the German desire for war. According to Trotter, Kaiser Wilhelm II was a wolf leader who had to continually find a new prey for his pack to prevent the German nation from falling back into a jumble of individual states, as it was before Bismarck unified them.

On the German side, this viewpoint was presented by Isaak Spier in a series of articles in 1916 for *Die Gegenwart*, a magazine that was later to become a forum for fierce criticism of rapidly advancing Nazism. A still excessively active instinct for hunting and killing explained 'the English policies in the Boer War, the English policy of attrition, the Belgian atrocities in the Congo, the German retaliation to the Belgian *franc-tireurs*, the Russian Jewish pogrom, Russia's war tactics in Prussia, the French war propaganda in the press, and the French treatment of prisoners of war.'[28] Although war always brought out the worst in people, among the Allies and especially the people of rural England, the process was particularly quick. They still had many remnants of their wild prehistoric nature, which were awakened at the first mortar fire. It was therefore not surprising, according to Spier, that the enemy resorted to excessive atrocities. What Spier seemed to forget all too easily was that when the First World War broke out Austro-Hungarian troops committed mass killings in Serb villages. The Swiss criminologist Rodolphe Archibald Reiss wrote that these atrocities had been driven by bloodlust.[29]

Such war propaganda mixed with science was very predictable. There is no objectivity in war. Yet Spier did go somewhat further than his British counterpart Trotter. He provided his readers with an insight into the mechanism by which that prehistoric instinct for hunting and killing was passed down through the generations. Since the conviction that humans are by nature predatory was so widely held and the belief that those wild instincts still survived in modern man so strong, how was it possible that this nature and these instincts were not always on the surface and clear for everyone to see? How could a hereditary character trait lie dormant in the human organism for millennia without showing itself, except when stimulated by an appropriate incentive, such as war? Even the greatest proponent of hereditary explanations, Gregor Mendel, admitted that we need never wait too long for inherited characteristics to show themselves. If the characteristics of a parent were not present in all their children, it would always be visible in some. How this happened is explained by Mendel's laws, rediscovered around 1900, which calculated the likelihood that inherited traits would manifest themselves in the next generation. Moreover, those traits were never forms of behaviour, feelings or ideas that manifested themselves suddenly, but stable physical characteristics. There was no discussion about whether it were possible to inherit the health issues of a parent, but that a German or English soldier could owe his exhilaration on contact with blood to a hunting prehistoric ancestor was a different matter. Spier gave the following explanation:

> When half-civilized peoples suddenly lose control of their senses during times of war – despite having been compelled to suppress and keep dormant their instincts for cruelty for so long – and resort to arson, lasciviousness and slaughter, this can be explained by their not so remote wild past. Such atavisms are difficult to eradicate. The engrams of relatively recent barbaric times have not yet been worn away by time or covered and replaced by new ones. They break through new tribal memories which may have been inherited as engrams in their brain cells but which are still too fresh, and thus cause such deeds.[30]

Spier found this explanation – and the term 'engram' – in two books published by German biologist Richard Semon in the first decade of the twentieth century. In a systematic and analytical way, Semon defended a hypothesis that had already been popular among a widely diverse group of thinkers for half a century, but which had never been thoroughly worked through in German. 'Engram' and other new terms were devised to inject fresh scientific élan into this old theory. The basic principle of the theory was that heredity was a kind of memory.[31] What memory did for the individual, storing a record of a conscious experience so that you could later recall it, heredity did across generations. Just as a gramophone record stored music, a photographic plate images and a brain individual memories, engrams stored experiences that we passed on to our descendants. This extended the time frame of the memory from the individual to successive generations. Instead of only our own personal identity, hereditary memories accumulated the experiences of all previous generations. Engrams gave us a collective memory and a mental heritage. Of course, not all experiences were eligible for hereditary transfer; not all memories became engrams or hereditary memory tracks. It helped if you did something very frequently or repeatedly over a long period of time. Just as a pianist only masters a complex sonata after endless practice, it is to be expected that only deeply rooted habits, actions vital for survival and widely shared experiences will become part of our biological heritage. 'Nature has no time for games,' Spier warned us.[32] Fads leave no engrams behind. It also helped if the stored experiences were old. New experiences were too fresh and easily 'forgotten'. Like overly light tiles on the roof of an old house, they would easily blow away in a storm, while the older layers – the foundations – would withstand all kinds of weather.

Explaining precisely how these genetic memory tracks were formed proved a more difficult task than coming up with the analogy between heredity and memory. How were behaviour and experience converted into engrams? How did these engrams change not only our brain cells but our reproductive cells (back then, scientists spoke of 'germ plasma')? How were these cellular carriers of genetic information created? Semon admitted that he did not know, but was not worried by this ignorance. What theory of heredity did know the answers to these questions? Every theory of the time had its speculative 'biophors' (Weismann), 'micellae' (Von Nägeli), 'plastidules' (Haeckel), 'ideoblasts' (Hertwig) or 'genes' (Johannsen), which carried the genetic material in the germ plasma.[33] None of these candidates had ever been observed. There were some who were pleased that scientists were unable to give any precise details. For British idealist philosopher James Ward, such hereditary information was grounded in qualitative changes that were far too complex for biochemists to understand. It comes as little surprise that blood was the mysterious liquid that accommodated this complexity.[34] The French pioneer of modern psychology Théodule Ribot had contempt for such haughty ignorance, beneath which a dualist or vitalist agenda was always to be found hiding. He had no doubt that memory traces complied with all the conservation laws in physics. Not a single byte of information was ever lost: there was always a trace of even the minutest unit; information always remained as energy and matter. It was simply possible that stronger memories overpowered weaker ones. Like a narrow path through the woods, these smaller memories were no longer to be found in the thick forest of our consciousness. But Ribot preferred a different image: 'Every experience we have had lies dormant within us: the human soul is like a deep and sombre lake, of which light reveals only the surface; beneath, there lies a whole world of animals and plants, which a storm or an earthquake may suddenly bring to light before the astonished consciousness.'[35]

Other proponents preferred musical comparisons and saw the carriers of genetic information as rhythms, vibrations or waves that were reactivated by appropriate sounds, melodies or voices. Only the repetitive vibrating of a necessary habit carved a deep enough groove in the vinyl of our immortal germ plasma. The most advanced proposal came from the Italian polymath Eugenio Rignano, who suspected that cell nuclei contained an 'accumulator' that recorded electrical oscillations like a sensitive compass and stored those that were repeated. When the same oscillation recurred, the electrical circuit was reactivated. Long before the electronic revolution, Rignano saw living cells, and reproductive cells in particular, as 'microchips' that were flexible enough to store new experiences.[36]

These wild guesses were certainly not the strongest point of the theory of genetic memory, but nor were they its weakest. After all, no one knew how we inherited characteristics from our parents. Speculation on the biochemical carriers was inevitable. The appeal of the theory lay in the sense of continuity with our ancestors. The supernatural contact that had been lost since the Enlightenment was now restored in the form of a trans-historical connection. The theory did not satisfy a desire for unity with the higher world of gods, demons and souls, but did offer a communal tie with our distant forefathers which transcended time. Supernatural, magic happiness was replaced by evolutionary, naturalistic happiness. The theory allowed you to enjoy a collective identity not fragmented by divisions that forced different times, communities and people apart. The evolutionary thinking on which the theory was based offered comfort for the existential emptiness left behind by the disappearance of the magic world. For a modern intellectual, contact with the origins of humanity was as meaningful as mystic unification with God for a Christian or a Jew. Genetic memory was the greatest gift that Darwin had given us.

The pleasure we derived from this gift was expressed in many imaginative examples of atavism which we would laugh about today. They were, however, taken very seriously in their time, precisely because they established that much-desired link with the distant past. With each example, you can feel how much those who conceived of it wanted to believe it was true. Crime, vagrancy, socialism – they were all seen as remnants of a primitive existence as ape-like nomads in which property, labour and class were as yet of no significance. Prostitution and sadomasochism were seen as awakened genetic memories of rough prehistoric times typified by primal promiscuity and sexual slavery. One of the most original evolutionary explanations came from German gynaecologist Adolf Gerson, who believed that menstrual pain was caused by memories of prehistoric rape:

> Imagine the nature of the sexual act in primitive times, if men learned it only by raping women from other, hostile tribes. The hordes would rush at each other across the moonlit plains and fight each other furiously. When the men of one horde had defeated and driven off the men of the other, they would fall upon their women. If the women resisted, they would be beaten. So imagine what primitive women thought about the sexual act. It was a terrifying and painful experience. Their nuptial bed was a bloody field on which the bodies of their male relatives and their comrades lay. If modern man can inherit the experiences of their primitive ancestors, it is not inconceivable that these painful memories come back to haunt today's women during menstruation.[37]

As ridiculous at it may sound now, seeing menstrual pain as a remnant of wild times gave prehistoric depth to the present. Strange phenomena acquired a trans-historical significance. They were like caves that would lead you to a large, illuminated chamber where, in the flames of a big roaring fire, you would see prehistoric wall paintings and people who could tell you exactly where those phenomena came from.

Even in the modern world, there were still people, phenomena and experiences that were descended directly from a distant past, a past that was close to the moral zero. The deep link between present and past created a sensation that oscillated between awe, fascination and fear. It was these emotions that gave the theory of genetic memory its great appeal. This is expressed strikingly in a short text by Forbes Phillips in *The Nineteenth Century and After* in 1906. For Phillips, the theory above all offered a natural explanation for occult phenomena like déjà vu and reincarnation, which rational sceptics rejected as superstition. The feeling of having been to an unknown place before, preferably before you were born, was generally considered as nothing more than a short circuit in the brain. The theory of genetic memory proved that this scepticism was unwarranted because it explained how every child inherited not only certain character traits from its parents and grandparents, but the experiences of its ancestors, which would return as reminiscent flashes. There was thus nothing occult, illusory or poetic about this 'haunting of a pre-existence'; it was based on the idea of an ancestral memory that answered many of life's puzzles – and without the help of oriental theology. Phillips compared this ancestral memory with modern photography: ancestral memory cells took photographs of prehistoric experiences which were passed down to successive generations in the form of photographic negatives in the germ plasma, where – often damaged, censored or distorted – they were projected like slides on the big screen of the consciousness when the opportunity arose.

Phillips was relieved that science allowed him to give in to that delightful feeling of a 'haunting of a pre-existence' and to defend it openly. And he was delighted that he was no longer faced with the dilemma of either giving up his comforting belief that the past was always with us or abandoning the path of critical science and seeking refuge among paranormal fantasts. He did not have to align himself with anthroposophist Rudolf Steiner, who also dreamed of an eternal collective memory but refused to have anything to do with serious science. According to Steiner, those indestructible memories were stored not in our brain cells but in an occult spiritual substratum. Phillips could defend without hesitation the exciting theory that we are full of latent ideas and dormant images of a distant past. Science gave him a green light to believe in a world that was not limited to the surface of the present but reached back to the dark forests of our prehistoric past. Phillips himself expressed this saliently:

> Whether we believe in apparitions or not, this world is a haunted one. Our thought-world is full of deep undertones that roll in upon us from the past. As we lay our ear to the din of the present, we find its accompaniment to be the immeasurable murmur of the ages, as the voice of many waters . . . And the mind of man is a haunted one. Far-away generations have cut deep the channels of our memories until what was once a volition is now an involuntary movement. We say a man has formed certain habits, but how often they have been formed for him in the dim past.[38]

As well as in habits and memories, this haunted past – 'deep in the recesses of memory lies buried some impression of which the present is a reproduction' – also revealed itself in dreams, which Phillips called 'a kind of free play' of the ancestral memory. When he writes that dreams contain images of the adventures of distant ancestors that reach us 'through the avenues of a *subconsciousness* which always held the records of such deeds',[39] the proximity of Freud can be felt, whose psychoanalysis cannot be separated from the theory of genetic memory. Freud had a lifelong passion for classical history, folklore and archaeology and liked to see himself as a kind of Heinrich Schliemann who, rather than the ruins of Troy, exposed the human subconscious. He was intimately familiar with the theory of genetic memory. He was, however, very critical of Semon's analysis, preferring the more subtle prose of Hering, Ribot, Butler and Haeckel. With the latter, he shared the widespread belief that each individual life passed through the phases of the collective past. Ontogeny repeated phylogeny. There were remarkable similarities between children and primitive humans, which you also found in people whose normal development into a civilized adult had been disrupted in some way. While the Italian doctor Cesare Lombroso applied this to born criminals and criminal lunatics, his Austrian counterpart preferred to focus on neurotics who did not repress the infantile desires that we all have, or did so but in the wrong way. Neurotics were not capable of giving those wild desires an acceptable place in civilized life.

In Freud's view, every modern child still wished to act like primitive man at that moral zero. In the primitive horde, you were not satisfied with the women that Gerson saw being raped in the moonlight but, as a young man, also wanted to have sex with your sister and mother, which your jealous father would prevent as long as he had the strength to do so. That was nature's way of preventing inbreeding, just as with horses and cattle. A lustful stallion was expelled from the herd and would go looking for a mare from another one. Freud was impressed by a variant of this rough basic scenario devised by James Jasper Atkinson – cousin of famous Scottish collector of folk and fairy tales Andrew Lang – in his *Primal Law* (1903). Atkinson did not exclude the possibility that mothers who loved their sons dearly – and especially the youngest – persuaded their husbands not to expel them like young stallions when they were sexually mature but to keep them in the herd. After all, the men could make good use of their virile sons to hunt and wage war. The fathers, susceptible to this line of reasoning, agreed, but only on condition that the young men stayed away from their mothers and sisters. According to Freud, it was not long before the sons broke this agreement – the first family law contract in history – and had sex with their mothers and sisters, and killed their fathers and ate them. For Freud, this was self-evident: 'Of course these cannibalistic savages ate their victim,' he tells us in *Totem and Taboo* (1913).[40] Later, they would feel remorse at their patricide and would sacrifice an animal, solemnly pledging to restrict their sexual desires to women from outside the tribe. People are not horses or cattle, but cultured beings with respect for religion, law and morals.

This primal scenario would repeat itself in the freshly awakened mind of every growing child. In *The Future of Illusion* (1927), Freud wrote that among the instinctual wishes which 'are born afresh with every child' are 'incest, cannibalism and lust for killing'.[41] Not only our childish desires, but our dreams, sexual perversions and neuroses, remind us of life in primitive times when we gave ourselves over to unbridled and taboo-free sex, murder, cruelty and perversion. It was the task of psychoanalysis to decipher these hereditary memories that resurfaced in our consciousness deformed, damaged and censored. Beneath all kinds of behaviour, thoughts, expressions and utterances which, to an inexperienced analyst, hardly deviated from the norm, lay desires, urges and yearnings that, in a primitive past, could be given free rein. In the confines of civilized society, however, they could lead to malaise, frustration and neurosis. The whole of psychoanalysis rested on the theory of genetic memory and greedily drank its fill from the comforting and blissful thought of a past that still haunted us all. Like Forbes Phillips, Freud believed that this intoxicating notion was not simply an occult dream but was solidly founded on scientific certainty. Thomas Mann, with whom I started this part of the book, was also fascinated by speculation that dreams were a throwback to the past. Hans Castorp's cannibalistic vision was more than a personal experience. Mann admired Freud, Schopenhauer and Nietzsche, who believed that 'in dreams time and space are suspended, and that prophetic dreams can therefore very occasionally afford insight into the past or the future'.[42] In his vision in the snow, Castorp's consciousness took him back to that moral zero. On the way, he passed medieval witches, Greek sacrificial temples and maenadic rituals. The further you went back in time, the more bloody survival became and the more bestial characteristics mankind took on.

The future of that idea was less bright than Freud had hoped. No matter how comforting the theory of genetic memory was and how much magic a subconscious full of ancestral impressions contained, it proved untenable. August Weismann made short work of this pseudoscientific Atlantis. Not only did the analogy between heredity and memory rest on a false analogy, there was also no evidence at all that you could inherit experiences from the past, no matter how often you experienced them. Although no one knew exactly what information the germ plasma contained, there were no unambiguous examples of inheritance of acquired characteristics. According to Weismann, hereditary transmission could best be explained by blind natural selection. Random mutations in the germ plasma – and not environmental influences on the brain or other body cells – changed our hereditary nature. Women may have been frequently and cruelly raped in primitive times, but that pain was never etched out in their germ plasma, and menstrual pain was certainly not a memory of that suffering. Evolution ran from below to above, from reproductive cell to body cell, and never vice versa. If this was the only direction in which heredity moved, the package of inherited characteristics was much smaller than had been hoped – and it most certainly did not include conscious experiences, no matter how surprising, sudden and enticing they were.[43]

Weismann's criticism did not convince everyone. Although he was an uncommonly sharp polemist who could tear every argument and counter-argument to shreds, he made no secret of the fact that he was waging an intellectual war against the principle of the heredity of acquired characteristics. His supporters thought the fanaticism with which he attacked every publication founded on this principle courageous, but his opponents thought it timid, unhealthy or at least suspect. Anyone who believed in genetic memory had to accept Weismann barking at them like a fanatical watchdog. He could drive everyone to distraction, but he had his uses. Science must be critical. As his

criticisms acquired increasing support and more details of biological mechanisms were discovered, it became more and more
difficult to ignore his barking. While Isaak Spier could still claim
in 1914 that the principle of inheritance of acquired characteristics was 'unquestionable evangelism', a quarter of a century later
Ernest Jones begged the now aged Freud to scrap a passage from
Moses and Monotheism (1939) because 'no responsible biologist
regarded [the principle] as tenable any longer'.[44] Freud refused
and continued to insist that anyone who rejected the theory was
wrong. Although this is only an anecdote, it says much about the
status of the theory during the interwar years, and about Freud.
Serious biologists who believed in heredity had long known that
no progress is made if speculative philosophical ideas are taken
as the truth, no matter how comforting and enticing they are.
Real science had nothing to gain from such illusions. Progress
was only possible through meticulous experimental research in
the footsteps of the rediscovered laws of Gregor Mendel. There
was greater insight into heredity to be gained from the study of
peas, evening primrose flowers, fruit flies or locusts than from
the archaeology of the human subconscious.

Bestial bloodlust fitted perfectly with this evolutionary philosophy. If people became intoxicated by blood in angry mobs, at
fights, during exhausting hunting parties or in slaughterhouses,
it was a remnant of a prehistoric experience that drove our
ancestors to hunt, kill and tear their prey to shreds. Bloodlust
did for meat and battle what sexual arousal did for reproduction – it provided the motivation. Seeing, smelling and tasting
blood brought the promise of approaching pleasure that gave
us the strength and energy to track down, attack and kill prey
or enemy. The experience of bloodlust made for better hunting
and killing. Bloodlust fitted in perfectly with the evolutionary
image of memories of a moral zero where man was a predatory
animal. The philosophical *curée* of belief in bestial bloodlust
thus consisted of four ingredients: the moral zero, a predatory

nature, the hunting instinct and the genetic memory. Not every ingredient was necessary. William James, for example, rejected the idea of genetic memory, despite leaving us one of the most striking evolutionary descriptions of bloodlust. Although that theory made the stained-glass window complete, not every shard of glass was required to see the full, colourful picture. Bloodlust could reach the germ plasma of modern man in a different way, not as an inherited memory but as a coincidental adaptation, like sex. Although this allowed bloodlust to escape the sharp criticisms aimed at genetic memory, it was on shaky ground for different reasons. While no one doubted the existence of prostitution, vagrancy or even menstrual pain, the occurrence of bloodlust had never been proven. Despite the many stories, the number of reliable testimonies was minimal. And even if it was no longer a wild myth but a real phenomenon, how was the exhilarating response to blood to be explained? Could people smell blood, like wolves, tigers and dogs? What exactly was in blood that excited us and linked us to our hunting forefathers? These are questions I will return to in the next chapter.

CHEMOSIGNALS

We agreed to meet on the terrace of a bar, halfway between her village and mine. She didn't have a lot of time as, less than a week later, she was starting a busy period of exams. She was running a long way behind because of illness and injuries, and had postponed exams for some of the more difficult subjects until the resits, because she could still not study for longer than half a day at a time. She had to rest a lot and got tired quickly. Yet she was willing to talk to me and to help me with my research, though the help would, of course, have to wait until her exams were out of the way. In the meantime, we could meet up for an introductory chat. It was not immediately clear from how she parked her car on the village square and walked over to meet me that she was in less than tip-top condition. Physical inactivity had made her a little heavier than you might expect an ardent sportswoman to be, but her tread was forceful and decisive. A jersey to keep her warm against the evening chill danced around her broad shoulders. She gave me a firm hand-shake and addressed me as 'sir'. No matter how casual I had resolved to be with her, she preferred to keep things somewhat more formal. She always closed her emails – very unusually for today's students – with 'yours sincerely'. By keeping a distance, though never being cool, she was making it clear that the reason for meeting me in the village bar on this sunny evening was not her as an individual, but her story.

She told me that she had experienced bloodlust herself. On a number of occasions, blood had caused her to fight more wildly, more enthusiastically and with fewer inhibitions. I was not familiar with the combat sport that she practised. But I did know that, in English boxing, referees would stop a match if a fighter was bleeding too profusely from the nose, eyebrows or elsewhere. There were various reasons for that. Stopping the fight gave the seconds a chance to check that the wound was not too serious, to treat it and stop the flow of blood. That would prevent the opponent from coming into contact with the blood, or at least to a lesser extent. Contact with other people's blood can have its risks, but an oft-heard reason for preventing it was that contact with blood made the boxers very aggressive, so that they fought much more ferociously, more than was allowed by the rules. I heard an example of this recently during the report of a regional boxing competition in Ghent, Belgium. Two boxers started to bleed heavily and the referee temporarily stopped the fight. The commentary team agreed with the decision, as they believed that blood gives you extra strength. If you bleed, they said, or if you see or smell blood, you start fighting like a wild animal. It was an old story. You can find it in books on duels with swords and daggers. In these fights, it was essential that blood flowed. Without blood, you could not win or lose a duel. It was not always necessary to kill your opponent; fighting until he bled was sometimes enough. Handbooks warned that anyone who continued to fight until the first blood was spilled could be driven into a frenzy by contact with the blood and would want to fight until the bitter end. In the words of one commentator, 'Once first blood was drawn, a berserk rage could take hold.'[1]

In my student's combat sport, mixed martial arts (MMA), a bleeding nose or eyebrow is not enough to stop the fight, unless the fighter can no longer see because of the blood or if the wound needs urgent attention. MMA is a full-contact sport fought in an octagonal cage and which, as the name suggests, combines a variety of fighting traditions. The fighters use English boxing, karate, kick-boxing and Muay Thai (Thai boxing) to attack, and defend themselves with Graeco-Roman wrestling, Brazilian jiu-jitsu and

Israeli Krav Maga. Protection is minimal. They wear no helmets, fight in bare feet and wear light gloves, leaving their fingers free. Only gumshields and crotch protectors are compulsory. The fights are short – fifteen minutes at most – but are fierce and with few rules. Only biting, hair pulling and intentionally poking an opponent in the eye are forbidden. A jury of three decides on who wins and loses if this is not clear from a knockout or submission. Points can be won for technique, control, domination and aggression. During competitive fights, you fight against a single opponent, but in training there are often more than one, which tests to the maximum your physical fitness and command of the different disciplines.

It was during these training fights against more than one opponent that she experienced bloodlust. One of the boys she was fighting caught her eyebrow, and she tasted her own blood in her mouth and smelled it in her nose. She felt as though she had tapped into an extra battery full of energy. She suddenly started fighting more ferociously. The same happened to the boys; when they saw the blood on her face, they immediately fought more aggressively. Another time, a girl she was fighting against started bleeding after a blow from a fist, making the boys who were fighting together with the girl suddenly very aggressive, as if the flowing blood had reminded them of their duty to protect her. The blood gave them a signal that they had to deal with whoever had hurt their girl, even if the attacker was herself a woman. The student suspected that blood revived old attacking instincts that were useful in hunting and war, and protective instincts for defending your own group against enemies.

The lectures I gave on blood at Ghent University placed her experiences within a bigger picture. She was not the only one to have experienced bloodlust and there were credible theories that explained the phenomenon. In the safe cocoon of serious science, she was willing to discuss her experiences and help me with further research. She came to see me after one of the lectures and we stayed in contact. It was not an easy step for her to take. She missed her sport, which had kept her fit and given her self-confidence, although she knew it took a heavy toll on her body. A bad fall, an overly tight hold, an unexpected kick to the shoulder or head, could put a final end to the sport she loved so much. Full contact meant full risk. The sport itself didn't make it any easier: MMA has a bad reputation. The combination of few rules and little protection suggests a level of brutality that alarms the authorities. People amusing themselves with violence is totally at odds with the modern ideal of civilization. The fact that MMA fights take place in a cage is also damaging for the sport's image. Although a cage is actually safer than a boxing ring, which the fighters can fall out of, it seems more of a place for fighting animals than for sportsmen and women – more like a *ratodrome* than a sports arena. It is important to be careful when talking about bloodlust because it emphasizes the bestial nature of MMA, putting the sport in an even worse light. If I wanted to speak to fighters, I had to be aware that they might not all speak the truth. They might not want to talk openly, if at all, about their responses to blood, for fear that it might make the sport they love seem barbarous. I had to ensure that the questions remained purely scientific, avoiding any hint of moral or ideological disapproval, and display genuine interest in their sport.

After the exams, which she fortunately passed, she put me in touch with around sixty local fighters, more than half of whom trained several times a week. The majority had been fighting for some years. Although not all of them practised MMA, they were active in at least one of the disciplines that it encompassed and most of them combined more than one. My questions showed that they by no means all shared the experience of my student. This was surprising. Only twelve had experienced something similar and, for seven of them, it had been more than three years previously. One seasoned fighter, who had been practising full-contact combat sports for more than seventeen years, was so surprised when I asked about the effect of contact with blood that he immediately asked me to explain the phenomenon. And he was not the only one for whom it was completely new. Most of them had never heard of bloodlust (66 per cent), had never witnessed it (68 per cent), had never experienced it themselves (77 per cent) and had never spoken to anyone else about it (79 per cent). And even more surprising, while the great majority were not familiar with the effect of blood, a similar large majority (66 per cent) did believe that an effect existed. Although they had never experienced it themselves or heard anything about it, they were certain that it occurred.

Only a quarter of those I interviewed thought that bloodlust in combat sports was purely myth. Among the rest, opinions differed about whether it had mental or physical causes. A mental cause could be, for example, the appearance of blood signalling that victory is close and providing an additional shot of energy to finish the job. In that scenario it would make no difference whether it is real blood or another red liquid. Those who thought that bloodlust had a physical cause believed that blood contained substances that made fighters more aggressive and less inhibited.

The most striking finding was that bloodlust was a relatively unknown phenomenon in the kind of environment that you would most expect to find it. Although my student suspected the opposite, my questions showed that few combat sportsmen and women had experienced or witnessed bloodlust. She had of course warned me that I should take the answers with a pinch of salt. There was a taboo on everything that could place combat sports in a bad light. She had done her best to motivate and reassure the respondents. She herself had found my questions sufficiently objective and neutral not to arouse suspicion. Everything was of course anonymous. This did not exclude the possibility that the taboo was so strong that the fighters did not give honest answers. But the results do not confirm this suspicion. Anyone who wishes to deny that a phenomenon occurs will not only insist that they have never experienced it, but reject the suggestion that it occurs in their sport at all. If they want to distance themselves from a phenomenon that they consider incriminating, they will claim that it is purely a myth. Only a quarter of the respondents said they that thought bloodlust in combat sports was a myth. The rest, with the exception of a small group who had no opinion on the matter, believed it existed, occurring worldwide and also among animals. They considered it to be caused both by one's own blood and that of the opponent, especially through a combination of smelling, feeling and seeing. They believed it to be little known both within and outside combat sports. A quarter of the respondents said that it was taboo to talk about this subject, but almost half stated emphatically that it was not. If bloodlust really occurred but was taboo, you would expect different answers.

What should I conclude from what my student and the other twelve fighters who claimed to have experienced bloodlust told me? Had they imagined it? Was it pure coincidence? On the one hand, there was the tradition of stories about the exhilarating effect of blood, examples of bestial bloodlust aplenty to show that there was nothing new in the fighters' accounts. On the other hand, there was the imagination. Blood stimulates our love of fantasy. Some people go into raptures if they find traces of the prehistoric predator in modern man. Those traces link our fleeting present with a deeper past. Others are critical of these remnants of a wild past, as they remind us too much of untenable evolutionary theories, like that of genetic memory. Everybody seems to have an opinion about it.

Because I was getting nowhere with all the anecdotes and theories, it was time for a scientific approach, especially as it seemed there had been little serious research on the subject of blood rush. There were a few publications on animal behaviour on contact with blood, but whether humans became aggressive or excited by contact with blood – and if so, how this could be explained – remained a mystery. In that void, I started to think about experiments that would enable me to test the reality of bestial bloodlust among people under controlled scientific conditions. I had had enough of the stories for the time being and hunkered after solid facts. How could it be determined definitively whether, when confronted with violence, aggression and danger, people were sensitive to the extraordinary effect of contact with blood? Ever willing to help, my student offered to translate the questionnaire into English so that she could send it to her American contacts in the hope of producing greater clarity. But I had made my mind up to move on to the next step and conduct a series of experiments. We took our leave and I wished her a speedy return to her beloved sport.

THE FIRST EXPERIMENT

A few years earlier, I had started an experiment aimed at answering a different question. I wanted to know how well people could detect blood. Then, too, I was tired of all the stories: hospital staff who believed you could smell human blood as clearly as coffee or herbal tea, even to the extent that some nurses claimed that each patient's blood, like their sweat, had its own distinctive smell;[2] some went a step further, saying that you could tell by the smell of a patient's blood what they were suffering from. A lot of the stories were about the smell of menstrual blood. No matter what perfumes, eaux de toilette or deodorants women used to disguise the fact that they were menstruating, there were people who claimed that they could smell it. Macho men, pregnant women and orthodox Jews shared this remarkable gift. One of the stories I heard came from a colleague in Amsterdam who had invited her Surinamese cleaning lady to dinner. The cleaner accepted the invitation on the condition that the hostess was not menstruating. My colleague thought this was pure superstition and, though she was indeed menstruating, decided to take the chance that the cleaner would not smell it. Her guest had hardly entered her apartment when she exclaimed, 'You're having your period, I can smell it!' She refused to stay for dinner, despite the delicious aromas from the kitchen.

A historical tale about smelling venal human blood that immediately made me sceptical took place in the chemical laboratory of the Faculty of Medicine at the Sorbonne University of Paris in the early morning of Monday 7 July 1834.[3] Several men stood around an open wooden chest addressed to the Crown's prosecutor in Paris, deep in discussion about how to conduct the experiment. They included Mathieu Orfila, one of the founding fathers of forensic toxicology, who at that point had been the dean of the medical faculty for some years. Jean-Pierre Barruel was also there, the chemist and experienced dissectionist at the same faculty, who had become convinced after countless dissections that the blood of every animal had its own scent, or bouquet of scents. In humans, that bouquet even varied from individual to individual, depending on their diet and living circumstances. The smell of a person's blood betrayed how they lived. Five years previously, Barruel had developed and described a method for isolating the scent of blood, so that anyone with a normal sense of smell could perform the blood test.[4] The method entailed mixing two-parts blood – or bloodstains dissolved in water – with three-parts sulphuric acid and heating the mixture gently until it started to evaporate. By then smelling the vapour that was released, it was possible to tell, according to Barruel, whether the blood came from a woman or a man, or from an animal. After much experimentation, he was able to distinguish the blood of cows, horses, sheep, dogs, rats and even chickens, ducks, turkeys and pigeons. He could tell the colour of the hair of human donors. Orfila, who denied the value of microscopes in analysing blood and bloodstains, promoted the smell method and defended its use in all kinds of murder cases in which the suspects claimed that the blood on their hands or clothes came from slaughtering chickens or rabbits and not from the murder victim. Other colleagues, including the chemist François-Vincent Raspail, were sceptical. Scent was too fleeting an impression of a too subjective sense to prove that anything was fact, especially if the suspect was likely to lose their head under the guillotine. He preferred to wait for a reliable chemical or microscopic test.

The wooden chest contained a number of sealed packages that Barruel and Orfila wanted to use to prove the validity of their theory. The packages were all labelled *Vêtements saisis sur le garde Hochet*, clothing found on Constable Hochet. Charles Hochet had been found in a wood near Château-Thierry, between Reims and Meaux, stabbed to death with his own dagger. It had been rash of Hochet to take an afternoon nap in the forest.[5] For several months, he had been usurped as lord and master of the woods around Château-Thierry by the Boileau brothers. Together with one Victor Darez, the three brothers, led by Jean-Baptiste, the eldest, poached everything that moved and was fit to eat in the expansive forest. Their traps, dogs and guns had a particular liking for fat hares. Hochet, who had the thankless job of upholding the hunting rights of the nobility and high-ranking citizens, was no match for the four poachers, who could not conceive of a life without hunting. Their whole lives, otherwise totally lacking in excitement, were devoted to tracking down, catching and killing wild game. Without the aroma of marinated hare haunch and the taste of oven-roasted game pie, there was something missing in their lives, making them wonder why God had given them senses. Without poaching, life was dull and bland.

After the hated constable had confiscated Jean-Baptiste's gun and threatened him with a trial, the four partners in crime had had enough. Along with the hares and deer, Hochet became fair game. In the many bars in the villages around Château-Thierry, they would swear – after too much *eau de vie* – that it was 'him or us', that they had to 'get him before he got them', and 'the constable would be taken care of before Midsummer's Night'.

But they didn't wait that long. Early in June, they surprised Hochet during his afternoon nap, overpowered him, relieved him of his sabre and used it to run him through in several places. A few days later, alarmed by the unpleasant smell of a dead body, passers-by found the murdered gendarme with his sable sticking up vertically out of his belly. Footprints, the threats the four poachers had uttered all around the local area and the bloody clothing found at their homes left little doubt about the identities of the killers. Nevertheless, Jean-Baptiste insisted that the blood on his trousers was not human, and certainly not Hochet's, but came from a poached hare that he had been skinning. Unfortunately for Jean-Baptiste, his brothers and mother denied that he had recently caught a hare. It had been more than a year since he had surprised them with a delicious fat specimen.

For Barruel, this was the opportunity he had dreamed of to prove that his smell test worked. The experiment started promisingly. Assistants cut a fragment of cloth from Hochet's bloody shirt and soaked it in a bowl of water, which gradually turned red. Barruel then poured the red liquid, mixed with sulphuric acid, into a glass tube, which he shook forcefully and heated over a candle. When the liquid started to emit vapour, it was impossible to ignore the strong smell of male sweat. To make sure they would not forget the smell, Orfila and Barruel took another good sniff at the tube. Then they compared it with another sample, a blue cloth stained with blood found at the scene of the murder. But this one released the scent of menstrual blood and human excrement, so they concluded that it had nothing to do with the crime. But the smell test soon proved to have its limitations. A sample of bloody earth taken from beneath the body filled the Paris laboratory with the luxuriant scent of the forest, of rotting leaves and moss-covered brushwood. The scent was so strong that there was no trace of the smell of Hochet's sweat. Most disappointing was the test of the stains on Jean-Baptiste Boileau's trousers. The piece of cloth with the biggest stains was cut out and soaked in water, which promisingly turned red. But it was not possible to tell from the vapour that it gave off when mixed with sulphuric acid and heated whether the blood came from a human or an animal, and certainly not whether it smelled of Hochet's sweaty blood or the aromatic blood of a forest hare. More blood would offer greater certainty, Barruel and Orfila concluded in their report.

The jury at the courts of assizes in Laon did not need that certainty. In mid-February 1835, they sentenced Jean-Baptiste to the guillotine and Victor Darez and François-Alexandre Boileau to forced labour for life. The youngest Boileau brother, Jean-Louis, was a minor and was acquitted. The executioner in Laon carried out the death sentence on Jean-Baptiste at the end of March. The death sentence for Barruel's smell test did not come until later. In 1848 the German haematologist Karl Schmidt published the results of a study during which six test subjects had to identify the blood of various animals by its smell.[6] The results showed a complete lack of unanimity. The smell test was given its very last chance in 1852. A woman accused of murder defended herself by claiming that blood discovered at her home was not human but sheep's blood, which she used to purify wine. Because there was a large supply of blood available, the test could finally prove its worth. To ensure that the test was properly scientific, experts added other samples and gave them all a random number. But the blind test failed. The experts could not agree and concluded that, 'You should only use this method with the greatest possible restraint.'[7] In other words, it was useless.

That conclusion came as no surprise to my students, I had asked them whether people could recognize the nature of blood. They did not share the optimism of Barruel and Orfila. Only 15 per cent of the 235 students I asked thought that you could identify human blood by smell, without using any of the other senses. Seventy-one per cent believed that this was not possible, while the rest didn't know. For animal blood, which I did not specify further, the percentage was even lower. The same applied to identifying blood by touch or sight. My students did not believe that you can smell, feel or see blood if you cannot combine these senses with others. Taste was, however, an exception. Almost half (44 per cent) believed that you can recognize the taste of human blood, that if you tasted human blood while blindfolded you would identify it correctly. Only 28.5 per cent claimed that they would be able to identify animal blood, but were more hopeful of success if the use of more than one sense was allowed. A majority (63 per cent) thought they would be able to identify human blood if they could use all their senses; only half (51.5 per cent) thought the same for animal blood. The option of tasting blood considerably increased the chances that they would recognize it. Barruel and Orfila may therefore have been better off devising a taste test to identify blood, rather than a smell test.

These are only opinions. And there is often a wide chasm between opinion and reality. I therefore placed 72 dishes containing liquids in a well-ventilated space and asked some eighty test subjects to look at or smell them and tell me which of the liquids were blood.[8] They were not allowed to taste them. As the test subjects would only have been permitted by ethical committees to taste their own blood, that would have entailed taking blood samples from them immediately before or during the experiment – a laborious, though not impossible, process. Because I was primarily interested in the effect of seeing and smelling blood, I restricted myself to those two senses. Blood rush is supposedly invoked by seeing or smelling blood, and only to a lesser extent by tasting it. We did not reveal what kind of blood was in the dishes. We had obtained human blood from the Red Cross donor centre. It had been declared unsuitable for medical purposes but was approved for experimental research. A standard dose of citrate had been added to stop the blood clotting, which had no observable effects on its smell or colour. In addition, we had blood from sows, castrated piglets and a few boars that had been slaughtered in a local abattoir. Citrate was also added to this blood. The blood that was dripped into the 15-millilitre dishes using a pipette was no more than a day old, refreshed every two hours and kept at room temperature. The human and pig's blood were the only actual blood used. Despite all the stories about smelling menstrual blood, we decided not to incorporate this into the test. I was not particularly interested in the effect of menstrual blood on human behaviour; blood rush is aroused by seeing or smelling venal blood and not menstrual blood. As control materials, we used five odourless liquids that closely resembled blood: two kinds of fake blood used in films, red colouring used in baking, red watercolour paint and bistre, a colour pigment acquired by boiling the soot of burned wood, used for drawing and for staining floors. All of the control liquids were mixed with water and binding agents, so that they looked like blood and remained odour-free.

We divided the 72 dishes between the two senses. Half were transparent, so that the liquid they contained could be seen clearly. Anyone who thought it possible to identify blood purely on the basis of sight did not need to use their nose. The remaining dishes were black, so that their contents could not be seen. The liquid itself was difficult to see. We covered all the dishes with a lid, so that the odour remained in the pot. With each sample, the test subject had to fill in a questionnaire stating whether the dish contained blood and how certain they were. They lifted the lid, smelled or looked at the contents, recorded their verdict, and replaced the lid. We arranged the dishes in two ways. We placed 48 of them in groups of four, separated by partitions. One dish in each group of four contained blood, so each test subject had one chance in four of guessing correctly. To exclude the possibility of a lucky guess, we placed the other 24 dishes in two rows of twelve. In each row, six dishes were filled with blood, three with human and three with pig's blood. To determine whether a successful detection was related to a better sense of smell, each test subject had to take two validated smell tests. We also wanted to know what experience our subjects had had with blood. It seemed obvious that a butcher's son would recognize pig's blood more easily than the daughter of vegetarian parents.

Obvious or not, that expectation was not borne out by the experiment. The findings were clear. Our test subjects could recognize pig's blood but not human blood. Whether the dishes with human blood were black or transparent, set up in series of four or twelve, examined by people with a lot of experience with blood or sniffed by those with the nose of a wine connoisseur, the probability of them guessing correctly was never higher than chance level. The results for pig's blood were, however, the complete opposite. Although the test subjects recognized visible pig's blood slightly more easily than when it was not clearly visible, the level of correct detections in both cases was very high, at 83 per cent and 75 per cent respectively. The way the dishes were set up had no effect on the results – the subjects identified pig's blood just as easily from series of four as from twelve. And here, too, a better sense of smell or more experience with blood made no difference at all. Pig's blood was just as easy to recognize for those with an average, inexperienced nose. But human blood remained completely undetectable, at least in the relatively small quantity of 15 millilitres and using only sight and smell.

We now know what makes pig's blood so recognizable. Researchers at the universities at Linköping, Sweden, and Erlangen, Germany, isolated more than twenty odorous substances in pig's blood and discovered that one of them, E2D – in full, trans-4,5-epoxy-(E)-2-decenal – emits a metallic odour that we associate with blood.[9] The odour is found in the blood of all mammals, but the concentration is higher in pigs than in cows and humans. That is why we detect pig's blood more easily than human blood, which is virtually odourless to human noses.

CHEMOSENSORY CUES

Although we cannot detect human blood by smell, it can have an effect on us. It may work in a subtle way, affecting our behaviour and emotions unconsciously. The smell of blood sets all kinds of responses in motion without our being aware of it. We know that many animals receive information through their sense of smell about the sexual readiness of a partner, the aggressiveness of an opponent, the proximity of prey, and a familial relationship with another member of their species. While it is safe to assume that the animals in question are not aware of the exchange of information, urine, sweat, excrement, body odour and special glands contain odorous substances that transfer these messages. When these signal substances are typical for a group of animals, scientists speak of pheromones. If all the males of a certain species can smell when a female is sexually receptive, they receive that information through pheromones. This term is not used when animals receive individual-related information, such as when ring-tailed lemurs sniff at the genital, scrotal and lip glands of a lemur of the other sex to determine whether they are related by blood. The messenger substances that help to curb their sexual impulses and avoid inbreeding are not pheromones.

Whether there are human pheromones remains a matter of controversy.[10] We know for certain that humans do not have the special olfactory organ – known as the vomeronasal organ or Jacobson's organ – that many other animals, including snakes and lizards, use to detect odorous substances. This 'second nose' is present in human embryos but disappears during the later stages of foetal development. Nevertheless, there are quite a few mammals with no special olfactory organ, such as rabbits and sheep, which can detect pheromones using their normal sense of smell. In theory, humans could also produce pheromones that we could detect with our noses. Because, in the recent past, science has been rather quick to conclude that humans are sensitive to

all kinds of pheromones while it has proved exceptionally difficult to come up with any hard evidence for that assumption, the
criteria for a substance being recognized as a human pheromone
are now very strict. It is no longer sufficient to show that humans
can detect specific odorous substances that work as pheromones
among many other animals, as long as they do not also influence
our behaviour. A particular substance working as a pheromone
with one species is no reason to assume that it does so with
another. Nor is it enough to know that sweat, tears, body odour
or other secretions can change our behaviour unconsciously,
without knowing exactly what chemicals are responsible for
this effect. The active substance has to be isolated, replicated
synthetically and, when it is administered in a natural dose, a
physiological or behavioural response has to be observed. To
date, not a single substance has passed this test.[11]

There are, nevertheless, plenty of candidates. The most
promising include the odorous substances excreted by the glands
around a woman's nipples during breastfeeding. If this message
substance is rubbed under the nose of a baby, it will begin to suck
and search for a nipple to feed from. And, as would be expected
from any bona fide pheromone, it makes no difference which
mother is excreting the odour. There are other more spectacular candidates. An Israeli team discovered that women's tears
dampen a man's sexual appetite. If a sponge with women's tears,
collected during the sad ending of a tear-jerker, was fixed under
a man's nose, he would find young women less attractive, his
testosterone levels would be lower and the areas of the brain
relating to sex would be less active.[12] A team of Dutch researchers captured sweat from the armpits of men while they were
watching films that evoked fear or disgust. They then let women
smell the sweat while they were solving a simple task. Without
knowing what they were smelling, the women imitated the feelings of the men. When they smelled sweat caused by fear, their
eyes opened wide, and when the sweat came from men watching

scenes that evoked disgust, they were more likely to turn up their noses.[13] Other teams discovered that odorous substances betray a person's age or state of health. We find the body odour or sweat of a sick person unpleasant and it can even trigger our immune system.[14]

Although researchers are obtaining surprising results, it is essential to remain critical. Pheromones easily appeal to the imagination. It is spectacular to discover that people communicate with each other unconsciously. It places our unique status as humans in perspective and confirms our animal origins. Many like to believe these stories. One example is that women who live together eventually menstruate at the same time. This is known as the McClintock effect, after the American psychologist Martha McClintock, who first described it in *Nature* in 1971. She asked female students who lived together in student houses to keep a record of the first day of their menstruation for six months and noticed that the differences between the dates gradually declined. She also found evidence for this synchronization when she regularly rubbed sweat from the armpits of a menstruating woman under the noses of five women and noted that their menstruation period shifted towards that of the sweat donor. It proved difficult, however, to replicate this result. In student houses, it would sometimes happen and sometimes not. It did not occur among female basketballers, lesbian couples or Dogon women in Mali who spend their menstrual periods together, separated from the rest of the community. When American psychologist Jeffrey Schank discovered no effect after a large-scale study of 186 women he had monitored for a year, he calculated why the probability of their cycles converging was so low.[15] We know for certain that the length of a woman's menstrual cycle depends on her body weight and age, and the reserves of ova also play a role. In addition, the length of each woman's cycle varies unpredictably. Consequently, the cycles of different women can appear to coincide. But if you wait long enough, that illusion will disappear.

Is the effect of blood a similar illusion? Not immediately. No one doubts any more that contact with blood changes the behaviour of animals, though the changes may be subtle and you need to be sufficiently sensitive to detect them. Anyone who expects extremely fierce reactions will be disappointed. This happened to researchers in California in the 1920s.[16] Cattle farmers were convinced that their animals were agitated by blood. They panicked, galloped off or became aggressive and attacked people when blood was present. Anyone who brought the animals to the abattoir, tended to their wounds or sawed off their horns was warned. To test the stories, researchers placed buckets of fresh cow's blood in a meadow full of Hereford bulls, or hung sheets soaked in horse's blood next to a haycock from which Durham cows were feeding. Sometimes the blood was clearly visible, sometimes it was covered with straw or grass through which the animals could smell it. To their surprise, the cows responded with very little agitation, let alone panic or aggression. Some were curious or not entirely at their ease, while others licked at the blood with obvious pleasure. The researchers could not corroborate the farmers' wild stories. They concluded that the animals' agitation was caused not so much by the contact with blood as by stress, pain and fear resulting from situations in which blood also happened to flow, such as traffic accidents or being at the abattoir.[17] It was these situations, rather than the blood itself, that made the animals frightened, agitated or aggressive. Blood was not an alarm substance in itself.

More refined research with cows and horses only partially reaffirmed this negative conclusion. A French research team led by Claudia Terlouw taught Aubrac cows to eat hay in an internal space which they could only reach by way of a narrow corridor.[18] As they passed down the corridor, they inhaled the odour of dog faeces, cow's blood and the urine of stressed and non-stressed 'conspecifics' (members of their own species), dispensed through vaporizers. Nebulized water was used as a control liquid. The researchers observed no difference in the cows before they ate but, after feeding, the blood had a definite effect. They sniffed at the air more and stretched their heads forwards and downwards more often. Dog faeces and the urine of stressed conspecifics had the same effect, while water and the urine of non-stressed conspecifics did not. The test animals did not become accustomed to the scent of blood. The longer they passed through the corridor with vaporized blood, the more stress-related behaviour they displayed. A Scandinavian team found similar subtle changes among horses.[19] Like cattle farmers, horsemen and -women tend to easily believe stories about the agitating effect of blood on their animals. Horses are alleged to bolt as they pass abattoirs. The ancients also believed that blood could drive horses wild. Achilles witnessed raging horses attacking Amazons after eating raw human flesh. As flight animals, horses are always on their guard for odours that may signal danger. The reality is, however, far less spectacular. Twelve Danish Warmbloods were trained to eat from a haycock smeared with fresh blood from a stressed horse that had been slaughtered in an abattoir. The test horses only sniffed longer at the hay and ate less of it after it had also been smeared with the pelt of a wolf. Neither odour caused a special stress response separately and the reaction to the two together was limited, with no increase in the test horses' heartbeats. The odour of stressed horse's blood may have caused the test animals to be more alert, but an additional stress factor – such as the scent of a predator, a sudden sound or an unexpectedly moving object – was required to genuinely activate the alarm response. Blood contact is not enough on its own. Both studies confirm the observations of well-known cattle expert Temple Grandin on the effects of blood on cattle in abattoirs.[20] Sudden noise, shiny objects and unexpected movements cause stress and panic among cows and horses more often than confrontation with blood, injuries or dead conspecifics, though the scent of blood can make the symptoms worse. Horses and cows are sensitive to blood in a subtle way; it makes them more alert.

Mice and rats, on the other hand, respond much more clearly to the sight and smell of blood. Again, it tends to make them less agitated and more likely to avoid conflict or resort to flight, rather than more agitated or aggressive. Even the most aggressive mice, which will immediately attack when put together, lose their enthusiasm for fighting if the head or flank of their opponent is smeared with real mouse's blood.[21] They sniff more and wait longer before attacking than mice confronted with red-dyed conspecifics. David Stevens discovered in the 1970s that thirsty rats that had to pass the blood of other rats to get to a water dispenser became very nervous.[22] They squeaked, walked away or stood stock still, urinated or defecated, and even bit Stevens on the hand. They only did this after contact with rat's blood, and not with the blood of a guinea pig, which did not interest them at all. Stevens did not exclude the possibility that the blood of non-stressed rats did not have the same effect as that of stressed rats. He referred to the Austrian ethologist Eibl-Eibesfeldt, who had observed that you could reuse a rat trap only if it killed the rat outright and no blood flowed. Otherwise, other rats would stay away from the trap.[23] As yet, there has been no research to discover whether it is only the blood of nervous or panicky rats that sets off the alarm bells. We do know, however, that the urine of calm and stressed rats brings about different reactions.[24]

The blood of rats and mice contains alarm substances, causing them to avoid contact with blood. Researchers have also discovered this response among white-tailed deer, chicks, Nile tilapia, spiny lobsters and bees.[25] But blood also attracts some animal species. Predators respond with enthusiasm when they see and smell blood. Detailed experimental research is not easy to find, but anyone who watches the National Geographic Channel now and again knows how greedily sharks respond to blood. Their reaction may often be exaggerated, but is impressive nonetheless.[26] Ten drops of blood in a volume of water large enough to fill a private swimming pool is ample to excite a shark. Wolves too are alleged to be able to smell blood at great distances – and therefore to find their way to the nearest abattoir – but I am not aware of any precise figures to back this up.[27] A rare example that investigates the blood response of predators is a recent study conducted among zoo animals, in which researchers dripped a small quantity (0.5 millilitres) of horse's blood onto wooden boards and observed how tigers and wild dogs responded to them.[28] They chose horse's blood because these carnivores were used to eating horsemeat. Conduct such as sniffing, licking, biting, growling and urinating was observed. The results were clear: the predators showed greater enthusiasm for the board with the blood than for boards with banana odours or no odour at all. The researchers also smeared a board with E2D, the substance that gives blood its metallic scent. Even though E2D is completely colourless, the tigers and wild dogs were as enthusiastic about this board as the one with horse's blood.[29]

Research has also been conducted to observe how bears respond to blood, and especially to menstrual blood. It was set up following a lethal incident in 1967 in which women camping in Glacier National Park, USA, were attacked by grizzly bears. It was suspected that the bears were attracted by the scent of the sleeping women's menstrual blood. In a brochure entitled *Grizzly, Grizzly, Grizzly*, the government advised women not to enter bears' habitats while having their periods. In a first experiment with polar bears, researchers found that the animals did indeed respond with great enthusiasm to tampons soaked with menstrual blood.[30] They ate them up as eagerly as toilet paper on to which seal oil had been dripped. They did not respond to tampons soaked in venal human blood, contradicting claims that polar bears – used to frequent food scarcity – will eat anything containing animal protein. For polar bears, menstrual blood smells and tastes better than venal blood. The researchers rightly noted that consuming blood is something different to bloodlust and the urge to attack. Even if polar bears like the taste of menstrual blood, it does not necessarily mean that they will kill for it. The bears did not molest female researchers who happened to be having their periods. This taste for menstrual blood was found only among polar bears; black bears, for example, showed no interest at all in it.[31] In tests, they always preferred food that contained no menstrual blood.

There is still much research to be done. It is known that chimpanzees will wait patiently under a tree to catch a few drops of blood.[32] The blood comes from red colobus monkeys, hunted, killed and torn apart by their fellows, who devour them high up in the trees. The chimps gaze longingly upwards, hoping for a morsel of meat, blood, bone marrow or even hair. It is unclear whether they do it for the blood itself or to take part in the exhilaration of the hunt and devouring of the prey. Chimpanzees do hunt, but to raise their sexual status rather than for food. They only eat meat that they have killed themselves, as an edible hunting trophy.

As for carnivores that reputedly want nothing else once they have tasted human flesh, I am not sure what to think. In mid-April 2013, photographs appeared in the media of a frenzied mob parading triumphantly through the streets of Kathmandu, Nepal, with the bloody body of a leopard. The animal had attacked fifteen people in a suburb of the city, including three police officers and two forestry officials. It had bitten its victims but had not mortally wounded them. Yet the mob wanted to do more than tranquilize the leopard, put it in a cage and transport it to a less densely populated area. It had to die because it had tasted human blood, and would continue to do so. Young children were no longer safe. After a more deadly incident elsewhere in Nepal some months earlier, the director of Nepal's Department of National Parks had explained, 'Since human blood has more salt than animal blood, once wild animals get the taste of salty blood they do not like other animals like deer.'[33] There are similar stories about dogs and even ferrets that have bitten humans. Contact with human blood is considered a reason to kill animals, although no one knows whether the stories are true: tales about blood are not among the most reliable. I would not be surprised if this did not turn out to be yet another blood myth. Only thorough scientific research can bring certainty. The same applies to the latest story about male iguanas, which respond very aggressively to their menstruating keepers during the mating season. There is evidence aplenty to be found on the Internet. The iguana expert at my university had not yet heard of the phenomenon, but did not exclude the possibility that the male iguanas were confusing the menstrual blood with a pheromone that warns them of the proximity of a rival male. Males iguanas fight each other during the mating season and pheromones play a role in the rivalry. Iguanas have a vomeronasal (or Jacobson's) organ, which is mainly used to detect pheromones. Whether the scent of menstrual blood does indeed resemble that of these pheromones, and thus whether this explanation is correct, is a matter for science to determine. For now, all I have is anecdotes.

THE RED EFFECT

So are people excited by blood? Let me start by examining the effect of the colour red, something we also know a lot about. Red makes women more attractive to men. Drivers are more likely to give lifts to female hitchhikers in red T-shirts. Male diners in restaurants give waitresses in red clothes or with red lipstick bigger tips. Profile photos of women in red attract more attention on social media. Men find women photographed against a red background more attractive, and women with a red laptop on their laps more arousing. All these preferences disappear if you dress the same woman in a different colour, omit the lipstick, picture her against a white or green background or replace the red laptop with a black one – and if women judge the images rather than men. Women do not find red more attractive, even if the subjects are men. Furthermore, men do not find women in red more honest, intelligent or friendly – just sexier. There is clearly a good reason why brothels burn red lights.[34]

In the case of food, red suppresses the appetite. Test subjects drink less from a red beaker than a blue one and are less likely to take snacks from a red plate than from a white or blue one. Our team experienced a similar phenomenon during an experiment on blood recognition. Afterwards, the test subjects were given a snack and a soft drink. For the drink, they had a choice between original Coca-Cola in a red can and Lipton's lemon ice tea in a yellow can. We were surprised at how popular the ice tea was. Very few of the test subjects quenched their thirst with cola in a red can after the blood experiment. Although the difference could have been attributed to current trends, we wondered whether our subjects avoided food or drink in red packaging because they associated it with the blood in the experiment. Research has shown, however, that such an association is not necessary. Food and drink in red packaging is in itself less attractive.[35]

Of greatest interest to us is the observation that the colour red stimulates aggression, dominance and physical performance. That was illustrated during the now renowned study by Russell Hill and Robert Barton from 2005, published in *Nature*, in which they concluded that competitors who took part in wrestling, boxing and taekwondo at the 2004 Olympic Games in Athens had more chance of winning if they wore red.[36] In these combat sports, one fighter wears red and the other blue. The fighters do not choose their colours themselves – that is left to chance. In 2008 the same research question was applied to English football.[37] The researchers looked at the results of clubs from eight English cities over a period of 55 years. They discovered that clubs with red shirts – for example, Manchester United – finished higher in the various competitions than clubs with shirts of other colours. A Spanish study did not, however, confirm these results.[38] Moreover, it is not clear what exactly causes the better performances. If the 'red effect' does exist, there are three possible, not mutually exclusive, explanations.

First of all, it is possible that red clothing makes a more positive impression on referees, who then make subtle decisions in favour of red clubs or competitors. A German study on Taekwondo confirmed this effect,[39] with referees giving more points to fighters in red. When the same fight was replayed on video, with the red fighter's kimono now coloured white, the referee gave him fewer points. Yet this is not the only explanation. In fights without a referee, competitors in red win more often. For three months a Romanian research team observed gamers playing the violent computer game *Unreal Tournament*, the object of which is to kill as many opponents as possible.[40] The gamers could choose between a red and a blue gladiator to fight against virtual people and animals. Again, the red fighter won more often. In *Unreal Tournament*, points are awarded by a computer program, not an impressionable human referee.

A second possibility is that competitors may be unnerved by the red of their opponents and perform less well. The opposite is, of course, also possible: you might become more aggressive yourself on being confronted with an opponent in red. The French researchers who monitored responses to hitchhikers and waitresses in red T-shirts and with red lipstick also conducted an experiment in which they obstructed drivers at traffic lights.[41] When the lights turned green, they blocked the road with a test vehicle that stalled and refused to restart. They kept this up until the drivers behind them started hooting their horns, flashing their lights or shouting. Red test cars came off worst. The hooting and flashing started more quickly than with cars of another colour. Red cars may invoke a more aggressive response, but they don't cause more accidents. It is much more dangerous to drive a black car, especially at night.

Lastly, wearing red might give you extra energy, so that you become more aggressive, more dominant and perform better. Studies are finding more and more evidence of this effect. They have found that red can also improve performance when there are no opponents involved. Test subjects asked to squeeze a hand-grip strengthener as hard and for as long as they could performed better if they were given a red pen or a red participant's number, or instructions printed on a red background.[42] A German research team came up with elegant evidence of increased desire to fight among competitors wearing red.[43] They asked handball players to fight each other with long sticks with hard, round cushions at each end with which they could hit their opponents but not hurt them. All the competitors wore blue or red helmets, gloves and chest protectors and their cushions were of the same colour. Competitors who suffered more hits than they gave lost the match. Before the match, the pulling power of the competitors was measured with a dynamometer, a short chain that they had to pull on as hard as possible. Their heartbeats were monitored during the match. The pulling power and the heartbeats of the red competitors proved to be higher than those of their blue opponents. Although it cannot be concluded from this that red fighters are better than blue ones, they certainly have more desire to fight.

All these studies tell us something about the effect of red, but not the effect of blood. A few studies do that, but have focused on the effect of blood in computer games. Their objective was to determine to what extent virtual blood affects the moral behaviour of the players. Would a ban on red blood in games, or replacing it with something green or pink, help to keep the aggression of gamers under control? The researchers found that red virtual blood indeed had an effect on gamers.[44] They played more aggressively during the game and also responded with more hostility to an insult made by a confederate afterwards than a control group that had only seen blue blood or none at all.

It is unclear whether that can be attributed to the blood in the game. Violent games with no blood or blue or green blood are so unrealistic that they spoil the fun of the game.[45] Gamers who are used to being rewarded with blood have to become accustomed to this alternative. And blood sells. The bloody version of *Mortal Kombat* sold seven times better than the bloodless version.[46] As long as there are no realistic games without red blood, there is no control situation that can be used to study the effect of virtual blood.

THE SECOND EXPERIMENT

Does real blood have an exhilarating effect on people? Are there odorous substances that we pick up unconsciously that can make us agitated? Did my student smell something in blood that made her less inhibited when she was cage fighting? Was there something in the hare's blood that gave me blood rush in that cellar? It is high time to answer that question. Because there are no studies that directly address this topic, I decided to tackle it myself. Together with a colleague who had experience measuring heartbeats, breathing and sweat secretions – parameters that indicate excitement – I devised a second experiment. We asked 120 young men to play a violent computer game. We chose a scene from *Unreal Tournament* in which the gamers had to shoot down as many opponents as possible in an empty factory. If they were shot by an opponent, they were unconscious for a few seconds, but then they could start again. They used the mouse to move, shoot, select weapons, accumulate more ammunition and get a fresh shot of adrenaline. Through their earphones they could hear shots, screams of pain and fear, and a lot of loud, inflammatory beat music. The test subjects had a quarter of an hour to get used to the game, master the rules and learn how to do everything with the mouse. The difficulty level adjusted automatically to their performance in the practice round. We then attached electrodes to their hands (to measure the sweat), chests (breathing) and feet (heartbeat). We fitted an odour mask under their noses and outside their field of vision, with a perforated tube into which we inserted a cotton wool bud soaked in liquid. We performed a simple odour test to see whether there was anything wrong with their sense of smell. Participants with a good sense of smell then played three rounds of the game, each lasting five minutes, during which they inhaled three liquids: human blood, fake blood and water. We did not tell them which of the liquids they were inhaling, as this would defeat the object of the test. If they knew what they were smelling and why, they would be able to prove what they themselves believed. To conceal our intention, we adopted a more subtle approach.

We did not mention blood at all to half of the test subjects, only that we wanted to test the effect of certain pheromones on human behaviour. We explained that we were not allowed to reveal what pheromones they would be subjected to. We could tell them – since they could it see for themselves – that the pheromones were dissolved in a red liquid (this was in reality human or fake blood) or a colourless liquid (water). That enabled us to determine whether blood itself had an impact on their behaviour while playing the game. If human blood contained odorous substances or chemical signals that caused excitement, we would see a difference compared to the other liquids. We took account of a possible alternative explanation: perhaps the exhilarating effect of blood has nothing to do with chemicals and is purely psychological. It is not the blood itself, but the awareness that you can smell blood that stimulates the pleasure of playing the game and the desire to fight. We told the other half of the participants that the pheromones were dissolved in blood or water. We avoided giving them the impression that the test was about the blood and not about the pheromones by saying that the blood was used simply to keep certain pheromones active – nothing more, nothing less. We told them that other pheromones remained active in water. This approach was a success. All participants except one believed that we were interested in the pheromones and not the blood. Each player inhaled one of the liquids in random order during the three rounds of play. We measured their pleasure, excitement and desire to fight in different ways, including their scores, their own estimation of how they had done after they had finished, and the fluctuations in their heartbeats, breathing and sweat secretions. We could tell when they suddenly started playing more intensely.

But we found nothing – or at least not what we were expecting to find. The scent of blood did not make the gamers more excited, and the real or imagined presence of blood did not enhance their gaming pleasure. On the contrary, in fact. The sweat secretions fell among the group who had been told that the pheromones were dissolved in blood. And their scores in the game were significantly lower than those of the group who knew nothing about blood being involved. The other parameters remained the same. The first group did not themselves feel that they had played with any less enthusiasm, and their breathing and heartbeats remained just as strong as those of the other group. Their scores and sweat secretions fell during all three rounds of play, including the one where they inhaled water. Despite all these nuances, it seemed that, rather than having a stimulating effect, blood was suppressing the gamers' pleasure. When they were told that they were inhaling the scent of blood, they were less enthusiastic about playing rather than more. That was an unexpected outcome. We would never have predicted that blood would suppress the pleasure of playing a violent computer game.[47]

Is bestial bloodlust nothing more than a myth? That cannot be concluded from this one experiment. Perhaps a virtual fight is not the same as a real one. Although the gamers enjoyed playing and their breathing, sweat and heartbeat values were significantly different from the baseline, it was not a real boxing match or cage fight, and certainly not a real hunt or a bloody fight. As a researcher, you do not have much room for manoeuvre. If you want to measure all kinds of bodily processes with electronic equipment, the test subjects cannot move too much. And if you want the approval of the ethics commission, the level of admissible violence is very low. Another factor is the blood that was used. Again, it came from blood transfusion centres, where a small quantity of anti-coagulation agent had been added. It was no more than a day old, at room temperature and in quantities of 8 millilitres. Would more blood, with more E2D, without additives and from stressed donors have produced a different effect? That possibility cannot be excluded. There may also be reservations about our test subjects: they were not butchers, hunters or combat sportsmen who experienced the 'savagery' of contact with blood, but well-behaved young men studying for 'civilized', intellectual professions. Perhaps blood only stimulated trained instincts, not dormant urges that you will never arouse with 8 millilitres of human blood. Or perhaps we would have had better results with women? After all, I started this part of the book with tales of maenads who found themselves in a Dionysian blood-induced frenzy.

These are all justified comments that deserve to be explored. But my conviction was gone. I no longer believed that my blood rush could be attributed to chemicals in the blood that unconsciously stimulated my senses. That naturalistic explanation had become a myth to me. Bestial bloodlust was founded on so many uncertainties that I had lost my faith. That my experiments had led to nothing only reinforced those doubts. If I looked at the big picture, it was all very clear. We liked to believe that bloodlust was a wild remnant of our primitive existence, but in reality none of that was true. Although the idea gave us a wonderful sense of historical continuity, bloodlust did not link us to a distant past that still haunts us in the present. Bloodlust gave the masculine identity substance, in which physical aggression, brute force and power over life and death were meaningful virtues. And that gave men a rather dubious pleasure in committing violence against other humans and against animals. Bloodlust fed our malaise with modernity, which saw people and society as things that we could mould and make as we see fit. Beneath the veneer of the ideal man lay a still-bestial nature. Now I had examined all these stories, theories and findings in detail, it had become clear to me that this explanation was founded on desire, hope and fantasy, and was not borne out by biological reality. There are no chemosignals in our blood that arouse our ancestral instincts. Blood contains nothing that excites us. It was time to say farewell to the illusion. It had had its time and I could no longer hold on to it. Bestial bloodlust was just as much a fiction as the idea of a moral zero, belief in predatory human nature and the fantasy of genetic memory. They were all attitudes from a time when real men still hunted wolves.

So how could I explain my blood rush? Blood was not a liquid with magical properties, nor did it contain chemosignals. I had also seen that, for many people, blood had a suppressing and restrictive, rather than an exhilarating, effect. That was clear not only from my second experiment, but from the reactions of the British soldiers whose officers had poured abattoir blood over them to make them more bloodthirsty. For a long time, I thought that this repellent response was irrelevant for my research purpose. I was interested in bloodlust, not in blood phobia. But I started to realize that it could help me to explain my blood rush. Perhaps the opposition between attraction and aversion was just what I needed. I found myself on the track of a third explanation: was it perhaps possible that my blood rush was caused on the one hand by fear and disgust and, on the other, by the fact that I could decide for myself whether to continue the blood contact or to stop it? That is why the fear and disgust did not overwhelm me. The distance remained sufficiently great. I was not averse to blood because I was not showered with it. On the other hand, something in the blood attracted me. The contrast with that clean cellar in that clean house was marked. Sensitive as I was to unmodern ideas, something dark came at me from that dripping blood. It was not powerful enough, not scary or disgusting enough, to make me afraid. And yet it aroused sufficient aversion to fascinate me. I enjoyed the bestial darkness that contrasted with the enlightened modernity that held sway in my parents' house. I compared my blood experience with watching a horror film in which forgotten demons suddenly disturb the peaceful life of a happy family. The pleasure did not come from the blood itself, but from the thoughts it invoked. The pleasure had a 'horror-aesthetic' cause. I will examine this romantic fantasy in the third part of the book.

PART THREE
BLOOD AESTHETICS

BLOOD HORROR

This final part of the book also begins with the murder of a child, though – strangely enough – the deed is later undone. The murdered child turns into an immortal vampire who, every night, hunts for fresh blood. We have now fully entered the world of fantasy. The resurrection takes place in the 1976 best-seller *Interview with the Vampire*, by Anne Rice, an American writer with Irish roots. In a moment of weakness, good vampire Louis – played by Brad Pitt in the 1994 film of the book, directed by Neil Jordan – drinks the blood of five-year-old Claudia, played by a young Kirsten Dunst. The young girl has spent days mourning at the side of the rotting corpse of her mother, who was killed by the plague. Louis is a vampire with principles – he has not tasted human blood for four years, only that of rats and chickens. But the child's pounding heart and the fresh blood flowing through her veins is more than he can withstand. He bites her and sucks her blood until her strong little heart almost stops beating. Lestat – played in the film by Tom Cruise – a psychopathic vampire who thinks Louis' moral scruples absurd, gives the child his own blood to drink. She greedily sucks the vampire blood from Lestat's wrist until she has drunk enough to die as a mortal and be reborn as a vampire. Lestat had given Louis eternal nocturnal life in the same way four years earlier. Claudia becomes their blood-sucking daughter, and a child's murder becomes a kind of adoption.

Rice, who suffered from severe depression after losing her daughter to leukaemia, borrowed this baptism by blood from Irish author Bram Stoker's 1897 classic *Dracula*, which also starts with the murder of a child. The first horrific scene witnessed by newly qualified solicitor Jonathan Harker in the castle of Count Dracula is a captive child in a large bag destined for three mysterious vampire women – the 'Sisters' – who also live in the castle. The following day the desperate mother, who had been begging for her now bloodless child to be returned to her, is ripped to pieces by Transylvanian wolves. In Stoker, there is no vampire blood for this anonymous child, nor for the flirtatious Lucy Westenra, Dracula's first victim on English soil. The intelligent Mina Murray – now Harker's wife – is, however, more 'fortunate'. Having been the donor on several occasions, she drinks from an open wound in Dracula's breast, held by the count 'in that terrible and horrid position'. For Mina, this baptism by blood is even more gruesome than having her own blood drunk by vampires. She feels dirty, adulterous and impure now that vampire blood flows through her veins like poison. As gruesome as it is, Stoker never makes it clear whether drinking vampire's blood is necessary for victims to become vampires themselves. Being bitten is sufficient, as with Lucy, who gives blood but does not seem to ingest vampire blood herself and still turns into a vampire. In Rice's book, one bite is not enough. If you do not want nocturnal life to be full of vampires in search of blood and wish to avoid complete vampire epidemics, as in novels like *They Thirst* (1981) and films such as *Vamp* (1986) and *Innocent Blood* (1992), you have to restrict access to this form of eternal life. The 1979 vampire comedy *Love at First Bite* introduced the option of having to be bitten three times, but why not simply go back to Stoker's baptism by blood, which was omitted from early stage and film versions of his story because it was too immoral? In Rice, you can only become a vampire yourself after drinking vampire's blood.

Rice is also clearer than her Irish precursor about other vampire rules. While Bram Stoker does not elucidate, Rice repeats over and over again that a vampire only drinks living blood, never the blood of human or animal corpses. She jettisons all the traditional traits of vampires – lying buried in the earth of their homeland; being invisible in mirrors; only dying from a stake through the heart; fear of the crucifix, the Host, holy water, garlic and incense – as superstition, but remains resolute about the lethal effect of cadaver blood and the fact that vampires burn up in daylight. 'You don't drink after they're dead! Understand that,' Lestat warns Louis firmly.[1] When Louis and Claudia have had enough of the inhuman Lestat and want to get rid of him, they trick him into tasting the blood of two dead boys by telling him the boys are in a drunken stupor. The dead blood poisons Lestat, but he does not drink enough to kill him. Although it is fiction, the ban on drinking dead blood is logical: it no longer contains any life force, there is no oxygen left in it and the red and other blood cells die. Nevertheless, this is curious considering how much vampires have to thank cadaver blood for. Without it, they would never have existed, never mind become the popular horror figures they still are to the present day.

The idea of vampires has been around for centuries. Stories of the dead roaming around at night and feeding themselves with the blood of living people and animals are to be found everywhere. Those who had died in suspicious circumstances, such as murder or suicide, or whose bodies had not been treated correctly, could find no rest and wandered the earth or wreaked vengeance on those who had wronged them. While waiting for death to come for them for good, these restless souls changed into revenants – ghosts who nourished themselves with living blood. In many cultures, including in pre-modern Europe, there was no absolute division between life and the hereafter. The living influenced the eternal fate of the dead, and the dead the temporal fate of the living. People who had died found themselves in limbo between life and death. They seemed dead, but were not yet. It is remarkable how widespread this belief in a continuum between life and death, in the vengeful power of revenants, was in the past.[2]

Popular belief in blood-drinking revenants was therefore nothing new. But vampires as we now know them in literature, films, comics, opera and theatre date back to real events in the first half of the eighteenth century.[3] The term 'vampire' first appears in official reports of actual events. The Habsburg authorities received requests from Serb farmers, who had recently been incorporated into the monarchy after the Ottoman troops had been driven out, to open up the graves of the dead to determine whether they had changed into vampires. If so, they had to be killed again. The reason for these post-mortem requests was the sudden deaths of a number of young people who had repeatedly complained of dreaming of dead people at night. In the winter of 1725, the townspeople of Kisilova asked for permission to open the grave of a man called Peter Plogojowitz after the suspicious deaths of nine villagers, and in the winter of 1732, a request was received from the town of Medvedia after a soldier called Arnod Paole had died following a fall from a hay wagon. When he was still alive, Paole had been troubled by vampires and drank vampire blood to discourage them. The request called for Paole's body to be exhumed, as four people who had dreamed about him had died suddenly. The local authorities were urged to grant the request, otherwise the petitioners would do it themselves illegally or leave the village. The local officials were not sure how to respond to such a strange request and asked advice from their superiors in Belgrade and Vienna. Official reports found their way to the editorial desks of Austrian and German newspapers. Intellectuals, scientists and writers picked up on the newspaper reports and discussed them at length in literary salons, academies and cultural societies. By the end of the century, the number of treatises, essays and opinion articles on vampirism were beyond count.

A recurring theme in all of the reports was the dark-red, liquid blood that flowed from the nose, mouth and ears of the dead bodies, staining the shroud and the lining of the coffin, and sometimes forming pools on the bottom of the open casket. The bodies bled from all orifices, and blood spattered in all directions when the villagers drove a stake through the heart or asked local gypsies to behead them. To them, liquid blood proved that the deceased was not really dead. They did not expect a dead body to contain fluid, uncoagulated blood. I did not expect to find it on the hare in my parents' cellar, either. I found it mysterious that blood continued to drip from the hare and did not clot in the white bowl underneath the animal's snout. For me, too, that blood was still alive. The Serb villagers had a similar experience. It was not normal for a corpse to bleed weeks or months after death. That blood still dripped from its mouth required an extraordinary explanation, and nocturnal feeding with fresh blood offered a satisfactory solution. Belief in vampires can thus be traced back to the belief that blood always coagulated after death. In other words, what happened to live people also happened after they were dead. Their blood coagulated and, if it didn't, there was something strange going on.

Unfortunately, not a word of this is true. That blood coagulates after death is just another blood myth which even forensic medicine took a long time to shake off. Until only a few decades ago, medical guides stated that fluid blood did occur in corpses, but only in the case of sudden death. Belgian experiments with dogs showed that this was the case with drowning, for example.[4] And blood proved not to coagulate after death by electrocution, being struck by lightning and shock. Nevertheless, liquid blood in corpses remained something unusual that was not to be expected in cases of death under 'normal' circumstances. Because sudden death was often also suspicious, the liquid blood in the corpse was immediately of forensic interest. Today, court and police doctors no longer derive causes of death from the fluidity of the victim's blood. As early as 1948, after investigating 61 autopsies, the British pathologist R. H. Mole called for the traditional view to be reversed: 'The existence of large clots in the main blood vessels is thus not the normal phenomenon, as would have been expected from blood *in vitro*, but the abnormal phenomenon. Emphasis on the fluidity of the blood as characteristic of any special cause or mechanism of death is probably misplaced.'[5] Mole discovered that blood only coagulated after death in the case of certain infectious diseases, like pneumonia, and illnesses that deplete the body's resources, such as cancer. We do not yet understand fully why cadaver blood sometimes remains fluid and sometimes coagulates. It is for future biochemical research to unravel these secrets. But to claim that blood normally coagulates after death or that fluid cadaver blood indicates a specific cause of death is completely outdated.

Eighteenth-century scientists did not know this.[6] Giovanni Battista Morgagni observed liquid cadaver blood while conducting an autopsy on a murder victim in *The Seats and Causes of Disease* (1769). He concluded that the blood was fluid because the man had been drunk when he was stabbed. In *A Treatise on the Blood, Inflammation, and Gunshot Wounds* (1794), John Hunter suspected that blood only remained fluid in the event of sudden death caused by epileptic seizure, electrocution, lightning, rage or a blow to the stomach. Augustin Calmet was convinced that the post-mortem bleeding of vampires had a natural cause, but his imaginative explanation in *Dissertations sur les apparitions des anges, des démons et des esprits* (1746; *The Phantom World*, 1850) proved only how extraordinary he considered liquid cadaver blood to be.[7] Because no one knew that it was not at all unusual for cadaver blood to be liquid, and that only the graves of people suspected of being vampires were opened, it was highly likely that blood would flow from the nose, mouth or ears of the corpse and that liquid blood would be found in the chest cavity or on the bottom of the coffin. In reality, the blood around the mouth and nose would come from the lungs, where the many blood vessels release more and more blood. The blood is forced out of the body through the windpipe by the accumulation of gas in the abdominal cavity during the decaying process. Blood from the leaking veins would also find its way to the lowest parts of the body and form blisters, which would then burst, fill the coffin with blood and stain the shroud dark red. For today's forensic scientists, these are normal post-mortem symptoms. For people in times when autopsies and dissections were rare or illegal, however, they were curious phenomena which, in panic situations, called for an exceptional explanation. What science did not have the answer to, people explained on the basis of the centuries-old belief in blood-slurping revenants.

Serb vampires did not yet bite their victims in the neck but in the chest, and were not white like corpses, but blood-red. Nor did they have the now familiar sharp eyeteeth. And Russian vampires used their pointed tongues, not their teeth, to puncture the skin and suck the blood of their victims. There are many differences between folklore and fiction, but what they have had in common from the beginning is their desire for earthly immortality, a sceptical attitude to modern science, the ambivalent attraction of the sinister and gruesome, and fear of the animal power of sex. On the latter, the report on the case of Peter Plogojowitz noted that, besides liquid blood, other 'wild indications' had been observed on the corpse. In other words, when they exhumed Peter's body, he had an erection. Out of respect for the deceased, the report gave no further details, but that only aroused people's curiosity even more. All of these themes and details appealed to the imagination of writers who were tossed back and forth between the Enlightenment and Romanticism, between scholarly treatises and encyclopaedic premises on the one hand and Gothic novels and rediscovered folklore on the other. From the second half of the eighteenth century and continuing today, an unprecedented vampire industry emerged, with early prototypes like Ossenfelder's poem 'Der Vampire' (1748), Goethe's ballad *Die Braut von Korinth* (1797) and Polidori's story *The Vampyre: A Tale* (1819), mass products like *Varney the Vampire* (1847), which introduced the pointed eyeteeth, and less well-known pearls like the novella *Carmilla* (1872) by Sheridan Le Fanu, in which the female Austrian vampire was exemplary company for her victims during the day and enjoyed simple human pleasures like good food and a glass of wine.

Published in 1897, Bram Stoker's *Dracula* put all of these earlier efforts in the shade. It is not easy to say why this was. *Dracula* was a large book, but not as voluminous as the eight-hundred-page *Varney the Vampire*. Besides the title figure, based on a real-life aristocrat from Wallachia who was known for his thirst for blood during his lifetime but not after it, *Dracula* offered little that was new. All of Stoker's themes, details and types are to be found in earlier vampire stories. And yet it is safe to say – under the permanently watchful eyes of the Dracula Society and the *Journal of Vampirism* – that this book is very thorough. *Dracula* gathers all the elements of vampirism that occur summarily and are widely disseminated in the earlier literature and weaves them together into a single story. Furthermore, it is a story that reads well and, with its modern narrative style, contrasts sharply with the more old-fashioned prose of its predecessors.

DRACULA

There is a passage in *Dracula* to illustrate practically every topic discussed in the earlier chapters of this book. Conversely, I could present the book as a series of footnotes to Stoker's masterpiece. The story needs no introduction. Count Dracula has purchased a number of properties in the centre of London, for which solicitor Jonathan Harker needs the count's signature on a number of documents. He travels to Transylvania, where he meets the count in his sinister castle in the remote Carpathian Mountains and is taken prisoner. After giving Jonathan to the vampire Sisters, the count travels to England by boat. The intention is that Jonathan never returns to England alive, but he escapes and ends up in

Budapest. Dracula meanwhile has arrived in England in an empty ship – he has drunk the blood of the entire crew – and has set his sights on the voluptuous Lucy Westenra, with whom no less than three men are in love: psychiatrist John Seward, American millionaire Quincey Morris and aristocrat Arthur Holmwood – later Lord Godalming and the one whom Lucy herself wishes to marry. Mina Harker, Jonathan's wife, watches desperately as her frivolous friend Lucy becomes weaker every day as the result of a mysterious illness. Seward calls in Abraham Van Helsing of Amsterdam, a 'philosopher and metaphysician, and one of the most advanced scientists of his day'. Van Helsing attributes Lucy's sickness to the bites of a vampire and the hunt for Dracula begins. The first victories, however, are for the count. Four blood transfusions are not enough to save Lucy. To make matters worse, the four gentlemen pierce her heart and decapitate her to halt her thirst for blood. The next victim is Mina, who undergoes the baptism by blood, but also establishes contact with the mind of the count. The men – now five, since Jonathan's return – set about tracking him down. Thanks to Holmwood's aristocratic network, they are able to enter the houses in London where he spends the daylight hours in a chest full of earth he has brought from Transylvania. As they destroy his hiding places one after the other, Dracula has no choice other than to return home. Just before he arrives, he and the Sisters are caught by Mina and the men. Of the mortals, only Quincey Morris dies in the ensuing fight. Dracula himself is killed, lifting the curse from Mina, who is once again pure and unsullied.

Bloodlust is one of the first themes found in *Dracula*. Vampires not only like to drink blood, they find it irresistible. When Jonathan cuts himself in the neck while shaving, the count grabs him by the throat in a demonic fury. He becomes calm again after touching a crucifix. Every film version of the story depicts Dracula's bloodlust differently. In *Nosferatu* (dir. F. W. Murnau, 1922), Jonathan cuts himself with a bread knife and in

Dracula (Tod Browning, 1931) – the film that made Hungarian actor Bela Lugosi world famous overnight – he pricks himself with a paperclip. Francis Ford Coppola's *Bram Stoker's Dracula* (1992) returns to the original but adds the brilliant detail of the count licking the razor. This has almost the same effect as the scene in Luis Buñuel's *Un chien andalou* (1929) in which the main character cuts through an eyeball with a razor. The count is obsessed with blood. Before forcing Mina to drink blood from his breast, he helps himself to some of hers, saying, 'First, a little refreshment to reward my exertions.' Even crazier about blood than the vampires is the strange figure of R. M. Renfield, a psychiatric patient in Seward's institution who has telepathic contact with Dracula. Renfield gets a kick from killing and feeds himself with anything that contains blood. He uses sugar to capture flies, which he then feeds to spiders to, in turn, attract birds. He wants a cat that will catch the birds. Seward describes him as a 'zoöphagous' (life-eating) and homicidal maniac. Renfield also applies the evolutionary principle of 'eat or be eaten' to people, if he gets the chance. After attacking Seward, he laps up the blood dripping from the psychiatrist's wounded wrist, like a dog.

The novel is also full of magical elements. Dracula turns into a dog, a bat, a lizard, a bird, a rat and even a mist and, as long as it is not over water, he can move at lightning speed for short distances. He could suddenly appear behind you. Unlike the expressionistic *Nosferatu*, he casts no shadow. The laws of nature do not apply to him. Through Van Helsing, Stoker takes folk tales, folklore and magic very seriously. He does not arrogantly condemn vampirism as unscientific nonsense. On the contrary, as a true scientist Van Helsing remains constantly aware of the limits of empirical knowledge and scientific research methods. It is those who think that science can explain everything that are superstitious. An open mind sees no division between science and faith. If he thinks that it will be more beneficial, Van Helsing falls back without prejudice on traditional practices (garlic) and

Christian symbolism (the Host, crucifix, missal), and emphasizes the power of prayer and the importance of religious devotion. Van Helsing is a philosopher and scientist who both embraces Enlightenment thinking and rejects it as too narrow minded because it closes its eyes to all kinds of occult wonders. By admitting magic to a *fin de siècle* society full of technological innovations and scientific discoveries, Stoker voices that ambiguous feeling about modernity. What we had gained in progress, we were in danger of losing in tradition, mystery and meaning. This is encapsulated in a passage from Jonathan Harker's journal: 'the old centuries had, and have, powers of their own which mere "modernity" cannot kill'.

That magic also contains blood. In *Dracula*, blood is not just a source of life, it is the seat of the soul. After biting their victims for the first time, vampires can manipulate their minds. They make them tractable and obedient through dreams, hallucinations, sleepwalking and hypnosis. After undergoing the baptism by blood, Mina knows what the count thinks and sees. Blood contact unites minds. And blood is not an anonymous bodily fluid but contains personal qualities that can be transferred to another body through transfusion. Stoker retains a very nineteenth-century view of blood transfusion. The young blood of Miss Lucy makes the count more youthful, as can be seen from Jonathan Harker's great surprise when he encounters Dracula again in London. This is not the only way in which Stoker's perspective is typically nineteenth century. Van Helsing refuses to use blood from domestic personnel to save the dying Lucy. British blood should remain divided according to class and status. Vulgar blood must not flow through noble veins. Because, in those times, blood was considered to be as personal as sperm, Dracula's transfusions are always penetrations in disguise, with the associated erotic insinuations. Holmwood, who gives his future wife the first transfusion – this *droit du seigneur* almost goes to Seward but Holmwood arrives just in time to claim the right – does not hear until later that Seward and Morris have also given her blood after him. Van Helsing does not want to tell him at first, to avoid any 'understandable' feelings of jealousy and infidelity at such an adulterous deed. Blood was then not yet the impersonal fluid it was to become a century later.

Such blood magic is also to be found in the historical and geographical setting for *Dracula*. The count had been living since the fifteenth century in a remote corner of Christian Europe, which had been fighting the advancing Ottomans for centuries and where the Church had the greatest difficulty in converting Huns, Scythians, Slovaks and other heathen peoples to the True Faith. In Christian eyes, Transylvania was a wild region where belief in Christian teaching was very precarious. Pagan rituals, perverse ideas and barbarian customs could soon be expected to prick through the veneer of Christianity. Stoker does not say it explicitly, but it takes little imagination to see Dracula as the modern equivalent of a heathen sacrificial demon. In times without human or animal offerings, demons could no longer lick the blood from the sacrificial altar, so quenched their appetites by sucking blood from human and animal bodies at the dead of night. Vampirism was heathen magic living on in Christian times, hence vampires' acute fears of Christian symbols. Having already lost their pagan cult of sacrifice, they now faced losing their hearts and heads. In a moment of despair, Van Helsing asks himself, 'Is there fate among us still, sent down from the pagan world of old, that things must be, and in such way?'[8]

But *Dracula* is also full of elements that belong in a naturalistic perspective on bloodlust. In the twisted mind of psychiatric patient Renfield, evolution is reversed in the direction of a more primitive life. The count himself, with hair on the palms of his hand, eyebrows that meet across the bridge of his nose, pointed ears and razor-sharp eyeteeth which you can hardly see beneath his luxuriant moustache, looks like an animal. He most resembles the wolves with which he has a strange affinity. Like a conductor, he directs the howling of the 'children of the night' and, like the leader of the pack, he orders them to attack all those who betray him. Dracula is a wild animal from a primitive region that, through permanent war, unstable Christendom and retreating civilization, is at a moral zero. Van Helsing believes that the count is what Italian criminologist Cesare Lombroso would classify as 'of criminal type'. His childlike brain is 'imperfectly formed' and has no place for noble or moral feelings that are of no evolutionary use at all in such a primitive, godforsaken place. Transylvania is the imaginary home of cruel warrior races such as the Huns, the Lombards and the Scythians who, disguised as dogs and wolves, were engaged in a war of all against all and were renowned for being bloodthirsty, fearless and cruel. Stoker refers on several occasions to the Berserkers, the Norse animal-warriors who instilled their enemies with terror, partly because they drank blood and ate raw flesh. The wolf that escapes from London Zoo in the story is called Bersicker.

To capture and kill Dracula like a wild wolf, hunting and fighting instincts come in very useful. Holmwood, Seward and Morris are 'real' men who still have enough barbaric masculinity to abandon themselves entirely to the ultimate hunt. This is no place for women. At first, they leave Mina at home. She might have the brain of a man, but she still has the heart of a woman. Only after it becomes clear that she has contact with the count through hypnosis is she allowed to join the vampire hunt. The three men share a passion for hunting. They have chased after animals all over the world with the intention of killing them. They also have experience with hunting wolves, and know that a Winchester is the best gun to shoot them with. For fox-hunting in England they have packs of hunting dogs, including terriers, the perfect dog, as in a *ratodrome*, to chase off the count's rats or bite them to death. Thanks to their hunting experiences, the men know what a blood rush feels like. Once the hunt for Dracula has started, Seward notes that he now knows 'what men feel in battle

when the call to action is heard'.[9] At such moments, the hereditary killing instinct springs up and demands enemy blood. Even
in the most strait-laced of Englishmen there still lurks a beast.

In the details, too, there are similarities with earlier themes:
horses that become frightened at the scent of wolves; Indian
tigers that will settle for nothing else once they have tasted
human blood. *Dracula* also makes use of two by-now-familiar
explanations for bloodlust – magical and bestial. Stoker sees
blood as a liquid that offers access to both the higher (supernatural) and the lower (animal) worlds, and the book contains
countless references to both. But it also does something else: it
is not necessary to believe in either the supernatural existence
of vampires or the evolutionary reality of bestial bloodlust to
enjoy this novel. *Dracula* is not intended to persuade readers
but to make them shudder in fright. It is not a philosophical
treatise, but a horror story. It was so popular because readers
were genuinely afraid and shocked. They dared not read what
would happen next, covering their mouths and even fainting at
the horrific story. Film versions had a similar effect. This was
not an unfortunate side effect, but exactly what Stoker wanted.
His readers were supposed to be horrified at his Gothic novel.
Together with the decaying corpses, the snuffling rats, the sinister graveyards and the deserted castles and abbeys, blood was
the ideal means to scare readers. In this way, *Dracula* throws
light on a third explanation for blood rush or bloodlust. Although
blood may not have a direct effect on us, in that it contains no
substances that unconsciously change our behaviour, it may well
affect us indirectly. Blood repels us, scares us and arouses our
revulsion but, in certain circumstances, also acquires something
appealing. That attraction drove people to the bookshops and
the cinemas.

Who knows, perhaps that combination of repulsion and attraction is a better explanation for the rush and/or lust that people
experience on contact with blood. Better than suspect theories

about the supernatural or naturalistic impulses. I shall begin my exploration of this explanation with the repellent effect of blood.

BLOOD PHOBIA

In 1881 the Russian immunologist Élie Metchnikoff, whom we encountered in the first part of the book, fell into a deep depression, caused by his second wife's typhoid, his own heart problems and his suspicions that, after the assassination of Tsar Alexander II, the political authorities would turn their attention to his liberal friends. He injected himself with a sample of blood from a patient with *febris recurrens*, or relapsing fever, a bacterial disease caused by a bite from a louse or a tick. If he died from the transfusion, it would be clear that the disease was transmitted via the blood, and his meaningless life would after all have been of some use. But the prominent scientist at the Institut Pasteur in Paris survived his desperate deed – and his wife was cured of typhoid. He did, however, become seriously ill and drifted between life and death in a feverish limbo for several weeks. It was clear from the remarkable similarity of the symptoms to those of the patient that the bacteria that caused *febris recurrens* was transmitted via the blood.[10]

Febris recurrens is only one of the countless diseases that can be contracted through contact with blood. Contact with the blood of others is not healthy. People knew that in the past, too. That is why fear and revulsion for blood is normal and universal. *Horror cruoris* is not a recent phenomenon but has always been with us. Epileptics who went to gladiator fights and executions in search of human blood retched as they drank the magical liquid. Christian authorities warned that overenthusiasm in equating Communion wine with human blood, even though it came from Christ, could fill believers with revulsion.[11] Most people have only a mild fear and revulsion for blood, though among children it is a little more marked. But a small group of people – about 2 per cent of men and 4.5 per cent of women – suffer from blood phobia, or what is described in psychiatric bibles such as the American Psychiatric Association's *Diagnostic and Statistical Manual of Mental Disorders* (DSM-5) as 'blood-injection-injury phobia'. This condition is considered a specific phobia, like fear of spiders or snakes.[12] It starts at around the age of nine among boys and seven and a half among girls, becomes less severe with age and can be temporary, for example during pregnancy. A significant number of pregnant women (7.2 per cent) cannot bear contact with blood.[13] Besides fear and disgust, blood phobia manifests itself through sweating, yawning, going pale, dizziness, nausea, ringing ears, visual disorders and fainting, with temporary loss of consciousness on contact with blood or even the thought of it. More than 80 per cent of blood phobia sufferers have fainted on contact with blood, real or imaginary. The rest have developed avoidance mechanisms. And yet, fainting at the sight or thought of blood is not unique to blood phobia. It can happen to most of us. Dutch research has shown that one in ten medical students have fainted at some point during their studies.[14] An estimated 1 in 1,000 to 1 in 300 blood donors faint while giving blood. That does not seem many, but with 27 million people donating blood ever year in Europe and the U.S., that is between 30,000 and 80,000 cases annually. And these are not people with blood phobia – they do not dare to give blood. Blood donors rarely faint when the needle pricks into their vein and the first blood flows through the rubber hose, but are more likely to do so when it is removed and they stand up. A glass of water before the needle is placed or some physical movement afterwards before standing up slowly can help. As the fear of fainting scares off many potential blood donors, scientists are trying to find ways of doing something to help them. Every case is one too many.

Fainting (*vasovagal syncope*) through emotion is a remarkable phenomenon. It is easy to explain why people faint as a result of physical triggers like pain, heat, sudden movement, alcohol or drugs, but that simply seeing blood, needles or wounds, or even the thought of them, can have such a dramatic effect remains remarkable. Few other external stimuli have the same impact. Being afraid can make the heart beat faster, cause screaming, cause sweating. It can make the person go rigid or start to run. Someone who feels revulsion might turn their nose up, stick their tongue out or retch, which can cause vomiting. It is unusual to faint from fear or revulsion. Unlike other phobias, blood phobia causes an initial rise in blood pressure and heartbeat, followed by a sudden fall in both (hypotension and bradycardia, respectively), which leads to fainting (syncope).

While an evolutionary explanation for the exhilarating effect of blood is not very plausible, it is easy to argue that the repellent effect of blood is related to evolution. Scientists believe more and more that blood revulsion is a product of natural selection.[15] Humanoids who possessed mechanisms for avoiding contact with pathogenic substances or, if there had been contact, neutralizing the consequences as quickly as possible, were more successful than other members of their species who did not possess such mechanisms. Fear acted as a primitive warning system and revulsion was a kind of inborn sickness prevention. The stimuli that these natural systems responded to were, given the differing environments in which humanoids lived, largely a matter of parental instruction – though that instruction was made easier by the fact that these stimuli tended to be imposing, noisy, sinister, powerful or quick in the case of fear, or slimy, sticky, liquid, smelly or wriggly in the case of revulsion. Anything that could enter the body through sex or food was always suspect. And if a member of the group was affected by something harmful, humanoids had the cognitive powers to recognize the unique feeling of infection and to combat the contamination by means of ritual. Our ancestors felt revulsion for those who came into contact with repugnant substances. After all, many diseases proved able to jump from one organism to another.

It should come as no surprise that blood disgusts us, considering the high quantity of pathogens it contains.[16] Given that blood can be drunk or that it can enter the body through sex (or Stoker's equivalent, transfusion), after contact with blood we experience a feeling of contamination and a need to be purified. Worse than being bitten by vampires is having to drink their blood, like Mina Harker during her baptism by blood. Only Dracula's death saved her. Our aversion to blood is of the same order as the revulsion we feel for other bodily fluids, such as sweat, urine or mucus. Nor is it so strange that blood inspires fear in us. It is the same fear we feel when confronted with other things that can cause us pain or threaten our lives. Where blood flows, you are likely to feel pain, lick your wounds or feel sorrow at injured or killed fellows. Both responses have their origins in hereditary mechanisms that are very easily triggered by blood. For people who suffer from blood phobia, the threshold for triggering these mechanisms is lower.

Scientists cannot agree on the value of fainting at the sight of blood. One recent theory, proposed by Stefan Bracha and Paolo and Marco Alboni, suggests that fainting is a radical way of feigning death.[17] Many animals, including roebucks, opossums and squirrels, do not fight or flee when faced with danger but stand or lie stock still, in the hope that a predator will not see them or think they are already dead (many carnivores do not eat carrion). Bracha and the Albonis believe that our vulnerable ancestors used this trick to deceive predators or other, violent humanoids. Among humans it leads to loss of consciousness. There may be two reasons for that. Our enemies may have been able to detect prey or other humanoids that pretended to be dead but were still conscious. That gave actual fainting an adaptive advantage. Second, loss of consciousness can be caused by the fact that we walk upright. The sudden drop in heartbeat and blood pressure leads us to faint.

A second theory, put forward by Rolf Diehl in 2005, links fainting to the fact that blood leaving a wounded body coagulates more quickly.[18] We know that animals lose consciousness if they lose more than a quarter of their body's blood. Loss of blood can be reduced by a reduction in blood pressure and a slower heart-beat. The blood then coagulates more quickly, so that the animal does not bleed to death. For Diehl, fainting is a risky trick of nature to prevent animals from bleeding to death by stimulating coagulation. There is of course a greater risk of the animal dying even more quickly by losing consciousness because it cannot escape from the predator. Diehl argues that, among people with blood phobia, the fainting-to-stimulate-coagulation response occurs much too early – a small quantity of blood, or even the thought of blood is enough to bring on a faint, without the victim being genuinely wounded or losing a lot of blood.

There are a number of issues with both of these theories and neither has been proved empirically. One objection to the defence theory of Bracha and the Albonis, the plausibility of which depends on how much our ancestors benefited from fainting, is the infrequency of blood phobia. If their claims are true, why is blood phobia not more widespread? An objection to Diehl's coagulation theory, the plausibility of which depends on how effective fainting is as a defence against bleeding to death, is that people faint not only at the sight or thought of blood, but in situations where blood does not flow at all. Medical students tend to faint more often in warm rooms or after an evening spent binge drinking than as a result of contact with blood, injection needles or open wounds. So why is fainting not more specific?

Why do some people suffer from blood phobia when others do not? That, too, is unclear. If you are a woman with a low education and blood phobia in the family, your chances are somewhat higher. Moreover, blood phobia does not occur in isolation. More often, it is one of a number of psychiatric disorders. But these hard statistics do not help much in identifying the real risk factors. One original and somewhat bold theory is that people with blood phobia have a greater fear of death and find it more difficult to accept their mortality, of which blood is a reminder. They are more sensitive than other people to the existential void that death confronts us with. They have fewer buffers that allow them to banish that unbearable mortality from their lives. This idea goes back to the influential theory devised in the 1960s and '70s by cultural anthropologist Ernest Becker, but has its roots in the psychoanalysis of Sigmund Freud, Otto Rank and Gregory Zilboorg and the existentialist philosophy of the Dane Søren Kierkegaard. Although Becker was an inspiring teacher and successful author – his *Denial of Death* won the Pulitzer Prize in 1974 – his theory found little resonance in academic circles because the abundance of Freudian speculation was backed up by very little empirical evidence. At the end of the 1980s, American psychologists Sheldon Solomon, Jeff Greenberg and Tom Pyszczynski launched a scientific counteroffensive by making Becker's theory, which they renamed terror management theory (TMT), empirically testable. Since then, the theory has been enriched by dozens of experimental studies published in prominent psychology journals. After more than 25 years of research, TMT has become a smoothly run business that is effective in spreading its theory, despite many of its principles, findings and generalizations still being controversial. Nevertheless, TMT has a certain intuitive appeal. It can be used to explain a lot of phenomena and many possible applications can be seen. Because it also has interesting things to say about the way we deal with blood, it is worth looking at more closely.[19]

FEAR OF DEATH

Have you ever wondered why freshly laundered clothes, a clean house or a warm bath make you feel good? Or why a squalid house, a stinking toilet, a freaked-out drug addict or a slurring drunk make you feel depressed? There is more to this than just liking cleanliness and being disgusted at filth. Cleanliness cheers you up and revulsion makes you feel despondent. Why is that? According to TMT, death is the greatest taboo. While, like all animals, humans are programmed to survive, we already know that the battle is lost. Sooner or later, the moment comes that we are no longer here. Although we have an intense desire to stay alive, we know only too well that this desire is an illusion. Our lives are finite and our stay here is temporary. This awareness is the downside of our human intelligence. As far as we know, we are the only animal that suffers from this cosmic joke. According to TMT, living in full awareness of our mortality is unbearable. The fear of dying, of no longer existing, to realize that, in the end, everything will have been for nothing, is so overwhelming that we arm ourselves against it. We have to, otherwise we will find ourselves in an existential crisis, overcome by a paralysing emptiness and the 'worm in the core' – as William James so graphically called death – will eat away at our joy at being alive. If we want to escape this *horror vacui*, fear of the void, we need buffers. Some people find comfort in belief systems about man and/or the world. Many religions assure us of life after death. Philosophy structures our reality so that we can understand it and death becomes little more than a metaphysical detail. Ideology carries us along on a social project that transcends individuals and generations. Others strive for personal fame, wealth, power or prestige to help them forget the futility of this temporal life. Ambition creates the illusion that everything has not been for nothing. Yet others take satisfaction from the warmth of a happy family. Their own existence is part of an extended genealogy that defies the passage of time. Everyone has their own strategy to protect themselves from the unbearable lightness of being.

What many of these buffers share is that they erect a solid fence between humans and animals. We hold eulogies to our human supremacy and avoid being reminded of our animal origins. Knowing that we are animals is knowing that we are mortal beings. We use art and culture to elevate ourselves above animals, which are only concerned with satisfying their primary needs. Some people hunger more for art than for calories. Cosmetic products disguise our bodily odours and give artificial colour to our nails, cheeks, lips and other parts of our bodies. We have special furniture to make sleep, preparing food, urinating and defecating look and feel more 'human'. We have cutlery to avoid touching our food or having to rip meat from the bone with our teeth. Clothes protect us from bad weather and hide our naked bodies. We shave and remove our body hair and make regular visits to the hairdresser to stop us looking like hairy mammals. Behaviour that we tolerate among animals – such as passing wind in company or belching after eating – fills us with revulsion in humans. Only erotic arousal, which is very selective, medical emergencies and intimacy with those we love can overcome the aversion we normally feel to intimate contact with other people's bodies. But again, for TMT, evolution explains more than just our aversion. It is not only our bodies that benefit from hygiene, politeness and respect, but our mental health. They help us avoid the existential crisis of being confronted by our animal origins. This explains why we cheer up at the sight of a tidy apartment and feel depressed by a dilapidated house that offers less comfort than a cowshed. We feel good when we do not have to think about our mortality.

Blood seeps easily through the cracks in those mental buffers. There are few things, with the exception of corpses and cadavers, that so strongly emphasize our animal past and our finite future. And that is why we prefer not to come into contact with blood. We have a mild fear of and revulsion to it. If the contact lasts for too long or is too intensive, it can depress us. Think of the British soldiers whose officers wanted to make them bloodthirsty by showering them with blood. Instead, they lost all their desire to fight for their country. Among people with little self-confidence and little cultural protection, that normal reaction can lead to blood phobia, even at the slightest contact with blood – with the paradoxical consequence that they are afraid to go to a doctor or dentist, have blood taken for medical tests or even to get pregnant – which means that they are more likely to shorten rather than extend their lives or those of their children. On the other hand, people who are tired of life and would rather die tend to lose all their horror of blood. Depressive Élie Metchnikoff apparently had no qualms at all about injecting infected blood into his veins. He was more afraid of living than dying. TMT explains all this very elegantly, while it sometimes seems that horror literature simply applies the theory's insights. To get its readers and viewers shivering with fear, it reminds them of things that emphasize our mortality. Take Stoker's *Dracula* again: there is not only a trail of blood running through the whole novel, it is also saturated with the smell of stinking corpses from graveyards, deserted buildings, tombs and coffins. The stench is so penetrating that 'it conveyed irresistibly the idea that life – animal life – was not the only thing which could pass away.'[20] Emerging from the vault holding Lucy Westenra's coffin, John Seward records 'how sweet it was to breathe the fresh air, that had no taint of death and decay. How humanizing to see the red lighting of the sky beyond the hill, and to hear far away the muffled roar that marks the life of a great city.'[21] Besides dread and revulsion, *Dracula* also invokes our fear of death. There is no horror more terrifying than one that penetrates our existential comfort zone.

TMT is tempting. But that is not enough to make it a successful theory. There is justified criticism of its basic principle that, in full awareness of our mortality, life is unbearable. Everyone is afraid of a painful death and regrets not being around to experience things that happen after we have gone, but that is not fear of death as such. Fear of death implies that the awareness that we are only here temporarily fills us with despair. That our existence is founded on a mental drama that we do not dare to think about. TMT has never proved that this fear is universal.

It has only presumed that this is the case, on the basis of dubious philosophical assumptions from existentialist philosophy and psychoanalysis. Furthermore, to explain the fact that many people do not suffer from fear of death – carers who assist dying people at home or in hospitals rarely encounter the phenomenon – TMT uses a trick that is familiar from the heyday of psychoanalysis: these patients are not afraid of death because they have suppressed it so effectively. But how can we tell whether someone has suppressed something or simply that it is not there in the first place? Although it may not be the case in strongly religious countries like the U.S. and Israel, in increasingly secular Western Europe, there is a growing group of people who know that there is no life after death, settle for a small family and attach relatively little importance to fame, fortune and power. What are they repressing? Is it not easier to believe that the fear of death is not universal? Then there is no longer any need to reduce all forms of cultural expression to a buffer against fear of death.

This is not the place to subject TMT to a thorough critical analysis. Other publications have already done that.[22] What surprises me is that TMT offers no explanation for the appeal of the horrific. We do not always avoid things that we find frightening, which are related to death or remind us of our animal origins; we also seek them out, to enjoy the horror and the fear. TMT takes no account of the fact that horror is a popular genre. That light-hearted flexibility clashes with the cast-iron universality in which TMT believes. In that sense, *Dracula* is also an ironical illustration of this theory. Stoker uses elements of it to horrify his readers even more. Be careful, he warns us, reading this book will lead to an existential crisis! But, in the end, this is no more than a rhetorical manoeuvre, a literary device to give the reader a sublime experience. The more horrific you imagine death to be, the more fun it is to flirt with it. That paradox is a basic law of horror-aesthetics, which explains the horror, as well as the excitement, of blood.

SUBLIME BLOOD

Very early one morning, a guide leads a group of culinary dreamers, including cookery journalists and restaurant chefs, through a national monument. It is not a hunting lodge or a game park, but Rungis, the world's largest fresh food market. Here France toils away every day, from two o'clock in the morning, to bring its highly praised cuisine to the rest of the world. Rungis, named after and now part of a commune to the south of Paris, is the Valhalla for foodies. In its more than forty halls, covering an area larger than Monaco, they can obtain products, ingredients and recipes that are to be found nowhere else. Besides being a gourmet's paradise, Rungis also accommodates a place or two where you quickly lose your appetite. And it is to one of these chambers of horror that the guide takes his charges, decked out in white disposable jackets and plastic caps. He leads them through tunnels, corridors and halls where it is never warmer than 7 degrees Celsius. After passing through the picturesque fish halls and the luxuriant fruit and vegetable sectors, they come to the immense *Pavillon des viandes*. Between the hundreds of carcasses hanging on hooks from the ceiling, muscular men in white pelerines, caps and aprons made of shiny metal plates looking very much like medieval chain mail walk around and chuckle at the culture tourists. These butcher-knights, their belts dangling with knives with colourful handles, know what horrific attraction is soon to follow. They are a little embarrassed by their enjoyment of the shock their visitors are about to experience. They themselves are now accustomed to the horrific scenes, but they remember their first encounter with it as if it were yesterday.

The meat market in Rungis is the successor to the legendary La Villette, the slaughterhouse complex in the northeast of Paris. Besides an abattoir, it also contained livestock and meat markets, and was known affectionately but poignantly to the local people as *La Cité du Sang*, the City of Blood.[1] The complex, dating from 1867, was one of the municipal projects of Baron Georges Haussmann, who radically redrew the map of nineteenth-century Paris. La Villette was one of his least radical projects, simply continuing the centralization of slaughtering activities in Paris initiated by Napoleon sixty years previously. There was already no space left in the centre of the city for small private butcheries, known as *tueries particulières*, of which there were still more than 350 in 1810. At the beginning of the nineteenth century every butcher in Paris slaughtered his own meat, in the cellar below the shop or in an outhouse at the back, accessible via a muck-covered inner courtyard. If Paris – which already had three-quarters of a million inhabitants – wanted to do something about the stench of rotting meat, clotted blood, manure and slaughter waste that hung over the city and floated on the Seine, the many accidents with panic-stricken animals, the sickly quality of uncured meat and the less tangible influence of the loose morals of the butcher-folk on young people, the only solution was to establish large public abattoirs on the outer margins of the city, safely hidden behind high walls and with medical services and an industrial infrastructure. The project started in 1818 with five slaughterhouses spread around the city. The crowning jewel was the Rochechouart abattoir in Montmartre. The original classical design by Bellanger referred back to Graeco-Roman sacrificial ritual but the eventual result was banal and utilitarian. The final stage of the project, completed in 1867, was the centralized slaughter and meat market complex in La Villette.[2] At that time, La Villette was a rough, working-class district with a terrible reputation for crime, unemployed immigrants and industrial experiments that cared little for the environment, security or social rights. Nevertheless, the district was easily accessible by rail and water, and had an ample supply of cheap labour willing to do dirty, heavy and dangerous work to keep their heads above water in the bustling metropolis. La Villette was the ideal place for Paris-Bestiaux. And, only a stone's throw away in neighbouring Aubervilliers, was Monsieur Gustave's famed *ratodrome*.

In the century that followed, La Villette grew to become a legendary abattoir. In 1929 the surrealist photographer Eli Lotar took pictures of sawn-off calves' legs that appeared in the magazine *Documents*, published by philosopher Georges Bataille. Twenty years later, film-maker Georges Franju documented life in the abattoir in *Le Sang des bêtes*, which was once shown by accident to an audience of young children at the Venice Film Festival. Fortunately, they thought the film very funny. Jean Lorrain, the ether-sniffing Belle Époque novelist, turned the morning visits of anaemic women who went there to drink fresh calf's blood into decadent vampire stories.[3] The reality was less decadent: because the ladies found the blood repugnant, their assistants added salt or sugar before they drank it. La Villette was an attraction: partly because of the picturesque abattoir workers, who spoke of the animals in their own jargon, so incomprehensible that even professors of anatomy did not know what they were talking about; but also partly because of the architecture. People came from all over Europe to see this French model public abattoir that was, after all, something completely new. There had been no public slaughterhouses since Roman antiquity. The abattoir had to reinvent itself.

The French model was unique in two respects. Although Paris separated the slaughter and the sale of meat, everyone in the city knew what went on in La Villette. Back then, the slaughterhouse was not an anonymous business, barely distinguishable from a furniture factory on an industrial park. It had a clear, self-confident and proud profile, accentuated by its entrance. Anyone approaching La Villette or Vaugirard, the slaughterhouse in the southern part of the capital, could see the monumental bronze or cast-iron statues of animals, girls driving cattle and even slaughter scenes. There were also plenty of living animals around La Villette, on their way to be slaughtered. They walked from the railway station, where they were unloaded from wagons, across a bridge over the tracks and the canal into the abattoir complex. Around the complex were double rows of muddy carts and trucks, the smoky bars and restaurants were full of noisy livestock traders, and there were all kinds of shops selling the most unimaginable wares. No matter how much the city planners had wanted to banish the whole slaughter business from the urban environment, it remained a very visible part of the city. And that failure was understandable. In times before industrial refrigeration, the distance between the breeding, slaughter, sale and consumption of meat had to be kept as short as possible. One gigantic meat centre was unavoidable. What you cannot hide, so thought the planners of Paris, you can better make into a real spectacle.

Another unique feature of the French-style abattoir was its division into a large number of slaughtering rooms, known as *échaudoirs*. The French were not interested in a single industrial slaughtering hall, like those to be found in America from the middle of the nineteenth century, and which had inspired automobile manufacturer Henry Ford to develop the first mass-produced car assembly line. In Paris, every master slaughterer (*chevillard*) had his own rented room in the abattoir where he would instruct his team to slaughter some twenty cows or thirty pigs a day, depending on supply and demand. He would then have the carcasses hung along the outside wall of the slaughtering room to wait for interested buyers. Although this system led to great diversity in products – each room had its own speciality – it was unhygienic and inefficient. It was impossible for meat inspectors to see what happened in the closed-off rooms. What their American colleagues could achieve in two or three days on the production lines in their slaughtering halls in Chicago took the French slaughterers a year. That pushed the price of French meat up to unprecedented heights and made it cheaper for French butchers to buy meat from abroad.[4] La Villette ultimately lost its battle against modern industrial slaughtering methods and closed in 1973 after a series of political and financial scandals. Since the 1990s, La Villette has enjoyed renown as a Parisian music temple, an extremely refined cultural institution where avant-garde jazz now resounds through the renovated *Grande Halle aux boeufs*.

The *Pavillon des viandes* in Rungis bears the scars of that modern evolution. In France, too, animals are now slaughtered in American-style privately run industrial abattoirs, with production lines rather than *échaudoirs*. Every animal passes through the same process, from life to death, from unclean to clean, from steaming, warm living animal to deep-frozen meat. Refrigeration technology means that there is no longer any need for a central complex where livestock market, abattoir and meat market are all in the same place. Everything is now as widely dispersed geographically as before 1818, even more so now that butcher and slaughterer are separate professions. In Rungis, too, there is no longer an abattoir or a livestock market. The *chevillards* buy their animals from breeders and have them slaughtered in private abattoirs. After BSE, swine fever and avian flu, no one wants to go back to the old livestock markets, which proved the most efficient way to make healthy animals ill. As a result of that division of labour, consumers are now completely unaware of the whole slaughtering process. We no longer see how the beef cattle in the meadow end up in bite-sized pieces wrapped up in cellophane on our supermarket shelves. Even cattle trucks look increasingly like normal lorries. Only the ventilated sides betray the fact that they are carrying live animals.

Although the *Pavillon des viandes* is now nothing more than a large meat market for wholesalers, it is still possible to find traces of the old La Villette in Rungis. There are a few *échaudoirs* where things happen which only occur in an abattoir, in that strange, hidden place where living animals are turned into tasty cuts of meat. Those are things which we prefer not to associate with the comfortable environment of a meat market, no matter how famous it may be.

Time to go back to the horrific scenario awaiting the foodies on their guided tour. One journalist described it as follows:

'Come on, let me show you my favourite spots!' Isabelle, our guide, lures us to a corridor full of open trays of lungs, pigs' and calves' heads and knocks on the door of a small workshop. Behind the door is a hallucinating scene: two burly men with razor-sharp knives are skinning calves' heads at lightning speed. They throw the remains – a mess of bone, meat and eyeballs – into a waste bin. Then they roll up the still intact outer part of the head, snout and all, until you can no longer recognise it as coming from a calf, and push it into a net, ready for use. 'Boiled calf's head,' Isabelle tells us. 'A traditional delicacy in salads.'[5]

Anyone who ever enjoyed watching the 1974 horror classic *The Texas Chainsaw Massacre*, about an American family that specialized in a gruesome form of home-slaughter after the father had lost his job in an abattoir, might just shrug their shoulders and say, 'Is that it? Have you seen this or that clip on the Internet?' It is undoubtedly possible to find even more horrific slaughterhouse scenes. But that is not what concerns me here. Everyone understands that the sight of calves' heads being skinned is hair-raising. You won't see many people with blood phobia in the *Pavillon des viandes*. The visible transformation from recognizable calf's head to a shapeless lump of meat, with two empty eye sockets still protruding from it, the blood and the slime that make us retch, the memories of our animal origins that supposedly make us live in mortal fear – there is no need for me to explain why such a scene fills us with fear, loathing and disgust. Of course, it could always be worse: there are no limits to blood and gore. What interests me more, however, is that this gruesome scene also has a certain attraction and beauty. It not only repels us but fascinates us, arouses our interest, stimulates and even excites us. It generates a sensation that is not entirely unpleasant and which contrasts with the disturbing emotions that it initially evokes.

This is not a perversity that I share with a handful of creeps. You can sense the same reaction in the journalist's description of her visit to Rungis. Her story did not appear in a trade journal for the meat industry. That journal's readers would be insulted to see an abattoir depicted as some kind of palace of horror. They would find the story too sensational and unprofessional. Nor was it published in a vegetarian activist magazine, whose readers would be annoyed at the lack of indignation. The story is too sympathetic to the slaughter scene it describes and fails to disapprove on moral grounds. The journalist reported on her visit to Rungis in the trendy weekend supplement of a quality Belgian newspaper that rewards its well-off readers on Saturday mornings, after a hard week at work, with stories that help them to forget the banal reality of their lives. These supplements entice us with myriad ways of spending the pay we bring home after long and stressful working days: on holidays, fashion, cars, designer items and delicious food and drink in restaurants or at home. It is all about generating an atmosphere. The weekend reader wants to dream, feel magic, experience sensation and feel a renewed lust for life. The skinning scene fits in perfectly with this leisure-time atmosphere. The story reads like an adventurous travelogue where the explorer journeys not through inhospitable regions full of dangerous animals and cruel tribes, but through an abattoir. It is a place that looks just as perilous as the untamed wilderness, with broad-shouldered slaughterers as contemporary headhunters.

In that context, the whole process of slaughter acquires a paradoxical attraction that is at odds with the filth, cruelty and fear of sickness and infection. In contrast to the step-by-step withdrawal of the unsavoury practice of slaughter from the proximity of everyday citizens, which started in the first half of the nineteenth century and ended with the anonymous slaughterhouses on industrial parks, there is a tendency to make the hidden facets of this industrial production process visible again. The slaughter of animals not only revolts us but excites us. These days, every self-respecting quality butcher will have a large display cabinet in which the expensive ribs of exclusive cattle breeds are maturing. They are shown off like a library full of richly illustrated manuscripts and folios. Stamped carcasses, large chunks of yellow-smoked bacon, cows' tongues and sucking pigs hang on gleaming metal meat hooks. In the shop window are shiny plucked chickens with their feet and feathered heads still attached. We are now again allowed to see, hear and smell how a skilled butcher chops, saws and cuts up animals and removes all the superfluous pieces. Sawdust or sand is spread nonchalantly on the floor to absorb blood and splinters of bone. None of this deters customers: on the contrary, it attracts even more of them. Although we cannot yet enjoy a good barbecue in an abattoir, caterers do now offer original culinary experiences with which to entertain your friends – in a cowshed, for example, amid rows of lowing cows with their necks through the railings, munching away at their troughs full of soya pulp.

While for some people the whole slaughter business cannot be far enough away from their sight and thoughts, others experience a paradoxical pleasure in being as close as possible to it with their senses. Their reasons are by no means always the same. Some are looking for 'the taste of the past', which was lost when the slaughterhouses were hidden away. Others are critical of the cowardice of meat eaters who no longer dare to look the animals they eat in the eye. Yet others link visible and transparent slaughter to a plea for less meat, and of a better quality. What all these self-aware carnivores have in common is that they see beauty in a form of food production that, no matter how you look at it, is dirty, cruel and inefficient. There is beyond doubt something deeply wrong with the way we produce meat and, even in the best possible meat world, these abuses cannot be completely banished. But instead of morally rejecting that production and combating it politically, some see it as an aesthetic experience that can be so deep and overwhelming that it generates excitement, pleasure, enchantment and happiness, rather than indignation or resistance. The skinned calves' heads give meaning back to our banal day-to-day lives. They contain a beauty and happiness that make life worth living. After such an invigorating weekend, the dull working week can start all over again.

THE AESTHETICS OF THE SUBLIME

This experience of beauty based on a confrontation between negative and positive feelings, of fear and revulsion that can lead not only to simple sentiments like excitement, pleasure or arousal but to more complex emotions like awe and passion, has been known since the Romantic era as the Sublime.[6] It is an old phenomenon revived in a new guise. The Romantics did not consider the slaughter of animals sublime, but found the sublime in mountains, deserts, oceans and wild open landscapes – perilous natural beauty that only an elite could protect themselves from. The intelligentsia did not need to put herds of sheep or goats out to graze, grow potatoes, maize or grain, or catch fish in ramshackle boats to survive. They also found the sublime in executions and gallows, criminals who made killing an art, and dangerous animals that tried to kill toreadors in arenas.[7]

Anything that inspired fear or which caused blood to flow could be a source of the sublime – but only if they, the only class that could permit itself the luxury of these aesthetic pleasures, were not directly involved in the events. Distance was crucial in order to enjoy the pleasure of the horror. An experience can only be sublime from a safe and comfortable vantage point. Anyone who passed by the countless *tueries particulières* of Paris on a daily basis was not receptive to the beauty of the abattoir. Like today's slaughterhouse workers, they could not enjoy the elevated delight of the slaughter. Their reaction was the same as that of the mountain farmer who could not fathom why rich people clambered up mountains for fun, or the fisherman who thought it insane that city folk would travel to windy coasts to dive into the cold water in their swimsuits. Only those who are not forced to expose themselves to the brutal reality, who can withdraw from it at will, have the luxury of enjoying the horrific, the threatening and the inhospitable. The sublime is the aesthetic experience of the tourist, the outsider or the dilettante. Anyone who skins calves' heads on a daily basis will not see the beauty in butchery. The sublime is the aesthetic of the leisure classes. Nevertheless, the experience must not be too non-committal. If the distance becomes too great, the aversion and fear become fake, there is no antagonistic pleasure and the promise of beauty is degraded to the level of a fairground attraction and a cliché. The sublime becomes a tourist trap. The modest distance that makes the sublime possible rests on a delicate and unpredictable balance between revulsion and attraction that does not appeal to everyone. What is sublime to one person may be simple horror or a cheap effect to another. Some may not be ready for it, others may have left it long behind. Nothing is sublime for everyone for all time.

All theorists of the sublime confirmed the importance of maintaining a modest distance. The Irish philosopher Edmund Burke wrote, 'When danger or pain press too nearly, they are incapable of giving any delight, and are simply terrible; but at certain distances, and with certain modifications, they may be, and they are delightful, as we every day experience.' Burke goes on to say, 'So it is certain, that it is absolutely necessary my life should be out of any imminent hazard, before I can take a delight in the sufferings of others, real or imaginary.'[8] For Immanuel Kant, too, the safety of the observer was paramount in enjoying the sublime in nature:

> Bold, overhanging, and, as it were, threatening rocks, thunderclouds piled up the vault of heaven, borne along with flashes and peals, volcanoes in all their violence of destruction, hurricanes leaving desolation in their track, the boundless ocean rising with rebellious force, the high waterfall of some mighty river, and the like, make our power of resistance of trifling moment in comparison with their might. But, provided our own position is secure, their aspect is all the more attractive for its fearfulness.[9]

That safety can be physical, for example a balcony behind reinforced glass, or virtual, as when watching or reading a tragedy, a thriller or a horror story, where you can always leave the theatre or close the book. But imitation horror is never as appealing as the real thing. To quote Burke again:

> Choose a day on which to represent the most sublime and affecting tragedy we have; appoint the most favourite actors; spare no cost upon the scenes and decorations; unite the greatest efforts of poetry, painting and music; and when you have collected your audience, just at the moment when their minds are erect with expectation, let it be reported that a state criminal of high rank is on the point of being executed in the adjoining square; in

a moment the emptiness of the theatre would demonstrate the comparative weakness of the imitative arts, and
proclaim the triumph of the real sympathy.[10]

As long as you are safe, real horror is simply much more exciting
than when it is staged or described in words. The imitation then
feels fake.

Why do we derive pleasure from the horrific? Theorists,
including contemporary thinkers and researchers, cannot agree
on that.[11] One of the oldest reflections on the horror paradox
comes from Jean-Baptiste Du Bos in 1719, who attributed the
pleasure to a bored elite that must continually seek new sensations.[12] The sublime became a trendy way to kill time. The more
emotional it was, the quicker a dull afternoon would pass and the
sooner it would be time to dine. To enjoy the sublime, it is essential to have the time and the means to seek it out and to maintain
the required safe distance. Boredom can certainly be one reason
for seeking the sublime. But that explains only that the sublime
can be a way to pass the time, not why the horrific can also be
pleasurable. There are many other ways to cure boredom. Sport,
a hobby, a comic book or a philosophical treatise are all ways of
passing the time, and some are more effective against boredom
than others. The similar explanation that we derive pleasure
from the sublime because we cannot tear ourselves away from
it, is equally inadequate.[13] It does not explain why we seek the
sublime in the first place, only why it has such a hypnotic effect
on us: because there is always a way out, we are in control of the
experience. Control is essential to the enjoyment of horror. But
being in control does not in itself explain why horror has such a
pleasurable effect on us. A lot of things that we can control leave
us completely cold. No one pays to go to a theme park where you
can open and close roller shutters with a remote control. And
the control is relative. Attractions in theme parks are exciting
because we can't switch off a hair-raising ride on a roller coaster.

No matter how hard we scream, we have to stay put until the terrifying ride is over.

The explanation that sees enjoying horror as a rite of passage also suffers from this weakness.[14] Young male adolescents, and especially those with a tendency towards sensation-seeking and high-risk behaviour, certainly make up the majority of the audience at cinemas showing the most hair-raising films. It makes them feel macho to laugh at or enjoy things that others find scary or unsavoury. Research also shows that the more a film scares the girls, the more the boys enjoy it. The more often girls put their hands in front of their eyes, leave the cinema or feel sick, the cooler the boys find it. For girls, it is the exact opposite: if they see that boys find it difficult to watch certain horror scenes, they enjoy the film less. These findings slavishly follow the stereotypical role patterns of caring girls and tough-guy boys. In the distant past, this division of roles may have been adaptive. In a dangerous situation, you have more chance of survival with a father who can deal with fear and a mother who can empathize with the needs and concerns of her children. Horror offers adolescent boys seeking status the opportunity to demonstrate that primitive talent. If you can watch *Evil Dead* or *Saw* all the way through and enjoy the horror, you are a real man.[15]

It also sounds tough to find the sight of big men with sharp, shiny knives skinning calves' heads exciting or beautiful. That aesthetic reaction shows that you can control your fear and repugnance. Finding gruesome things appealing raises your status as a fearless man, especially when there are women around. In modern times, however, with such great emphasis on hygiene, comfort and healthy living, it seems more likely that your status would fall. Rather than being a real man, the chances are you would be seen as a pervert or a weirdo. But whether enjoying horror raises our status or not, this explanation does not tell us why we can experience the sublime from horrific things, even when we are alone and no one else sees how much we are enjoying it.

Other explanations attempt to answer the pleasure question, but do so only for representations of the sublime and not for real experiences like threatening natural forces, genuine crimes or abhorrent abattoir scenes. American philosopher of art Noël Carroll believes that the pleasure comes from the cognitive attraction of the story within which the horror is embedded. Thrillers, horror films, disaster movies and whodunnits indeed shock and horrify us because they contain scenes that are scary and abhorrent, but those scenes are part of a narrative structure that makes us curious (Who is the killer? How will the hero catch him or her?), challenges us intellectually (Does the plot hold water? Can I predict the ending?) and contain characters and situations that make us think because they contrast so sharply with our daily experience and sensible idea of the world. According to Carroll, 'art-horror is the price we are willing to pay for the revelation of that which is impossible and unknown, of that which violates our conceptual schema'.[16] This cognitive pleasure overshadows the initial emotional revulsion. Almost three hundred years ago, Scottish Enlightenment philosopher David Hume came up with a similar answer to the question of why people find tragedies full of misery and suffering so attractive. According to Hume, it is not the observer's cognitive enjoyment that solves the paradox, as Carroll later thought, but the aesthetic satisfaction, which increases with the rhetorical richness of the tragedy. Imagery, rhythm, timbre, narrative composition and plot structure can make the story so fascinating that we no longer feel the misery and horror. A refined, elevated style compensates for the repellent content.

Although there is something to be said for all these theories, they share a clear shortcoming in that they each only relate to a limited number of sublime experiences. Many horror stories lack the cognitive stimulation and stylistic complexity that explain the enjoyment for Carroll and Hume; on the contrary, it is their shocking rawness and the direct confrontation that produce the aesthetic pleasure.

A more widely applicable theory seeks the answer in the satisfaction of gradually overcoming the fear stimuli.[17] Because the sublime is always experienced at a safe distance, you can explore danger without being in danger yourself. It is a game in which you can allow the fear to enter just a little, and return to your comfort zone if it gets too hot to handle. This game of taking a risk, feeling the danger and then withdrawing and seeing how it felt has a certain appeal. This can be seen with young children who find it exciting to keep going a little further when they are playing, but also with adults who learn to practise a dangerous sport step by step. By daring to go further and further, they gain more control over the challenges posed by the game or sport. Overcoming a new challenge gives pleasure, despite the initial fears, even if the risk – as the result of experience gained earlier, repeated practice and the permanent possibility of rescue in the case of a real emergency – is never that great. If you look at what you have achieved from the perspective of your starting point it can be thoroughly frightening to see what risks you take now. Experiencing the sublime is comparable to learning to deep-sea dive, glide or ride a horse. If we are confronted with fear in small, manageable doses, it does not necessarily feel unbearable. With the prospect of new challenges, fear acquires something stimulating and exciting.

This theory, too, is incomplete. It is unclear whether the satisfaction of gradually conquering fears also applies to aversion, which is an essential component of horror-aesthetics. Do you derive greater pleasure on seeing even more mutilated bodies than the time before? Does your excitement increase when you see more blood, mucus and excrement? I suspect not. With the exception of a few horror fanatics, people who are sensitive to the sublime do not experience horror as a gradual learning process comparable to mastering a high-risk sport or hobby. Horror does not work in degrees, licences and medals, but with surprise, shock and the creation of an atmosphere. Something that is unpredictable, appears suddenly and is shocking is by definition anything but gradual and has the potential to produce a pleasant sensation of fright. Step-by-step horror produces only boredom.

Researchers still do not agree on where that paradoxical horror-pleasure comes from. Perhaps there are different reasons for it and a single universal theory is infeasible. So it is better to examine what kind of horror we enjoy and what elements of horror we find fascinating or exciting. This can vary quite widely. While one horror fan may like true stories with no supernatural elements, another may prefer esoteric tales full of zombies, monsters and vampires. Horror is an aesthetic form with many subgenres.

DARK ROMANTICISM

One explanation that appeals to me – though I do not wish to claim that it applies to all lovers of the sublime – is that enjoyment of horror stems from a deeper insight. The horror-aesthetic confirms a sensation that gives us such pleasure that it overshadows the unpleasant feelings of fear and aversion. Because it touches us more deeply, we experience beauty in it. This idea is expounded by the American master of horror and fantasy fiction H. P. Lovecraft in his 1927 essay *Supernatural Horror in Literature*. The deep insight that all horror reveals to us, according to Lovecraft, is that the world in which we live is ultimately unknowable and consequently remains a dangerous universe that is all around us. All human achievements that suggest the opposite – he calls them 'materialistic sophistication' – such as scientific knowledge and technological comfort, as well as ethical and political arrangements like democracy, human rights and the rule of law, are nothing but a fragile island in a sea of chaos that knows no natural laws, certainties or civilization. Outside that island of order, safety and hygiene there is a universe full of confusion, lethal danger and squalor. If you come into contact with this world, you suffer unbearable fears and are consumed with disgust. But because we are on that comfortable island and because civilization has progressed so spectacularly in the past few centuries, we live in the illusion that the whole cosmos is just as neatly ordered. Horror breaks through that illusion, and scares us because it makes us aware that those achievements can disintegrate at any moment. That insight of vulnerability and powerlessness does not fuel normal fear but cosmic fear, which flows over into a sublime feeling of awe and admiration. Every overwhelming experience with that forgotten unknown can become an existentially deep experience full of beauty, delight and emotion – even if it begins with pure fear and revulsion.

This explanation bears some resemblance to terror management theory, which explained where our disgust – for blood, among other things – comes from. Things that we have in common with animals remind us of our animal origins and our mortal existence and fill us with fear of inevitable death. Lovecraft replaced TMT's universal fear of death with an instinctive fear of the unknown. Death is only one of the demons threatening the island of modernity. There are many other forces to be afraid of. Unlike TMT, Lovecraft does not wish to hide the fear of the unknown behind buffers. He does not consider the fear as purely destructive. At the right moment and in appropriate circumstances – distance remains important – the fear can offer unprecedented beauty. The sublime is the epiphanic reward for those who dare to think about the omnipotence of the unknown and to be aware that everything is fragile and relative. The idea of cosmic fear and awe of the unknown gives TMT a positive twist and gives the theory a broader application. Everything that is frightening can lead to a confrontation with the unknown and open the door to sublime beauty – including a few skinned calves' heads or a hare dripping blood in a dark cellar.

Lovecraft was indebted not only to the influential theory of Rudolf Otto of the sacred as *mysterium tremendum et fascinans*

– Otto was undoubtedly appalled that the interaction between attraction (*fascinans*) and repulsion (*tremendum*) was applied to horror – but to the core ideas of the Romantic era. This intellectual school of thought, which is still evident today in many everyday ideas – such as the belief that a good relationship should always be based on reciprocal romantic love – started as a resistance movement against the dogmas of the Enlightenment. The Romantics despised the Enlightenment concept of happiness. If reality can really be explained completely by science and controlled by technology, if there is nothing that escapes the straitjacket of cause and effect and everything that happens is based on material and physical processes – whether they be molecules or planets, thoughts or ideas, societies or cultures – then belief in unknown or higher forces that give that reality a deeper meaning is utterly pointless. For Romantics, so much demystification is completely intolerable. Not that they do not enjoy the comfortable progress that science and technology offer. Their horror-aesthetics make full use of that progress. But for the Romantic, there is more than fleeting happiness. Life offers more than a dive in a swimming pool followed by a delicious ice cream or a flirtation with a pretty girl or a cool-looking guy. They want more than sensual or erotic pleasure, or pleasant social contact. In the words of German poet Novalis, 'by endowing the commonplace with a higher meaning, the ordinary with mysterious respect, the known with the dignity of the unknown, the finite with the appearance of the infinite, I am making it Romantic.'[18] Romantics are not satisfied with the everyday. They romanticize reality with an atmosphere, a thought, an emotion or a fantasy so that it no longer feels banal but once again radiates magic. They cannot live with a plain and bare, illusion-free reality with no deeper purpose, ultimate essence or hidden plan. The notion that there is nothing that escapes the everyday makes them despondent. They consider the modern ideal of progress, which aims to improve people's lives, recklessly nihilistic, although they are well aware that this comes over as very elitist. Again, there must be food on the table before the sublime can be contemplated. In a world in which by no means everyone has the opportunity to achieve even superficial happiness, this romantic plea for deeper contentment sounds very detached from daily reality.

Furthermore, the Romantics have a feeling for history that is lacking among Enlightenment thinkers. For the latter, history is a scrapheap full of superstition, barbaric practices, incurable diseases, invincible plagues and permanent wars caused by a lack of reasoned control and a surplus of impulsive emotion. From history, we learn at best how not to do things. Preferably, Enlightenment thinkers would like to make a *tabula rasa* of the past, draw a definitive line between primitive times and the sophisticated future, and eagerly anticipate the emergence of the new man, who looks only forwards. The past has nothing attractive to offer and it is best forgotten as soon as possible. For Romantics, it is completely different. They see this faith in progress as part of a pendulum movement. They embrace the idea that everything comes back at some point and that nothing is ever lost or gained permanently. As well as new scientific theories and refined civilization, the future – just like the past – will have its share of irrationality and barbarity. Only those who do not know their history see progress. The past is not a dog-eared photo album with ghastly black-and-white pictures, but a book full of wisdom, forgotten ideas and lost beauty. In the ruins of the past lie many treasures waiting to be rediscovered. When, despite the immense success of industrial production, people today seek passionately for natural, craft-made, handmade or biological organic products, they are hoping to find historical treasure. Old-fashioned products had a taste, a quality or some other characteristic that make them worth saving. History itself is, incidentally, a Romantic invention. The Romantic era spawned disciplines like folklore studies that were founded on an enthusiastic belief in the value of history.

If you add to these properties of the Romantic era a preference for the darker side, the result is Dark Romanticism. The atmosphere, thoughts, emotions or fantasies that Dark Romantics impose on banal reality are not positive, but negative. They do not elevate reality to a harmonious and loving paradise, but to a frightening place. Reality is chaotic, unknowable, unsafe and uncontrollable. Humanity is bad, stupid, covetous, wild and superstitious. The children of the Enlightenment can, with the best will in the world, build a veneer of civilization, but it will remain unstable and vulnerable. A darkness full of crime, violence, tyranny and ignorance threatens to extinguish every flame of a flickering Enlightenment. Nothing can resist that dark side. It cannot be controlled and human rationality is powerless to stop it.

What is interesting about Dark Romanticism is that its negative universe is not depressing and does not incite militant resistance; on the contrary, it drives those who are susceptible to it into raptures. They derive enjoyment from so much misery. They find this frightening world sublime – as long as they do not have to experience it at first hand. Lovecraft's romantic explanation makes the paradox comprehensible. Horror causes an aesthetic experience because it confirms the Dark Romantic view of man and the world. The Enlightenment and modernity do not tolerate fear and aversion. Nothing is dirty, scary or taboo. The world of the future is clean, safe, peace-loving and clear. It is a brave new world. That we can still be frightened, that taboos continue to exist and that we are disgusted if someone breaks them, shows that we do not yet understand everything, cannot control it and, where necessary, adjust it. There are things that are beyond our control – things that we do not want to or cannot see but which scare us out of our wits or make us feel nauseous when they do show themselves. Horror is a philosophical protest against the pretensions of the Enlightenment.[19] Dark Romantics delight in rationalist overconfidence getting a taste of its own medicine. The world remains a frightening place and humankind is itself a terror. You cannot make a *tabula rasa* from that deep truth, enlightened ideals or not.

It is that anti-Enlightenment thinking that gives the horror genre its antithetical form. As well as darkness against light, there is the wilderness against the city, the Middle Ages against modernity, agriculture against industry, feudal nobility against the bourgeoisie, supernatural occultism against pure naturalism, historical against contemporary location. No single horror author consistently uses all the elements on the left side of these oppositions. In order to surprise – which is essential for horror-aesthetics – the horror must be well hidden and only revealed when the reader or viewer least expects it. Nevertheless, horror always questions the legacy of the Enlightenment and the achievements of modernity. No matter how much knowledge we possess, how many rights and resources we have, beneath that superficial happiness strange, mysterious and evil forces smoulder and rumble, like gas bubbles in a dark swamp from out of which a gigantic water monster will arise. Or, as British film critic and horror author Kim Newman once put it succinctly: 'the central thesis of horror . . . is that the world is a more frightening place than is generally assumed.'[20]

AESTHETICS OF HORROR

Although the slaughterhouse is a modern invention, it is a horrific place that falls outside the reach of modernity. It is a place that conceals the taboo of taking life, and what happens there is cruel, dirty and frightening. Hidden well away from meat-eating consumers, who want to know nothing of the origins of their steak or cutlet, the slaughterhouse is a Dark Romantic place full of negative forces that the Enlightenment only keeps under control with difficulty. A sudden confrontation with skinned calves' heads or dripping blood gives us a glimpse of the dark side of our existence. People with no romantic sensitivity prefer to forget such horrors as soon as they can. They feel distressed or angry because they were not warned in time. But for those of a romantic nature, such gruesome scenes confirm their deep suspicion that, despite all its progress, the world remains a frightening place.

Blood plays a central role in that horror-aesthetic framework. For those who still believe it, blood is a magical substance which establishes contact with a supernatural reality which Enlightenment thinkers ridicule but which romantics still take seriously. The horror genre is full of supernatural creatures and events. Blood is never just blood, but a carrier of strange forces, a vehicle for infection by evil, a substance that makes healthy minds crazy or sick. In this way, the long tradition of thinking of blood as something magical flows seamlessly over into modern horror literature. For those who still believe it, blood awakens the beast inside us. It makes us wild and bloodthirsty. Some still claim that the contact with blood makes slaughterhouse workers aggressive. If the anti-meat consumption books of Gail Eisnitz (*Slaughterhouse*, 1997) and Jonathan Safran Foer (*Eating Animals*, 2009) are to be believed, the scent of blood alone is sufficient to achieve this effect. 'Down in the blood pit they say the smell of blood makes you aggressive, and it does,' says an abattoir worker in *Slaughterhouse*.[21] It is now clear that this is not the case. That myth is founded on a belief in the non-existent bestial power of blood. And yet we like to believe it. For anti-meat activists, it confirms the cruelty of slaughtering animals. In an enlightened future, we will no longer eat meat, or at least only artificial meat. In Utopia, we will all be vegetarians or vegans, as in the Earthly Paradise. All cruelty, filth and inefficiency will have been brought under control or banned. The reason why Dark Romantics like to believe the myth, however, is completely different. That the scent of blood can still make us aggressive shows that we remain cruel predators who can never be fully civilized.

Piercing the veneer of civilization is a bloodthirsty animal that cannot be tamed. There will never be a Utopia, just as there was never an Earthly Paradise. Where bloodlust is a good reason for an Enlightenment thinker to stop eating meat and become a vegetarian, for a Dark Romantic it is the very reason to keep doing it. Bloodlust is proof that the Enlightenment has the wrong end of the stick. In the words of French philosopher Dominique Lestel: 'Vegetarians . . . never admit that life itself is dirty, bloody, repugnant, malodorous, unjust, cruel, and so on, even though it possesses immeasurable richness and great beauty.'[22]

Blood rush is then a sublime experience. Contact with blood may be frightening, dirty and dangerous, but it leads to pleasure, excitement and even ecstasy. Although Romantics like to think that the experience is caused by magical forces or chemosignals, they are aware that the excitement is a throwback to the aesthetic dynamics of the sublime and romantic doubts about the Enlightenment and modernity. Blood excites those who like to believe that it is something beyond the reach of our civilization and our control, and brings together all kinds of dark forces, like death, decay, violence and barbarity. This horroraesthetic explanation for blood rush sits alongside the two other explanations – blood magic and blood-thirst – but is also clearly compatible with the claims on which they rest. If blood did prove to contain magical or active substances that affect our behaviour in subtle ways, Dark Romantics would welcome the discovery. Such discoveries would reinforce their scepticism against the optimistic and rationalist dogmas of the Enlightenment.

If the other two explanations for blood rush cannot be justified, the horror-aesthetic explanation holds water. It is based on a large number of convictions that cannot easily be refuted. We examine two of them here. First of all, sublime blood experiences are often so personal that they defy scientific analysis. Science does not exclude the possibility that a few people will become bloodthirsty after smelling blood. We only know that it is not a widespread phenomenon based on a fixed mechanism. In addition, Enlightenment objections are often so general, vague and incontestable to the point of triviality – death and decay will always be with us – that scientific criticism cannot address them. Blood rush can be understood as a purely aesthetic experience that makes use of the natural aversion and fear that blood arouses and generates sublime pleasure through the clearly true message that there will always be things beyond our control.

The horror-aesthetic explanation is scientifically safe, in that we can enjoy blood rush without having to believe things that are clearly wrong. Although there are certainly romantics who dare to venture deep into the parallel paranormal universe – there are still people who hunt vampires, for example – it is possible to be sensitive to the sublime without having to surrender to occult charlatanism. You can go along with romantic doubts about the Enlightenment and modernity for quite a way without ending up in the opposite, anti-scientific camp. It is enough to take account of the sometimes destructive power of incontestable dark elements. Science, technology, law and morals will never have everything fully under their control. Natural violence, death, decay and crime will not be eradicated. It is a sign of wisdom to remain alert to every manifestation of superstition, barbarity, abuse of power or chaos. In that sense, the sublime is even a must. It protects us from arrogance. But why should we derive pleasure from these dark forces? Why should we become so excited or moved at so much misery? Why do we not resist it? Why do we not feel indignation? Why do we not use that anger to do something while it is within our power to do so? The moral justification of the sublime is a tougher problem. Is it not perverse to be attracted to something that we ought to be fighting against? Is it not shameful to become excited by something that should arouse our indignation? The final chapter explores this conundrum.

BLOODLESS

We already know what the ideal slaughterhouse will look like in the future. You drive your SUV to a restored farm on the edge of town. The farmyard is full of 'happy pigs', grunting and snuffling around until they die a natural death. The farm you have chosen specializes in Mangalica pigs, also known as 'sheep pigs' because of their thick woolly coats. Half a century ago, this race of pigs – originally from Hungary – was virtually extinct. As consumers increasingly demanded lean meat, the market for Mangalica meat, with its tasty layers of fat, almost disappeared. They were bred mainly as a hobby, but people who liked something a little different would find their way to this farm. Their friendly nature and curly fleece make the Mangalicas a favourite with children, who come to stroke them in the farmyard. But what makes this farm special is the animal-friendly way in which it produces meat. Every two weeks, the breeder takes a small piece of tissue from the back, belly, rump or some other part of a pig's body and places it, together with a growth medium, in a bioreactor in the pig shed. In the past, this serum was made from the blood of calf foetuses removed from the wombs of slaughtered cows. Now, artificial blood is used to make the muscle cells grow very rapidly and create a sloppy mass. Electrical pulses stimulate the strips of tissue until they become powerful muscles, which are woven together in an organic 3D printer to generate the desired consistency of meat. The printer combines muscle tissue with connective tissue, fat and bone in such an astonishing way that an artificial rib cannot be distinguished from a real one. For anyone who wants a leaner piece of Mangalica meat, the breeder simply turns the fat knob down a little.

Cultured meat was invented by the Dutch physiologist Mark Post who, in the summer of 2013, delivered a 'proof of principle' in the form of a test-tube hamburger. Although the burger was much too dry because it contained no fat and required masses of red colouring to compensate for the lack of myoglobin, it did taste like real meat and sizzled enticingly in the pan when fried at the presentation in London. Although the technology was still primitive and the result a little meagre, the media event was unforgettable. It heralded the dawn of a new era in meat production where the killing of young, healthy animals was not required. In the *Pavillon des viandes* in Rungis, the *chevillards* scratched their heads as they watched the images of the lab-hamburger on their television screens. It would be a while before it caught on, they reassured each other. Since then, the technology has advanced rapidly. It no longer takes three months to turn 20,000 strips of muscle tissue into a hamburger. After a week to produce the basic meat mass, the printer can transform it into a hamburger in only a few minutes. Chicken – even the exclusive Bresse Gauloise – only needs a few days in the bioreactor. And the hamburger no longer costs a quarter of a million euros, but only a little more than meat from animals that have undergone the torture of slaughter. For ethically aware meat eaters, the price is no longer an obstacle to making the change to cultured meat. It is, of course, not yet perfect. If the division of the stem cells can be increased in the future, the two-weekly tissue sample can be taken less frequently. Although it is spread over a number of animals and is no more painful than a diabetes injection, taking the tissue sample is still a moment of stress. It may not be comparable to the stress of the final journey to the slaughterhouse, but it is preferable to avoid it if possible. When we only need one sample from each animal, the ideal slaughterhouse will have become a reality. All animals are eligible for the production of cultured meat, even rare species such as pandas, ortolans or leopards – though few people would be able to confirm whether they taste like the original. The Belgian government recently approved legislation banning the cultivation of cultured human meat. Cannibalism is and continues to be forbidden.[1]

Cultured meat is a challenge for vegetarians. Once this ideal slaughterhouse exists, there is no longer any ethical reason not to eat meat, at least not if the suffering of animals was the main motivation. Test-tube meat can of course be dangerous, inefficient or unhealthy, but it is certainly not harmful to animals, so it is an alternative that can be eaten with a clear conscience. Those who are adventurous in their culinary habits almost owe it to themselves to try it. And cultured meat is a challenge for the traditional meat eater, too; there is considerable resistance to in-vitro meat. Research conducted for Mark Post's hamburger stunt showed that our first reaction to the thought of this freakish Frankenstein food is revulsion. Most respondents became less averse to the idea when they heard of its advantages and were assured that the meat is safe and healthy. They even became curious and wanted to taste it. Nevertheless, a quarter of the participants still found the idea of synthetic meat repugnant and said they wouldn't want it in their mouths.[2]

That minority is clearly not aware how their daily portion of regularly slaughtered meat is produced. If anything is repugnant, it is the living conditions of pigs in the agro-industry. They have been described in grisly detail many times, and filmed repeatedly by animal rights organizations, some of which give daily updates of the horror on their websites. But even in the small, animal-friendly farms breeding pigs that do not bite each other's tails out of boredom, are not castrated without anaesthetic and have sufficient room so that sows do not crush their own piglets, life is still miserably short. Meat piglets go to the slaughterhouse when they are about six months old. Utilitarian ethicist and animal activist Peter Singer finds this defensible.[3] If one happy pig is replaced with another, on balance, the level of happiness does not fall. Because pigs have no concept of the future, they are not being frustrated and, because they are granted a painless death, no suffering is added to their short but contented lives. And yet it would seem wrong if someone were to kill their perfectly healthy pet dog painlessly after three years and replace it with a new dog that is just as healthy, only to kill it in the same way three years later.[4] Killing a young, healthy animal, no matter how painlessly, does not sit well with most of us. In the slaughterhouse of the future, there will no longer be discrimination between domesticated animals and pets. Pigs will be able to live as long as our spoiled cats and dogs.

People are also opposed to cultured meat because it is not natural. They prefer natural things to synthetic things.[5] Children feel the same way, but are less fanatical about it than adults.[6] People love anything that is biological, craft-made or organic. Industrially manufactured products alienate us from our original, natural environment, which we feel is healthier, safer, tastier and more wholesome. The less products are artificially manipulated, the more authentic and better they are. This idyllic illusion aside, meat is far from being a natural product. All meat is artificial in the sense that it comes from overbred animals that either did not exist in their current form in their natural state or whose meat was inedible. Mangalica pigs are the result of centuries of breeding and refining wild Hungarian species by mixing them with other races. To produce tasty meat, feeding and care are just as important as genetics. The animals are given not only food, but vaccinations, medicines and protection that would not exist in their 'natural' habitats. The environment in which they live is as artificial as the cultivation of the muscle cells in a bioreactor. The only difference is that the latter takes place at a deeper level. And not to speak of how this meat is processed, stored, distributed and sold – all of which has to fulfil the strictest of hygienic standards. Meat is a biohazard that can only be kept safe with high technology. If you are not happy with unnatural production methods, then that objection applies to the whole meat production chain. If you want 'natural' meat, you have to go hunting yourself.

I can imagine that cultured meat will never be the same as meat from slaughtered animals. After all, margarine is not butter, synthetic leather is not real leather, and surimi – imitation crab sticks made from whitefish, eggs and flavouring – is not the same as freshly caught and cooked crab. It is very difficult to replicate or equal the taste and feel of a natural product in an artificial substitute. We are very quick to notice when something tastes or feels different. It is a myth that humans do not have a highly developed sense of smell or that our sense of taste is limited to four or five basic tastes (bitter, sweet, salty, sour and savoury or umami).[7] If you only taste with your tongue or smell with your nose (traditional or 'orthonasal' smelling), this is true. Our noses are nothing in comparison to the damp nasal organ of the dog. But retronasal smelling is something completely different. Retronasal means that aromas reach the nasal cavity via the mouth and the pharynx. This happens when we chew food or warm liquids in our mouths and mix them with saliva and air. Scientists recently calculated that humans can distinguish a trillion different scents.[8] That is many more than the few million colours and a couple of hundred thousand tones we are able to identify. Our fine sense of taste uses retronasal smell, which enables us to distinguish subtle variations. It allows us to tell the difference between Sicilian Ragusano cheese from grass-fed cows in the summer and hay-fed in the winter.[9] Anyone who can taste this difference, or that between farmed and wild sea bass, will certainly be able to tell slaughtered meat from cultured meat that comes out of the 3D printer.

Replicating our sense of touch is even more difficult. Despite our best efforts, there is still no synthetic leather or wood that feels exactly like the real thing. Blindfolded test subjects immediately know the difference.[10] To the great frustration of the porn industry, the field of teledildonics – the use of haptic devices to feel bodily parts realistically at a distance – is still in its infancy. In the words of a recent handbook on the future of artificial touch, 'Nothing will ever replace the tactile sensation of warm flesh.'[11] Touch remains the sense that enables us to distinguish real from fake. Doubting Thomas wanted to feel Christ's wounds before believing that he was still alive. It is feeling with our skin that ultimately tells us if something is genuine or not. No one is under the illusion that a thick, artificial entrecote will feel the same as a natural one. In this first stage of producing cultured meat, the focus is not on ensuring that it looks and feels like real meat, as it will be processed into a wide variety of meat preparations.

In theory, there is nothing to stop us making a perfect copy of natural meat. Anything can be replicated synthetically – blood, meat, blood sausage. But replicating always means changing, otherwise there is no point to it. You might want to replace an expensive or unhealthy ingredient with a cheaper or healthy substitute, or a dangerous or unethical process with one that is safe and acceptable. By doing so, you always lose or gain certain properties that can affect the sensual qualities of the original. It will taste or feel different. You can try and disguise the difference by adding new ingredients or new processes, but those additives and processes will again add or remove properties that will affect the taste or feel. The original taste or feel will never come back. The more differences you remove, the further you move from the original. Our sensitive senses are implacable: the imitation product feels and tastes different.

Although it is real meat, cultured meat will always remain something different. But that does not necessarily make it better or worse. The Dutch philosopher Bas Haring once pro-voked his readers with a eulogy to surimi. He said that he found surimi tastier than real crab and that he didn't trust anyone who thought real crab was better, because they didn't trust their own sense of taste. They allowed it to become obscured by nostalgic, conservative sentiments rather than focusing purely on the taste.[12] Haring can undoubtedly clearly distinguish between the tastes of surimi and crab and knows full well that there is surimi on the market that tastes more like plastic than fish, just as he knows that there is crab that smells of ammonia. His point is that crab is not by definition tastier because it is real, nor is surimi less tasty because it is fake. Whether or not something is the real thing is not a valid argument. The assessment of taste should rest on objective impression. The only way to find out if you like something or not is to taste it without knowing what it is. The image of a product must not affect your judgement. The crab is not better just because it has dangerous claws, it has been boiled alive, its round body contains yellow-green gunge that is mouth-wateringly delicious, and that a whole ritual has to be gone through with hammers, tongs and long, fine forks to get at its delicate meat. No, you have to distance yourself from all that. All that matters is the taste of the final product on your plate. Haring speaks consistently of 'stuff you eat'; he doesn't allow the image of a product to prejudice his choice of food.

But is it really possible to distance yourself from the atmosphere surrounding a product and concentrate purely on its objective qualities? And is it necessary? It is of course sad if you claim to prefer crab but cannot distinguish its taste from surimi, or may even choose surimi in a blind test. You make yourself look ridiculous. But is it such a bad thing if taste is all in your mind, is an expression of your identity and how you look at the world, and is part of an atmosphere that makes you happy? How do you make choices without taking that atmosphere into account? How do you choose a pullover, a sofa or a car by only taking account of their objective qualities? You cannot buy all the models that pass the objective test. After all, you want something that suits you. The same applies to meat and food in general and explains why some people who love the romantic idea of the sublime prefer the real thing. The fact that real meat is 'wrong' gives it an atmosphere that is paradoxically attractive. The death, the danger and the uncleanliness surrounding the breeding and slaughter of living animals imbue it with something exciting, a quality that is lost when meat is produced artificially in the controlled environment of a laboratory. The farm shed where the Mangalica meat is produced in the bioreactor is too clean, too safe and too controlled. The romantic misses the unbridled negative forces encountered in a real pig house.

The grocer in my village knows something that Mark Post doesn't. Every autumn, he transforms his shop into a forest. It is full of dozens of different kinds of mushroom and toadstool, including bay bolete and porcini. From the middle of November, these are joined by the first truffles. All of these specialities have a unique taste. We like to think we can tell them from regular cultivated mushrooms, but we mainly think they taste better because of the atmosphere surrounding them. They are wild and come from the forest, and that places them a little outside the civilized world. That wild image gives them extra taste, something my grocer understands instinctively. When I told him that Italian biologists had deciphered the genome of the black winter truffle, he was aghast, exclaiming, 'Are you serious? We have to keep some of the magic, don't we?' He knows full well that the sublime gives his products extra taste, even if it is imaginary. When I invited Mark Post to give a lecture, someone from the audience asked him whether he expected a lot of people not to eat cultured meat because it was not the real thing. He had difficulty understanding the question: if you know that cultured meat is animal-friendly and tastes like real meat, what's the problem? Consumers don't have some irrational, emotional bond with meat, do they? They don't follow a subjective image or a vague atmosphere, but make their choices on the basis of objective qualities. As much as I admire Post's work, it appeared he had never given any thought to this problem.

THE DANGERS OF THE SUBLIME

What is the problem if you find something better because of its image or the atmosphere it invokes? If you would rather have the original than an imitation? I don't think we can object to that on principle. But it is slightly different with the sublime. Is it not a little dubious to enjoy something that is gruesome? Criticism of the sublime on ethical grounds is as old as the sublime itself. As early as 1827, the English publicist Thomas De Quincey wrote an amusing essay on the subject, entitled *On Murder Considered as One of the Fine Arts*. In the essay, he argues tongue-in-cheek that everything has a moral and aesthetic side. These sides are separated only by time. Once morals have had their say, it is the turn of taste and the fine arts:

> When a murder [has been committed], and a rumour of it comes to our ears, by all means let us treat it morally. But suppose it over and done . . . what is the use of any more virtue? . . . Therefore let us make the best of a bad matter; and, as it is impossible to hammer anything out of it for moral purposes, let us treat it aesthetically, and see if it will turn to account in that way.[13]

Time makes the enjoyment of horror acceptable. No one will be worse off from events that can no longer be avoided. The same argument justifies fictional horror which, by definition, has no real victims. Although, in exceptional cases, an obsession with crime can lead to imitations in the real world, De Quincey is right in saying that morality and beauty can be perfectly combined. You might be irritated at the gratuitous violence in *Game of Thrones* or *Grand Theft Auto V*, but you cannot accuse their fans of sadism. People are generally good at distinguishing between fiction and reality, past and present, and what should and shouldn't be avoided. But if horror-aesthetics wishes to be more than purely a form of relaxation, it cannot limit itself to fiction and the past. The real world of the present day must always be a scary place. If horror is to retain its power, it must also be encountered in day-to-day reality. If it is not, it becomes a game in which it is not the fear and revulsion that are enjoyed, but the artistic rhetoric. The awareness that horror is real gives it its vitality. This is why authors and screenwriters go to great lengths to make the frightening events they portray as real as possible. Their stories are based on real events, contain amateur images of the victims (found footage), or are supported by 'scientific' discoveries or philosophical theories that promise to demonstrate the dark side of humanity and of reality.

Sublime horror can never be completely banished to fiction or the past. Although doing so has ethical advantages, because no victims are created, it does erode the aesthetic value. The horror becomes non-committal, clichéd and subcultural. But when there is a refusal to banish horror from the real present, the problems start. Horror-aesthetics has a bad reputation as a view on reality. Western history is one of exclusion: barbaric races, femmes fatales, born criminals, moral imbeciles, feeble-minded psychiatric patients, practitioners of infamous professions, maenadic crowds – they were all too cruel, too superstitious, too unclean or too underdeveloped to be a part of the civilized world. Humans and animals that fell into these categories were banished to a moral zero, until understanding began to grow that they were the victims of fantasies of savagery or that their wildness was due to poverty, misery, exclusion, colonization and/ or slavery. Bloodthirstiness and magic were popular elements in these dubious fantasies.[14] They illustrated the savagery of the primitive Other. Close up, civilized Westerners were afraid of these imaginary blood-driven maniacs but, from a safe distance, they enjoyed the bloodlust. It felt sensational when the refined West proved to have caves and grottos harbouring dangerous savages.

The sublime creates victims. It strips people of their dignity. It places them in a group of beings that are not real humans, so that they lose their personal identity. Scientists have played their part in this process of dehumanization. After stripping people down and measuring them, they exhibited and published articles and books on these 'semi-humans'. These so-called scientific publications not only contained facts that supported the researchers' belief in the primitive human, but revealed their gruesome fascination with their sensational subjects. There was no objective science to be seen. The scientists were susceptible to horror-aesthetics. How else can we explain the following anecdote?

On 18 December 1890, forensic psychiatrist and self-proclaimed anthropologist Jean-Louis Fauvelle showed a number of photographs of the hands of a rapist to the Anthropological Society in Paris.[15] After being fired from his job at the foundry at Hirson in northern France, Louis Saucourt raped the landlady of an inn where he had taken rooms. It is a story of poverty, unemployment, alcohol abuse and frustration.[16] But Fauvelle interpreted the events completely differently. He alleged that Saucourt was a member of a violent and brutal race of people who lived in villages and hamlets on the edges of the forest of Thiérache, in the foothills of the Ardennes. The pictures of Saucourt's hands, with their short thumbs and palms that were half the length of the index fingers, showed that the perpetrator was more ape than human. His short, squat body, broad jaw, pronounced eyebrows and abundant blond, slightly yellow hair, added to the speculation. As a scientist, Fauvelle did not wish his suspicions to be recorded in the official annals of the Society. Further research would be required to prove conclusively that Saucourt was a member of a criminal race. Yet he warned the Society in advance that 'anthropological research in Thiérache – a region that was extremely remarkable geologically and anthropologically – would be very difficult and perhaps even dangerous'.[17] Of course, Fauvelle did not say explicitly that he found this racist horror story exciting and framed his research in the context of a humanitarian mission to make the French Ardennes a little safer, but there is the feeling that such sensational accounts, no matter how serious their scientific tone, are driven more by the thrill they give the researcher than by a quest to find the truth. The danger was appealing: venturing into the macabre forest of Thiérache acquired the allure of a journey of discovery in one's own country into a domestic heart of darkness.

Enjoying horror makes us blind to the naked truth, which is even more gruesome. We give priority to a romantic illusion that creates victims above the prosaic truth that calls the perpetrators to account. There is an unacceptable aspect to enjoying real, current horror. Dark Romanticism generates or exacerbates exclusion. This is not an unfortunate side effect, but the essence of horror-aesthetics. It draws its sublime pleasure from that exclusion. Precisely because it attributes dark powers to nature, animals and humans, as a counter-offensive to civilization, it generates the aesthetic dynamics of attraction and repulsion. Something can only inspire horror if it is situated outside our civilized comfort zone and is therefore excluded. Horror by definition implies discrimination. It is a darkness that you cannot illuminate.

If our desire for sublime pleasure perpetuates that exclusion, then it is indefensible. Aesthetic pleasure cannot outweigh the legitimate desire of many people who now live in misery but hope for a more comfortable future. The same applies to slaughterhouse aesthetics. This pleasure, too, pales against the emancipatory struggle to give farmed animals a longer and better life. Good people do not like real horror; they do something about it. If they want to feel the excitement of vicarious fear, they watch a horror film, take a ride on a roller coaster, or read about the horrors of the First World War.

BLOODLESS

And yet it is not easy to say farewell to the sublime. For those who have it good, live comfortably and hygienically, are healthy and feel safe, participate in an efficient economy and enjoy democracy and human rights, modernity can be a little stifling. We can generally put up with it at work, but at weekends we want something different. We drive to our holiday homes in the country, where civilization is less oppressive. The elitism of this desire makes it no less real. Progress does not come without a price. Pressure to achieve is high; the fear of not keeping up with the rat race or losing status is enormous. There is much malaise with the reverse side of modernity. Has the ideal of modelling and controlling the society we live in not gone too far? Was a world with less comfort, more risks, less frantic obsession with economic prosperity not better? Romantic adventurers make a great fuss about turning their backs on this breathless rat race, only to return to it some years later, rested but somewhat disillusioned. Outside modernity, life offers little room for manoeuvre. Consumption seduces us, technology saves lives and the fear of no longer belonging causes panic. Yet, today, it is almost outmoded to be modern. Progress has lost its attraction. Industrialization is no longer an ideal. Technology should be invisible. Our schoolteachers no longer ask primary school children to draw a factory production line that produces one hundred winter coats a day, as their Russian colleagues did eighty years ago. Today's kids draw trees, flowers and animals (which also have good lives). Modernity is no longer a source of meaning, partly because it is all around us and partly because we now also see its less attractive sides.

Malaise and the need for variety keep the sublime alive. If modernity holds us too strongly in its grip, we yearn for a world that is still wild and where we are not under permanent control. Trends and fashions respond to that yearning. Top restaurants use ingredients they find in the natural environment, rediscover the taste of old-fashioned ways of storing and preparing food, such as fermentation, pickling, smoking and drying, and serve products that the modern diner finds disgusting, like rancid butter, smoked birch bark (which tastes like tar), bone marrow and crispy pig's ears. Wild products sell. Although Western Europe is now practically full to bursting with roads and motorways and it is even forbidden to drive off-road in some places, sales of suvs with four-wheel drive are higher than ever. No other kind of car has such spectacular sales figures. If anything is proof that Westerners buy their cars for completely irrational reasons, it is the mass purchase of suvs which, apart from being completely useless, also use more fuel and are more expensive to buy. You might spend hours in traffic jams and pay through the nose for fuel and taxes, but your suv gives you the illusion of adventure in risk-free modernity. That atmosphere of wild uncontrollability is also to be found in fashionable boutiques, which put their customers in the mood to spend money by filling their shop windows with sawn-off tree trunks, blocks of wood, bones and skeletons. Scandinavian fashions are popular because these countries, with their fjords, lakes and islands, suggest an image of a civilized wilderness.

References to the sublime can also help those for whom modernity and the Enlightenment do not go far enough. The concept store of the *Vegetarische Slager*, the 'vegetarian butcher' in The Hague, sells meat substitutes in an old butcher's shop which, with its white tiles, chopping block and sturdy scales, preserves the atmosphere of its original occupant. Even the shop's art deco logo – a young woman holding a bunch of carrots in one hand and a butcher's cleaver in the other – aims, despite the explicit irony, to maintain something of the romantic excitement surrounding traditional meat production.

The most telling example of our longing for the sublime is the policy of 'rewilding', giving land back to nature. In the

Netherlands, the government returned a 50-square-kilometre (19 sq.-mi.) area of marshland between the towns of Almere and Lelystad, originally destined for industrial development, completely to nature. In this area, the Oostvaardersplassen, nature was left to its own devices and an environment has developed that is intended to closely resemble the Netherlands as it was thousands of years ago. Herds of large grazing animals like red deer, Konik horses and Heck cattle roam free, and the white-tailed eagle, which has not nested in the Netherlands since medieval times, has returned. Public enthusiasm for this 'return to nature' has been enormous. A film about the area, *De Nieuwe Wildernis* (dir. Mark Verkerk and Ruben Smit, 2013), enjoyed unexpected success in the cinemas and opinion polls showed that people wanted more 'wild nature' like the Oostvaardersplassen and fewer parks. In an over-civilized land like the Netherlands, there is a great yearning for untamed nature. It is difficult to imagine just how liberating people find the idea of rewilding. Even wolves, which killed packs of hunting hounds in the nineteenth century, are welcome back in Western Europe. We need some element of risk to make our dull, controlled lives a little more interesting and exciting.

But that romantic yearning brings contradictions. Red deer were in the Netherlands thousands of years ago, but Konik horses and Heck cattle are modern attempts to reintroduce primitive species that date back less than a century. Moreover, Heck cattle are irrevocably linked to Socialism, whose leaders enthusiastically supported this eugenicist project of the Heck brothers to reintroduce racially pure cows on German soil. In the past, glorifying wild nature was particularly popular among reactionary dreamers. Progressive thinkers were not interested in the primitive past. We currently have a sublime fascination with the untamed wilderness, though not everyone shares it: a former inspector for the Dutch department of nature management called this experiment in rewilding a 'horror park' and refused to vote for progressive parties that wanted to allow untamed nature to run amok. A heated debate erupted following television images of wild animals dying of hunger at the end of the winter. A weakened deer hobbled away from the camera and stumbled into a pool, where it drowned in full view. People were outraged. Shouldn't we do something? Give them some extra food? Shoot them to put them out of their misery? And should we help only those that are dying, or also others, to prevent them from suffering? If you leave nature to its own devices, you soon find yourself faced with these brutal scenarios. It is wonderful to enjoy from a distance, even breathtakingly beautiful in its ruthless wildness, but miserable and sad if you realize how much the animals are suffering to satisfy our romantic fantasies. For surimi fan and anti-romantic philosopher Bas Haring, the solution to this horror is clear: cultivate all nature and make the wilderness into a park. It is complete lunacy to think that animals want to live in a wild, natural environment. Do we want to go back and live in the jungle?

I am under no illusion that this struggle between the Enlightenment and Romanticism will be solved in the near future. The more bloodless the former wants our civilization to be, the more the latter yearns for blood. The struggle also takes place within ourselves. Louise Fresco, UN agricultural expert and author of the excellent *Hamburgers in Paradise*, is vocal in her criticism of the elitist nostalgia of well-off consumers for small-scale, biological or biodynamic products that are produced so inefficiently that they are more of a threat to global food security than a serious alternative. But even the level-headed and rational Fresco is sensitive to the charms of an old-fashioned Italian farm where Mangalica pigs snuffle around the farmyard until they find their way into traditional meat recipes. If she is inviting friends around for dinner, she has no problem choosing between the efficiency of anonymous meat from the supermarket and respectfully produced meat with its own story from the local organic farmer.[18] Although there may be many reasons for endorsing that choice, our sensitivity for the romantic and the sublime is certainly one of them. We hide that preference under pretexts like the special taste, respect for diversity, openness to traditional values, the desire to be exclusive – or to fish for compliments about our good taste – but, deep down, we like the feeling that, just for a while, we are escaping the modernist illusion that we can model and control society to our own tastes.

The Enlightenment and Romanticism are the Western yin and yang. They are irreconcilable but, at the same time, inseparable. As long as we remain aware of their strengths and weaknesses, we do not need to choose between them. They correct each other's omnipotence, pretension and blindness. Ideally, they hold each other in equilibrium. One is more for the working week, and the other for free time and holidays. Though they are contradictory, we give both a place. In that way, we confirm the complexity of our existence. Let us try to be both enlightened and romantic: critically rational, yet acquiescing in our passions. Each at the right time and in the right proportions. Life should be neither bloody nor bloodless.

REFERENCES

INTRODUCTION

1 Schury (2001), pp. 183–8; Weiermair (2001).
2 Famulla (2009), pp. 81–3. The Schloss Moyland Museum in Cleves has a number of these bags in its collection.
3 Reiss (1916), pp. 184–5. For more on Reiss and his research, see Quinche (2009).
4 Gay (1993), p. 12; Jerome (1900), pp. 207–8.
5 Nye (1975), pp. 1–2.
6 Goethe (1806), Part I, 1740. This statement by Mephistopheles does not appear in Goethe's *Urfaust*, an earlier version of the work published between 1773 and 1775. I know of no articles or monographs dedicated to this well-known and widely used saying.
7 Spörri (2013), pp. 28–9.
8 Aristotle, *History of Animals* 3, 6; Owen (2001), p. 8. Aristotle believed that the blood of the deer, the roe, the antelope and the hare does not clot, or to a lesser extent, due to a lack of 'fibrous matter'. Rather than becoming stiff or jelly-like, it takes on the consistency of milk.
9 Ellis (1903), p. 102.
10 Hayes (2005), pp. 186–7.
11 Three (1984), p. 189.
12 I am certainly not the first to note that a general phenomenology of blood is no longer feasible. See Cazelles (1991), p. 1333.

PART ONE: **BLOOD MAGIC**
BLOOD MIST

1 Dölger (1934). More recent writers on this theme include Henrichs (1970), Rives (1995) and Lanzillotta (2007).
2 Henrichs (1970), p. 32.
3 Epiphanius of Salamis, Panarion, 25.5.5–6.

4 Lanzillotta (2007), pp. 98–102, sums up the proponents and opponents.

5 Ibid., pp. 101–2; Mahieu (2012), pp. 818–28.

6 Dölger (1934), p. 211. Translated by A. Brown.

7 Rives (1995), pp. 77–80.

8 Philostratus, *Life of Apollonius*, 7.18 and 8.5.

9 *Historia Augusta*, 8.1–2.

10 Johnston (2002) provides a good overview of the role of blood and sacrifice in magic. Faraone and Obbink (1991), Graf (1997) and Mirecki and Meyer (2002) are classic works on magic in antiquity.

11 Dölger (1934), p. 212. Knust (2010) gives more recent examples in which blood, preferably menstrual blood, is used in love potions.

12 Rüsche (1930), p. 95.

13 Zacharias (2008), pp. 58–60.

14 Dölger (1934), pp. 212–13.

15 Pliny, *Natural History*, 30:IV. Translated by Rackham et al. Harvard University Press, Cambridge, MA, and William Heinemann, London, 1949–54.

16 With thanks to Johan De Smedt, who researched this for me. This is not the place to discuss the controversies surrounding alleged discoveries of blood at prehistorical sites (Loy et al., 1990), or the blood symbolism of ochre (Knight, 1991).

17 Rüsche (1930), pp. 35, 78–9, 85.

18 Homer, *Odyssey*, 22.309, 24.185. Translated by Fitzgerald. Vintage Classics, London, 2007.

19 Rüsche (1930), pp. 57–61.

20 Homer, *Odyssey*, 10.24–31.

21 Plutarch, *The Life of Aristides*, 21; Pindar, *Olympian Odes* (*Carmen Olympicum*), 1.90.

22 Rüsche (1930), p. 57. Translated by A. Brown.

23 Plutarch, *The Life of Solon*, 21.5.

24 Rüsche (1930), pp. 75–6. For this practice of drinking the blood of executed criminals, also see Dölger (1926), Bargheer (1931) and more recently Moog and Karenberg (2003).

25 Schild (2007), p. 126. Translated by A. Brown.

26 Dölger (1926).

27 Tertullian, *Apologeticum*, 9.10. Translated by T. R. Glover. Harvard University Press, Cambridge, MA, and William Heinemann, London, 1977.

28 Clement of Alexandria, *The Paedagogus*, 3.3.25.2.

29 Moog and Karenberg (2003) defend this explanation.
30 Pliny the Elder (*Natural History*, xxviii, pp. 4–5), Aretaeus of Cappadocia (*Treatment of Chronic Diseases*, vii/4, pp. 7–8) and Caelius Aurelianus (*On Chronic Diseases*, i, p. 130) completely rejected this blood treatment. Caelius Aurelianus regarded this cure as 'detestable, barbarous and inhuman'. See Moog and Karenberg (2003), p. 139.
31 Augustine, *Confessions*, 6.8. Translated by Henry Chadwick. Oxford World Classics, 1991.
32 Homer, *The Iliad*, 22.70 and 22.76. Translated by Robert Fitzgerald. Oxford World Classics, 2008.
33 *Geoponica*, 19.2.3.
34 Philostratus, *Heroicus*, 218. Translated by Ellen Bradshaw Aitken and Jennifer K. Berenson Maclean. Society of Biblical Literature, Atlanta, GA, 2001.
35 See Herodotus, *Histories*, 4.106, on the drinking of human blood by the Scythians; Isidor of Seville, *Etymologiae*, 9.82 and Ammianus Marcellinus, *Res Gestae*, 27.4.4, on the Thracians; Tacitus, *Annals*, 1.31 and Procopius, *De Bello Gothico*, 2.15, on the Chatti; Paul the Deacon, *History of the Lombards*, 1.11 and Marcus Velleius Paterculus, *Compendium of Roman History* 2.6, on the Lombards; and Pausanias, *Description of Greece*, 10.22.3, on the Gauls.
36 Galen Last (2015), p. 147.
37 Aeschylus, *Eumenides*, 858.
38 Ammianus Marcellinus, *Res Gestae*, 28.6.13.
39 Ibid., 31.16.6. Translated by Thayer, Loeb Classical Library Edition, 1939.
40 Euripides, *Heracles*, 965. Translated by E. P. Coleridge. Perseus Digital Library, www.perseus.tufts.edu.
41 Rüsche (1930), p. 63; Kadletz (1978).
42 Pausanias, *Description of Greece*, 2.24.1.
43 Pseudo-Apollodorus, *Bibliotheca*, 1.9.27. Aeson was not the only one to die after drinking bull's blood. Midas and Themistocles suffered the same fate.

SACRIFICIAL BLOOD

1 Pollan (2013), p. 51.
2 Thomas (1991), p. 295; Steintrager (2012), p. 170.
3 The clearest of these claims are made by Graf (2012), pp. 45–6.
4 Straten (1995).

5 Burkert (1983), pp. 3–7.

6 Ekroth (2007). These animals were probably taken to the temple after they had been killed. Their meat would supplement that of the sacrificed animals.

7 Frankfurter (2011).

8 Lambert (1993).

9 Stowers (1998).

10 Ekroth (2007).

11 Scheid (2007).

12 For more on Jewish ritual sacrifice, see Klawans (2001), Stowers (1998), Biale (2007) and Gilders (2007, especially 2004).

13 See, for example, Ullucci (2012).

14 Girard (1977), p. 21.

15 Graf (2012) provides a summary of the criticisms.

16 McCarthy (1969, 1973) and more recently Ekroth (2002), pp. 247–51 and Ekroth (2005) doubt the religious status of blood in Greek sacrifice. For a criticism of this standpoint, see Stowers (1998).

17 Homer, *Odyssey*, 27, 44–9. For an overview of Greek blood dishes, see Ekroth (2002), pp. 247–51. For the vase paintings, see Ekroth (2005).

18 The classic work on this issue is De Vries (1958), I, pp. 406–28. More recently, there is Bray (2008). Wagner (2005), pp. 329–431, is more informative on the sacrifice of horses.

19 Gilders (2004); Gilders (2007).

20 This criticism is based completely on Gilders (2004).

21 Vervenne (1993), p. 460; Gilders (2004), p. 16; Biale (2007), p. 19.

EVIL BLOOD

1 See www.magentzedek.org, accessed 2 July 2019.

2 Vervenne (1993), p. 469.

3 Tertullian, *De Pudicitia*, 12. 3–4; Cyril of Jerusalem, *Catecheses*, 4.28.

4 Biale (2007), p. 21.

5 Astour (1967); Grintz (1966); Milgrom (1991).

6 For all nuances of early Christian attitudes towards ritual sacrifice, from tolerance to demonization, see Ullucci (2012).

7 Tertullian, *Apologeticum*, 22.6. Translated by T. R. Glover. Harvard University Press, Cambridge, MA, and William Heinemann, London, 1977.

8 Ibid., 23.3–5.

9 Jones (2014), pp. 34–46.

10 Origen, *Contra Celsum*, 7.5. Translated by Frederick Crombie. Christian Literature Publishing Co., Buffalo, NY, 1885.

11 Pliny, *Natural History*, 30.12.

12 Nagy and Prescendi (2013), pp. 9–10.

13 Strabo, *Geographica*, 4.4.5; Julius Caesar, *De Bello Gallico*, 6.16.2. Diodorus of Sicily 5.31.3–4. For more on this, see Kaenel (2013).

14 Tacitus, *Germania*, 12 and *Annals*, I.61. See also Jordanes, *Getica*, v.41, Procopius, *De Bello Gothico*, 2.15 and Orosius, *Historiae*, 5.16. For Germanic human sacrifice, see de Vries (1958), pp. 409–14.

15 See, for example, Plutarch, *De Superstitione*, 13; Diodorus of Sicily, 20.14; Tertullian, *Apologeticum*, 9.2–3. For more on this, see Rives (1994).

16 Xella et al. (2013); Smith (2013).

17 Brunaux (2008); Kaenel (2013).

18 There is also some evidence that the Greeks and Romans actually practised human sacrifice. The Greeks sacrificed Persians before the Battle of Salamis (480 BC) and the Romans had the tradition of *devotio*, where military officers sacrificed themselves to ensure success in battle. An example was consul Decius Mus in the Battle of Vesuvius (339 BC).

19 Nagy and Prescendi (2013), pp. 3–10, reject the continuity between human and animal sacrifice argued by Alfred Loisy in his *Essai historique sur le sacrifice* (1920). For a recent discussion on this issue, see Kolakowski, Nagy and Prescendi (2013).

20 Varhelyi (2011).

21 See Henrichs (1970), pp. 33–5, for a comparison of the different versions.

22 Porphyry, *De Abstinentia ab Esu Animalium*, II.42. For this Neoplatonic criticism of ritual sacrifice, and for the claim that sacrificial blood summoned demons, see Young (1979) and Bradbury (1995).

23 Plutarch, *Moralia*, 5.417. Translated by F. C. Babbitt, Loeb Classical Library, 1936.

24 Athanasius of Alexandria, *Contra Gentes*, 2.25. Translated under supervision of P. Schaff and H. Wace. T&T Clark, Edinburgh, 1891.

25 See Jones (2014), pp. 24–33, Salzman (2011), Shlosser (1991) and Barnes (1984) for an overview of the legislative initiatives. Stroumsa (2009) provides a wider, cultural description of the evolution to a religion without ritual sacrifice.

26 Bradbury (1995) and Belayche (2001) provide a detailed discussion of this revival during Julian's reign.

27 Harl (1990) describes the late remnants of animal sacrifice in Byzantium.

28 Tertullian, *Apologeticum*, 9.14. See Jones (2014), p. 69, for details of this compulsory participation in ritual sacrifice.

29 Prudentius, *Peristephanon*, 10.1011–50.

30 Cameron (2011), pp. 159–63. Earlier authors like Duthoy (1969) were also sceptical.

31 Jones (2014), p. 74.

32 For the Lombards, see above; for the Huns, see Ammianus Marcellinus, *Res Gestae*, 31.2 and Widukind de Corvey, *Rerum Gestarum Saxonicarum*, 1.18. For a critical study of this 'steak tartare', see King (1987), who argues that it makes the meat inedible.

33 Mohr (2005) and Fraesdorff (2005) are excellent studies on these 'barbaric' northern peoples.

34 Adam van Bremen, *Gesta*, iv.26–7, with its wonderful call for silence that only stimulates the curiosity. Quote found in Bray (2016), p. 129. For another source on Scandinavian human sacrifice, see Helmold van Bosau, *Chronica Slavorum*, p. 52.

35 See Samson (2011) for an exhaustive analysis of these mythical warriors, who gave us the word 'berserk'.

36 Samson (2011), pp. 232–5; Maurer (1856), ii, pp. 111–12.

37 *Vita Vulframni episcopi Senonici*, 8; *Lex Frisionum*, v. For more on this, see Siems (1980), pp. 334–69, 118–21.

38 Fadlan (2012), pp. 43–58.

39 See the excellent book by Guizard-Duchamp (2009) on the Christianization of the 'wild' Frankish world.

40 Bradbury (1995).

RED URINE

1 The best works on the Christian devotion to blood are Bynum (2007), Vincent (2001) and Rubin (1991). Kolb (1980) provides interesting illustrations. The subsequent paragraphs are based on these works.

2 Rousseau (2005) describes this growing tolerance for consuming products containing blood. Grumett and Muers (2010) also add a number of important details.

3 Classic works on this subject are Strack (1900) and Hellwig (1914).

4 Jori (2005).

5 Hippocrates, *Nature of Man*, 4. Quoted in Jouanna (2012), p. 230.

6 See Haak (2012) for more on this hypothesis, and criticisms of it.

7 The four fluids (blood, yellow bile, black bile and phlegm) were present in the blood. Blood was therefore a fluid in itself, and a mixture of fluids, including 'blood'.

8 Riha (2005) and Lenhardt (1986).

9 Rothschuh (1974); Seidler (1974); Debus (1977), pp. 512–19.

10 For the use of blood in alchemy, see Romswinkel (1974) and Thorndike (1934), III, pp. 78–84.

11 This anecdote is to be found in Knight and Hunter (2007). See Büttner (1987) for the importance of Boyle's *Memoirs*.

12 See Seidler (1974, p. 57) who claims that in '1818 entdeckte der Schüler Hunters, der britische Militärarzt Everard Home, die Blutplättchen' and refers to a paper that was published in 1820.

13 The various articles and the chronological overview in Boroviczény, Schipperges and Seidler (1974) provide a good review of these 'blood developments'. This remains the only comprehensive work on the history of haematology, with the exception of Owen (2001), which focuses on blood coagulation.

14 Jacob (1974).

15 Spörri (2013), pp. 53–5 summarizes this controversy. Silverstein (1979) and Sarazin (2007) provide a deeper analysis. See Tauber and Chernyak (1991) and Cavaillon (2011) on Metchnikoff.

16 Parmentier and Déyeux (1791), p. 2. Translated by A. Brown.

17 In 'Sang', Dechambre (ed.), *Dictionnaire encyclopédique des sciences médicales* (Paris: Masson and Asselin, 1878), série 3, tome 6, p. 443.

18 Harrington (1996), p. 12.

19 Hufeland (1837), p. 807.

20 See Wernz (1993), pp. 101–7, for more on this blood-balsam theory.

21 Hufeland (1795).

22 For a general treatment of vitalism, see Steigerwald (2013). For vitalism in eighteenth- and nineteenth-century blood analysis, see Coley (2001).

23 In 'Sang', Dechambre (ed.), *Dictionnaire encyclopédique des sciences médicales*, p. 456.

24 For more on this history, see Owen (2001) and Coley (2001). The most comprehensive contemporary works were John Hunter,

A Treatise on the Blood, Inflammation and Gun Wounds (1794) and Charles Turner Thackrah, *An Inquiry into the Nature and Properties of Blood* (1819). Jacobus Schroeder van der Kolk provided an excellent summary in his *Dissertatio physiologico-medica inauguralis* (1820).

25 Corrie (1791), pp. 84–7.

26 Steigerwald (2013), pp. 54–8.

27 Harrington (1996) and Lawrence and Weisz (1998).

28 Coley (2001), p. 2171.

29 It was Weber's famous lecture *Wissenschaft als Beruf* (Science as a Vocation). See Harrington (1996), p. xv.

30 For Steiner's influence on Beuys, see Famulla (2009).

31 Steiner (1906).

32 Spörri (2013), pp. 199–260.

33 See Maluf (1954), Pelis (1997), Webster (1971) and Starr (2000).

34 Starr (2000), pp. 3–18.

35 Pelis (1997).

36 Ibid., p. 357.

37 For illustrations of direct whole-blood transfusions, see Spörri (2013), pp. 333–5, and the painting by Dutch artist A. C. van de Lee (1933), now on display at Sanquin Research in Amsterdam.

38 These fantasies have been brought together in Hering and Maierhof (1991), Delaney, Lupton and Toth (1988), Buckley and Gottlieb (1988), and Meyer (2005), pp. 123–62.

39 Pliny, *Natural History*, 7.64.

40 Hering and Maierhof (1991), pp. 7, 165.

41 In 'Sang', Dechambre (ed.), *Dictionnaire encyclopédique des sciences médicales*, p. 497.

42 Although Spörri (2005), p. 329, and Hering and Maierhoff (1991), p. 82, believe that Burger (1958) put an end to this discussion, that is not the case. The wave of publications that started in the 1920s did slow down for a long period, but renewed interest emerged as of the 1970s. Burger's contribution was by no means seen as the end of the debate.

43 Weber (1975), p. 96. Translated by A. Brown.

44 Despite historic summaries like those of Spörri (2005) and the reference in Buckley and Gottlieb (1988), p. 20, there is no thorough study of menotoxins. Weber (1975) provides the most complete contemporary overview.

45 The list of menstruating mammals is short: most hominids and primates menstruate, with the exception of lemurs and tarsiers. It has also been observed among certain fruit bats and shrews. Biologists do not consider the periodic blood loss of dogs and other mammals, indicating that the female is 'on heat' (the oestrus stage of the reproductive cycle), to be genuine menstruation.

46 Schick (1920).

47 Mommsen (1934), p. 1480. Translated by A. Brown.

48 Schick (1920), p. 379. Translated by A. Brown.

49 Macht and Lubin (1924), pp. 413–14.

50 Ibid., p. 463.

51 Zondek (1953), p. 1068.

52 Bryant, Heathcote and Pickles (1977).

53 For more information on this, see www.sanquin.nl.

PART TWO: **BLOOD THIRST**

HAEMOTHYMIA

1 Mann (1924), pp. 616–17. For more on Castorp's dream, see Robertson (2006).

2 Zika (1996), p. 102.

3 See Guthrie (1950), pp. 145–82, Henrichs (1978) and Bremmer (1984) for more on this cult.

4 Henrichs (1978) gives a detailed description of this ritual.

5 See Edmonds (1999) for the mythical background.

6 Segal (1973–4) elaborated on this opposition between the Dionysian ritual and classical animal sacrifice.

7 This was the opinion of religious historian Albert Henrichs (1978), p. 147.

8 Euripides, *The Bacchantes*. Translated by Edward P. Coleridge. University of Adelaide eBook, https://ebooks.adelaide.edu.au, 2014.

9 Zola (1895/1885). Translated by Havelock Ellis. The Lutetian Society, London, 1895. Barrows (1981), pp. 93–113, discusses this scene.

10 Barbey d'Aurevilly (1916/1852), p. 223; Marcandier-Colard (1998) discusses this fragment, pp. 180–82.

11 Zola (1895/1885).

12 Ibid. See Pick (1989), pp. 88–9 and Barrows (1981), pp. 20–21, on speculations about the reality of castrations during French strikes.

13 Barrows (1981), pp. 76–81; Pick (1989), pp. 71–2.

14 Nye (1975), pp. 1–2. See also the Introduction.

15 Barrows (1981) and Nye (1975) remain classic works on this subject.

16 Sighele (1892), p. 102. Translated by A. Brown.

17 Chantala (1907), p. 61. Translated by A. Brown.

18 Tarde (1892), p. 367.

19 Lombroso and Laschi (1892), I, p. 194. Translated by A. Brown.

20 Vandenberg (2014), pp. 131–49. With thanks for confirming this
    to me by email.

21 Bynum (2007), pp. 119, 184, 246, 306. This can be found in St John
    of Capistrano, *Tractatus de Christi sanguine pretioso* (art. 16, sext.
    B), and in a letter from him.

22 Bourbon del Monte (1877), p. 85. Translated by A. Brown. Other
    very bloody books about animals were Jacolliot (1884) and
    Delcroix (1882), which compares fishermen who kill dolphins
    with soldiers driven to a frenzy by blood (p. 376).

23 Lombroso (1895), I, p. 271. Translated by A. Brown.

24 See Thoinot (1898), Laurent (1903) and Ellis (1927) for all these
    'perversions'.

25 This last case is to be found in Peskov (1898) and the others
    in Ellis (1927).

26 Claye Shaw (1909).

27 Dr Earl Russel during a meeting of the Medico-Legal Society
    on 25 May 1909.

28 Ellis (1903), p. 73.

29 I found this story about the Duke of Beaufort in Moriceau (2011),
    pp. 162–3. Additional details come from Halna du Fretay (1891),
    Chabot (1898) and Chevallier-Ruffigny (1938).

30 Moriceau (2011), pp. 157–9.

31 Rousseau (2005), p. 252.

32 Ibid., pp. 248–52.

33 Fabre-Vassas (1982); Hell (1997), p. 58.

34 Halna du Fretay (1891), pp. 14, 16–17.

35 Chabot (1898), p. 360. Translated by A. Brown.

36 Mangan and McKenzie (2010), pp. 7–8, 24.

37 Hell (1997), pp. 30–35.

38 Ibid., p. 33.

39 Quotes from Ortega (1972/1942), p. 32. See Cohn (1999) for more
    on this text and blood ecstasy while hunting.

40 Pollan (2006).

41 An example is Cohn (1999).

42 See Agulhon (1981), pp. 83–4, for dog-fighting and the *ratodrome*; De Vroede (1993), pp. 134–5, for badger-baiting; and Turner (1980), pp. 20–22, for bull-baiting.

43 Nye (1993), p. 185.

44 Mangan and McKenzie (2010), p. 74.

45 Mangan (2013) provides an excellent description of the transition from blood sports to athletic sports.

WILD ORIGINS

1 Duysters (2002) describes the history of these stained-glass windows.

2 Ortega y Gasset (1972/1942), p. 46.

3 Hering and Maierhof (2002/1991), p. 22, with reference to Duncan. Baptist Verduc (1696) asked, tongue in cheek, what apes had done wrong to suffer the punishment of menstruation.

4 Hesiod, *Works and Days*, II, 121–39.

5 See Vandenberg (2014), pp. 299–345, on these cannibalistic monsters and peoples in antiquity.

6 Plato, *The Republic*, 9, 571. Translated by Desmond Lee, Penguin Books, Harmondsworth, 1974.

7 Aravamudan (2009) discusses these illustrations.

8 Dickason (1984), pp. 29–40.

9 Ibid., pp. 66–70.

10 Aravamudan (2009), pp. 43–53; Ashcraft (1972), pp. 148–54.

11 See Kuper (2005) and Stocking (1987) on this Victorian primitivism. For earlier forms, see White (1972) and Dickason (1984).

12 Lubbock (1865), p. 484.

13 Hart and Sussman (2009) defend this standpoint. See Verplaetse (2011), pp. 79–82 for a summary of the 'man-the-hunted' argument.

14 Crook (1996); Crook (1998).

15 Dart (1953); Ardrey (1976); Washburn and Lancaster (1968); Wrangham and Peterson (1997).

16 James (1904), p. 39; James (1910), p. 660. See also Crook (1998), p. 273.

17 Dart (1953), pp. 207–8.

18 Crook (1996), p. 21.

19 Darwin (1958), p. 54.

20 James (1910), p. 661.

21 James (1890), II, p. 412.

22 Ibid., II, pp. 412–13.

23 Moore (1933/1916), p. 106.

24 Mangan and McKenzie (2010), p. 175.

25 Bourke (1999), pp. 140–43, 403–4.

26 Crile (1915), pp. 20–21.

27 Trotter (1916), p. 237.

28 Spier (1916), p. 173. Translated by A. Brown.

29 See Introduction, p. 9.

30 Spier (1916), p. 172. Translated by A. Brown.

31 Otis (1994) and Schacter (2001) described this theory of genetic or organic memory in detail.

32 Spier (1916), p. 172.

33 Farley (1982) gives an excellent overview of the state of knowledge of genetics at the time.

34 Ward (1913), p. 43.

35 Ribot (1875), p. 48.

36 Otis (1994), p. 18; Schacter (2001), pp. 116–17.

37 Gerson (1920), p. 71. Translated by A. Brown; Hering and Maierhof (1991), p. 90.

38 Phillips (1906), pp. 980–81.

39 Ibid., pp. 982–3.

40 Freud (1919/1913), p. 235.

41 Quoted in Corbey (1991), p. 40, whose analysis of Freud I have used in previous and subsequent paragraphs.

42 Robertson (2006), p. 56.

43 Schacter (2001), pp. 127–35.

44 Otis (1994), p. 184.

CHEMOSIGNALS

1 Carroll (2006), p. 179. For the meaning of 'berserk', see Part I of this book, p. 85.

2 Hayes (2005), p. 4.

3 Golan (2004), p. 147; Orfila, Barruel and Chevallier (1835).

4 Barruel (1829).

5 *Gazette des Tribunaux*, 21 February 1835, provides details on the Hochet case.

6 Schmidt (1848).

7 Tardieu, Barruel and Chevallier (1853), p. 417. Translated by A. Brown.

8 See De Smet, Van Speybroeck and Verplaetse (2012) for a complete description of this experiment.

9 Nilsson et al. (2014).

10 Doty (2010); Wyatt (2015).

11 Wyatt (2015).

12 Gelstein et al. (2011).

13 De Groot et al. (2012).

14 Olsson (2014); Mitro et al. (2012); Moshkin et al. (2012).

15 Schank (2006), with thanks to Ellen de Visser, science editor
    at *De Volkskrant*, for this information.

16 Stratton (1923); Blodget (1924).

17 Stratton (1923), p. 386; Blodget (1924), p. 338.

18 Terlouw, Boissy and Blinet (1998).

19 Christensen and Rundgren (2008).

20 Grandin (1993), p. 292.

21 Sandnabba (1997).

22 Stevens and Saplikoski (1973); Stevens and Gerzog-Thomas (1977);
    also confirmed by Hornbuckle and Beall (1974).

23 Eibl-Eibesfeldt (1970), p. 236.

24 Mackay-Sim and Laing (1980).

25 March (1980) and Nunley (1981) for white-tailed deer; Jones
    and Black (1979) for chicks; Barreto et al. (2013) for Nile tilapia;
    Shabani, Kamio and Derbu (2008) for spiny lobsters; and Goodale
    and Nieh (2012) for bees.

26 Klimsley (2013), pp. 126–7.

27 Moriceau (2011), pp. 58–9.

28 Nilsson et al. (2014).

29 This has recently also been determined for wolves (Arshamian
    et al., 2017) and meerkats (Pettersson, Amundin and Laska, 2018).

30 Cushing (1983).

31 Rogers, Wilker and Scott (1991).

32 Stanford (1999), pp. 64, 199. See also Stanford (1998),
    with foreword by Richard Wrangham, and Newton-Fischer
    (2007).

33 *Daily Mail*, 10 April 2013. For earlier incident, see also: https://
    edition.cnn.com/2012/11/03/world/asia/nepal-leopard-deaths/index.
    html, accessed 2 July 2019.

34 For a summary of these studies on the 'red effect', see Lin (2014),
    pp. 202–3. Guéguen (2012) is a good example.

35 Genschow, Reutner and Wänke (2012).

36 Hill and Barton (2005).

37 Attrill et al. (2008).

38 For example, Garcia-Rubio, Picazo-Tadeo and Gonzalez-Gomez (2011).

39 Hagemann, Strauss and Leissing (2008).

40 Ilie et al. (2008).

41 Guéguen et al. (2012).

42 Elliot and Aarts (2011).

43 Dreiskaemper et al. (2013).

44 Barlett, Harris and Bruey (2008); Krcmar and Farrar (2009).

45 Jeong, Biocca and Bohil (2012).

46 Goldstein (1998)

47 Verplaetse and De Smet (2016). Very recent research with E2D confirms this suppressing effect. Gamers who inhaled E2D leaned back more, which the researchers interpreted as an evasive movement after contact with blood (Arshamian et al., 2017).

PART THREE: **BLOOD AESTHETICS**

BLOOD HORROR

1 Rice (1976), p. 31.

2 Van Gennep (1960).

3 The following paragraphs are inspired by Barber (2010).

4 Barber (2010), pp. 114, 208 refers to Ponsold (1957), p. 292, Glaister and Rentoul (1966), pp. 115–16, and Mant (1984), p. 139. The experiments with dogs are described in Owen (2001), p. 89.

5 Mole (1948), p. 424.

6 Owen (2001), pp. 88–9.

7 Calmet thought that liquid blood was fat and bone marrow fermented by the sun warming the earth of the graveyard. See Barber (2010), pp. 113–14.

8 Stoker (1986/1897), p. 134.

9 Ibid., p. 335.

10 Cavaillon (2011), p. 415.

11 Bynum (2007), p. 15.

12 Marks (1988) and Bienvenue and Eaton (1998) provide good summaries.

13 Lilliencreutz and Josefsson (2008).

14 Ganzeboom et al. (2003).

15 Curtis, de Barra and Aunger (2011); Oaten, Stevenson and Case (2009); Verplaetse (2011), pp. 125–30.

16 Curtis and Biran (2001), p. 24.

17 Bracha (2004); Bracha et al. (2005); Alboni, Alboni and Bertorelle (2008).

18 Diehl (2005).

19 Solomon, Greenberg and Pyszczynski (2015) provide a concise summary of this theory in book form. Hayes et al. (2010) also presents a good overview.

20 Stoker (1986/1897), p. 197.

21 Ibid., p. 209.

22 See, for example, the special issue of *Psychological Inquiry*, 4, 2006, which is devoted to discussion of TMT.

SUBLIME BLOOD

1 My description of La Villette is based on Claflin (2008), the history of slaughterhouses in the Netherlands and Europe on Koolmees (1997), and early nineteenth-century developments on Watts (2008).

2 See Lee (2008) for a discussion of these topics, and Hersey (1988) for the incorporation of ritual sacrifice elements (such as guttae) in architecture.

3 Bataille (1929). See Lowenstein (1988) for more on Franju's film and Vialles (1994), p. 53, for the anecdote on the children watching the film in Venice. For the blood-drinkers, see the stories by Lorrain (1898) and Rachilde (pseudonym of Marguerite Eymery-Vallette), and the painting by Joseph Ferdinand Gueldry (1898), to which Dijkstra (1986) devotes a number of pages (pp. 333–51).

4 Claflin (2008), p. 37.

5 *De Standaard*, 22 June 2014. Translated by A. Brown.

6 Classics on this theme are Monk (1935) and Kirwan (2005).

7 See Black (1991), pp. 13–15, 67–9, and Marcandier-Colard (1998), pp. 11–51, on the sublime and violence, murder and crime.

8 Burke (2015/1757), Section 7:40.

9 Kant (2009/1790), p. 91.

10 Burke (2015/1757), Section 15.

11 Smuts (2007) and (2009) summarizes the discussion.

12 Du Bos (1719). Livingstone (2013) discusses this theory.

13 Morreall (1985).

14 Clasen (2012).

15 Ibid.; Hoffner and Levine (2005).

16 Carroll (1990), p. 186.

17 Bantinaki (2012).

18 Novalis (1997), p. 60.

19 See the excellent introduction, 'Negative Aesthetics', in Botting (2014), pp. 1–19.

20 Quoted by Clasen (2012), p. 227.

21 Eisnitz (1997), p. 92; Foer (2009), p. 249.

22 Lestel (2016), p. 85.

BLOODLESS

1 I found inspiration for this utopia in Weele and Driessen (2013) and Weele and Tramper (2014).

2 Verbeke et al. (2015); Verbeke, Sans and Van Loo (2015).

3 Singer (2011), p. 386.

4 Visak (2011) is critical of this argument equating domesticated animals with pets.

5 Rozin (2005); Rozin (2006).

6 Lockhart, Keil and Aw (2013).

7 Shepherd (2012).

8 Bushdid et al. (2014).

9 Carpino et al. (2004); Rapisarda et al. (2013).

10 Overvliet and Soto-Faraco (2011); Whitaker, Simoes-Franklin and Newell (2008).

11 Gallace and Spence (2014), p. 227.

12 Haring (2011), p. 216.

13 De Quincey (2006/1827), pp. 12–13.

14 Besides Galen Last (2015), Dickason (1984) and Dudley and Novak (1972), see also Young (1995), McClintock (1995) and Jahoda (2009). Galen Last (p. 170) claimed that the idea of black soldiers committing violent atrocities gave white people sexual pleasure. McClintock also speaks of 'porno-tropics', which clearly goes further than enjoyment of the Sublime.

15 Fauvelle and Fauvelle (1890). Translated by A. Brown.

16 Le Courrier de l'Aisne, 6 November 1890.

17 Fauvelle and Fauvelle (1890), p. 958. Translated by A. Brown.

18 Fresco (2015), p. 242.

BIBLIOGRAPHY

Ancient Greek and Latin sources are not included in this list. I refer to the specific passage in the original work and to a modern English translation in the references.

Agulhon, M. (1981). 'Le sang des bêtes: le problème de la protection des animaux en France au xixe siècle', *Romantisme*, 31, pp. 81–109

Alboni, P., M. Alboni and G. Bertorelle (2008). 'The Origin of Vasovagal Syncope: To Protect the Heart or to Escape Predation?', *Clinical Autonomic Research*, 18, pp. 170–78

Albrecht, J., et al. (2011). 'Smelling Chemosensory Signals of Males in Anxious Versus Nonanxious Condition Increases State Anxiety of Female Subjects', *Chemical Senses*, 36, pp. 19–27

Aravumudan, S. (2009). 'Hobbes and America', in *The Postcolonial Enlightenment: Eighteenth-century Colonialism and Postcolonial Theory*, ed. D. Carey and L. Festa (Oxford: Oxford University Press)

Ardrey, R. (1976). *The Hunting Hypothesis: A Personal Conclusion concerning the Evolutionary Nature of Man* (London: Collins)

Arshamian, A., et al. (2017). 'A Mammalian Blood Odor Component Serves an Approach-avoidance Cue across Phylum Border – from Flies to Humans', *Scientific Reports*, 7

Ashcraft, R. (1972). 'Leviathan Triumphant: Thomas Hobbes and the Politics of Wild Men', in *The Wild Man Within: An Image in Western Thought from the Renaissance to Romanticism*, ed. E. Dudley and M. E. Novak (Pittsburgh: University of Pittsburgh Press), pp. 141–81

Astour, M. C. (1967). *Hellenosemitica: An Ethnic and Cultural Study in West Semitic Impact on Mycenean Greece* (Leiden: Brill)

Attrill, M. J., et al. (2008). 'Red Shirt Colour is associated with Long-term Team Success in English Football', *Journal of Sports Sciences*, xxvi/6, pp. 577–82

Bantinaki, K. (2012). 'The Paradox of Horror: Fear as a Positive
    Emotion', *Journal of Aesthetics and Art Criticism*, LXX/4, pp. 383–92
Barber, P. (2010/1988). *Vampires, Burial, and Death: Folklore and
    Reality*, 2nd edn (New Haven, CT, and London: Yale University Press)
Barbey d'Aurevilly, J. (1928/1852). *Bewitched* (New York: Harper & Brothers)
Bargheer, E. (1931). *Eingeweide: Lebens- und Seelenkräfte des
    Leibesinneren im Deutschen Glauben und Brauch* (Berlin: de Gruyter)
Barlett, C. P., R. J. Harris and C. Bruey (2008). 'The Effect of the
    Amount of Blood in a Violent Video Game on Aggression, Hostility,
    and Arousal', *Journal of Experimental Social Psychology*, 44,
    pp. 539–46
Barnes, T. D. (1984). 'Constantine's Prohibition of Pagan Sacrifice',
    American Journal of Philology, CV/1, pp. 69–72
Barreto, R. E. et al. (2013). 'Blood Cues Induce Antipredator Behavior
    in Nile Tilapia Conspecifics', *PLOS ONE*, VIII/1, e54642
Barrows, S. (1981). *Distorting Mirrors: Visions of the Crowd in Late
    Nineteenth-century France* (New Haven, CT: Yale University Press)
Barruel, J.-P. (1829). 'Mémoire sur l'existence d'un principe propre à
    caractériser le sang de l'homme et celui des diverses espèces
    d'animaux', *Annales d'Hygiène Publique et de Médecine Légale*, 1,
    pp. 267–77
Bataille, G. (1929). 'Abattoir', *Documents*, 6, pp. 327–9
Becker, E. (1973). *The Denial of Death* (New York: Free Press)
Belayche, N. (2001). 'Le sacrifice et la théorie du sacrifice pendant la
    "réaction païenne": l'empéreur Julien', *Revue de l'Histoire des
    Religions*, 218, pp. 455–86
Biale, D. (2007). *Blood and Belief: The Circulation of a Symbol between
    Jews and Christians* (Berkeley, CA: University of California Press)
Bienvenue, J. O., and W. W. Eaton (1998). 'The Epidemiology of Blood-
    injection-injury Phobia', *Psychological Medicine*, 28, pp. 1129–36
Bildhauer, B. (2006). *Medieval Blood* (Cardiff: University of Wales Press)
Black, J. (1991). *The Aesthetics of Murder: A Study in Romantic
    Literature and Contemporary Culture* (Baltimore, MD, and London:
    Johns Hopkins University Press)
——, and A. Green (1992). *Gods, Demons and Symbols of Ancient
    Mesopotamia: An Illustrated Dictionary* (Austin, TX: Texas
    University Press)
Blodget, H. C. (1924). 'A Further Observation on Cattle and Excitement
    from Blood', *Psychological Review*, XXXI/4, pp. 336–8

Botting, F. (2014). *Gothic: The New Critical Idiom*, 2nd edn
(New York: Routledge)

Bourbon del Monte, J.B.F. (1877). *L'homme et les animaux: Essai
de psychologie positive* (Paris: Germer-Baillière)

Bourke, J. (1999). *An Intimate History of Killing: Face-to-face Killing
in Twentieth-century Warfare* (New York: Basic Books)

Bracha, H. S. (2004). 'Freeze, Flight, Faint: Adaptationist Perspectives
on the Acute Stress Response Spectrum', cns *Spectrums*, 9, pp. 679–85

——, and A. S. Bracha et al. (2005). 'The Human Fear-circuitry and
Fear-induced Fainting in Healthy Individuals: The Paleolithic-threat
Hypothesis', *Clinical Autonomic Research*, xv/2, pp. 238–41

Bradbury, S. (1995). 'Julian's Pagan Revival and the Decline of Blood
Sacrifice', *Phoenix*, xlix/4, pp. 331–56

Bray, D. (2008). 'Sacrifice and sacrificial ideology in Old Norse religion',
https://openjournals.library.sydney.edu.au/index.php/SSR/article/
view/207/186

Bremmer, J. N. (1984). 'Greek maenadism reconsidered', *Zeitschrift
für Papyrologie und Epigraphik*, 55, pp. 267–86

—— (ed.) (2007). *The Strange Way of Human Sacrifice* (Leuven: Peeters)

Brunaux, J.-L. (2008). *Nos ancêtres les Gaulois* (Paris: Seuil)

Bryant, J. A., D. G. Heathcote and V. R. Pickles (1977). 'The search
for "menotoxin"', *The Lancet*, 8014, p. 753

Buckley, T., and A. Gottlieb (1988). 'A critical appraisal of theories
of menstrual symbolism', in *Blood Magic: The Anthropology of
Menstruation*, ed. T. Buckley and A. Gottlieb (Berkeley: University
of California Press)

Burger, H. (1958). 'Zur Steuerung des Menstruationszyklus', *Deutsche
Medizinische Wochenschrift*, 83, pp. 1991–7

Burke, E. (2015/1757). *A Philosophical Enquiry into the Origin of Our
Ideas of the Sublime and Beautiful* (Oxford: Oxford University Press)

Burkert, W. (1983/1972). *Homo Necans: The Anthropology of Ancient
Greek Sacrificial Ritual and Myth*, trans. Peter Bing
(Berkeley, ca: University of California Press)

—— (2011). *Kleine Schriften V. Mythica, Ritualia, Religiosa 2*
(Göttingen: Vandenhoeck & Ruprecht)

Bushdid, C. et al. (2014). 'Humans can discriminate more than 1 trillion
olfactory stimuli', *Science*, 343, pp. 1370–72

Büttner, J. (1987). 'Die physikalische und chemische Untersuchung
von Blut im 17. und 18. Jahrhundert: zur Bedeutung von Robert

Boyles "Memoirs for the Natural History of Human Blood" (1684)',
Medizinhistorisches Journal, 22, pp. 185–96

Bynum, C. W. (2007). *Wonderful Blood: Theology and Practice in Late
Medieval North Germany and Beyond* (Philadelphia, PA: University
of Pennsylvania Press)

Cameron, A. (2011). *The Last Pagans of Rome* (Oxford: Oxford
University Press)

Carpino, S. et al. (2004). 'Contribution to native pasture to the sensory
properties of Ragusano cheese', *Dairy Science*, 87, pp. 308–15

Carroll, N. (1990). *The Philosophy of Horror, or Paradoxes of the Heart*
(New York and London: Routledge)

Carroll, S. (2006). *Blood and Violence in Early Modern France*
(Oxford: Oxford University Press)

Cavaillon, J.-M. (2011). 'The historical milestones in the understanding
of leukocyte biology initiated by Elie Metchnikoff', *Journal of
Leukocyte Biology*, 90, pp. 413–24

Cazelles, H. (1991). *Sang: Supplément au dictionnaire du Bible*
(Paris: Letouzey & Ainé), pp. 1332–53

Chabot, A. de (1898). *La chasse à travers les âges: Histoire anecdotique
de la chasse* (Paris: Savaète)

Chantala, H. (1907). *Les folies de la foule* (Toulouse: Gimet-Pisseau)

Chevallier-Ruffigny, F. (1938). 'La chasse aux loups et la destruction
des loups à Poitou aux XVIIIe et XIXe siècles', *Bulletin de la Société
des Antiquaries de l'Ouest*, 3e série, XI, 1er trimestre,
pp. 599–601

Christensen, J. W., and M. Rundgren (2008). 'Predator odour per se
does not frighten domestic horses', *Applied Animal Behaviour
Science*, 112, pp. 136–45

Claflin, K. (2008). 'La Villette: city of blood (1867–1918)', in *Meat,
Modernity, and the Rise of the Slaughterhouse*, ed. P. Y. Lee
(Durham: University of New Hampshire Press), pp. 27–45

Clasen, M. (2012). 'Monsters evolve: a biocultural approach to horror
stories', *Review of General Psychology*, XVI/2, pp. 222–39

Claye Shaw, T. (1909). 'A prominent motive in murder', *The Lancet*,
4477, pp. 1735–8

Cohn, P. (1999). 'Exploding the hunting myths', in *Ethics and Wildlife*,
ed. P. Cohn (Lewiston: Edwin Mellen Press)

Coley, N. G. (2001). 'Early blood chemistry in Britain and France',
Clinical Chemistry, XLVII/12, pp. 2166–78

Corbey, R. (1991). 'Freud's phylogenetic narrative', in *Alterity, Identity, Image*, ed. R. Corbey and J. Leerssen (Amsterdam: Rodopi)

Corrie, J. (1791). *An Essay on the Vitality of Blood* (London: Elliot and Kay)

Crile, G. W. (1915). *A Mechanistic View of War and Peace* (New York: Rowland)

Crook, P. (1996). *Darwinism, War and History: The Debate over the Biology of War from the 'Origin of Species' to the First World War* (Cambridge: Cambridge University Press)

—— (1998). 'Human pugnacity and war: Some anticipations of sociobiology 1880–1919', *Biology & Philosophy*, 13, pp. 263–88

Curtis, V., and A. Biran (2001). 'Dirt, disgust and disease: Is hygiene in our genes?', *Perspectives in Biology and Medicine*, 44, pp. 17–31

——, M. de Barra and R. Aunger (2011). 'Disgust as an adaptive system for disease avoidance behavior', *Philosophical Transactions of the Royal Society B Biological Sciences*, 366, pp. 389–401

Cushing, B. S. (1983). 'Responses of polar bears to human menstrual odors', *International Conference on Bear Reservation and Management*, 5, pp. 270–74

Dart, R. A. (1953). 'The predatory transition from ape to man', *International Anthropological and Linguistic Review*, 1/4, pp. 201–19

Darwin, C. (1958). *The Autobiography of Charles Darwin* (London: Collins)

Debus, A. G. (1977). *The Chemical Philosophy: Paracelsian Science and Medicine in the Sixteenth and Seventeenth Centuries* (New York: Dover)

Delaney, J., M. J. Lupton and E. Toth (1988). *The Curse: A Cultural History of Menstruation*, 2nd expanded edn (Urbana, IL: University of Illinois Press)

Delcroix, V. (1882). *Histoire illustrée des animaux* (Rouen: Megard)

De Quincey, T. (2006/1827). *On Murder* (Oxford: Oxford University Press, Oxford World's Classics)

De Smet, D., L. Van Speybroeck and J. Verplaetse (2012). 'Why men do not make good vampires: Testing the ability of humans to detect true blood', *Annals of Human Biology*, 3, pp. 1–10

De Vroede, E. (1993). 'Beestige spelen: Dieren in het volksvermaak', in *Dieren in het volksleven*, ed. S. Top (Leuven: Leuvense Vereniging voor Volkskunde), pp. 125–53

Dickason, O. P. (1984). *The Myth of the Savage and the Beginnings of French Colonialism in the Americas* (Edmonton: University of Alberta Press)

Diehl, R. R. (2005). 'Vasovagal syncope and Darwinian fitness', *Clinical Autonomic Research*, xv/2, pp. 126–9

Dijkstra, B. (1986). *Idols of Perversity: Fantasies of Feminine Evil in Fin-de-siècle Culture* (New York: Oxford University Press)

Dölger, F. J. (1926). 'Gladiatorenblut und Martyrenblut: Eine Szene der Passio Perpetuae in kultur- und religionsgeschichtlicher Beleuchtung', in *Vorträge der Bibliothek Warburg. Vorträge 1923–1924*, ed. F. Saxl (Berlin: Teubner), pp. 196–214

—— (1934). '"Sacramentum infanticidii": die Schlachtung eines Kind und der Genuss seines Fleisches und Blutes als vermeintlicher Einweihungsakt im ältesten Christentum', *Antike und Christentum*, pp. 188–228

Doty, R. L. (2010). *The Great Pheromone Myth* (Baltimore, MD: Johns Hopkins University Press)

Dreiskaemper, D. et al. (2013). 'Influence of red jersey color on physical parameters in combat sports', *Journal of Sport and Exercise Psychology*, 35, pp. 44–9

Du Bos, J.-B. (1719). *Réflexions critiques sur la poésie et sur la peinture*, 2 vols (Paris: Pierre-Jean Mariette)

Dudley, E., and M. E. Novak (1972). *The Wild Man Within: An Image in Western Thought from the Renaissance to Romanticism* (Pittsburgh, PA: University of Pittsburgh Press)

Duthoy, R. (1969). *The Taurobolium: Its Evolution and Terminology* (Leiden: Brill)

Duysters, K. (2002). '"Das genügend bekannte, unerquickliche Kapitel": Helene Kröller-Müller, Arthur Hennig en de glas-in-loodramen in het jachthuis Sint-Hubertus', *Vormen uit Vuur*, CLXXVII/1, pp. 2–15

Edmonds, R. (1999). 'Tearing apart the Zagreus myth: A few disparaging remarks on orphism and original sin', *Classical Antiquity*, 18, pp. 35–73

Eibl-Eibesfeldt, I. (1970). *Ethology: The Biology of Behavior* (New York: Holt, Rinehart & Winston)

Eisnitz, G. A. (1997). *Slaughterhouse: The Shocking Story of Greed, Neglect, and Inhumane Treatment inside the u.s. Meat Industry* (Amherst, NY: Prometheus Books)

Ekroth, G. (2002). *The Sacrificial Rituals of Greek Hero-Cults* (Liège: Centre International d'étude de la religion grecque antique. Kernos Supplément 12)

—— (2005). 'Blood on the altars? On the treatment of blood at Greek sacrifices and the iconographical evidence', *Antike Kunst*, 48, pp. 9–29

—— (2007). 'Meat in ancient Greece: Sacrificial, sacred or secular?' in *Sacrifices, marchés de la viande et pratiques alimentaires dans les cités du monde romain*, ed. W. Van Andringa, *Food & History*, v/1, pp. 249–72

Elliot, A. J., and H. Aarts (2011). 'Perception of the color red enhances the force and velocity of motor output', *Emotion*, xi/2, pp. 445–9

Ellis, H. H. (1903). *Studies in the Psychology of Sex: Analysis of the Sexual Impulse. Love and Pain. The Sexual Impulse in Women* (Philadelphia, PA: Davis)

—— (1927). *Studies in the Psychology of Sex. Volume 3: Analysis of the Sexual Impulse. Love and Pain. The Sexual Impulse in Women*, 3rd edn (Philadelphia, PA: Davis)

Fabre-Vassas, C. (1982). 'Le partage du ferum: Un rite de chasse au sanglier', *Etudes Rurales*, 87–8, pp. 377–400

Fadlan, I. (2012). *Ibn Fadlan and the Land of Darkness: Arab Travellers in the Far North* (London: Penguin)

Famulla, R. (2009). *Joseph Beuys: Künstler, Krieger und Schamane: Die Bedeutung von Trauma und Mythos in seinem Werk. 2., neue bearbeitete Auflage* (Giessen: Psychosozial-Verlag)

Faraone, C. A., and D. Obbink, eds (1991). *Magika Hiera: Ancient Greek Magic and Religion* (Oxford: Oxford University Press)

Farley, J. (1982). *Gameten and Spores: Ideas about Sexual Reproduction, 1750–1914* (Baltimore, MD: Johns Hopkins University Press)

Fauvelle, C., and J.-L. Fauvelle (1890). 'Photographies de criminel', *Bulletin de Société d'Anthropologie de Paris*, pp. 957–9.

Foer, J. S. (2009). *Eating Animals* (London: Penguin)

Fraesdorff, D. (2005). *Der barbarische Norden: Vorstellungen und Fremdheitskategorien bei Rimbert, Thietmar von Merseburg, Adam von Bremen und Helmold von Bosau* (Berlin: Akademie, Orbis mediaevalis. Vorstellungswelten des Mittelalters, 5)

Frank, R. (1984). 'Viking atrocity and skaldic verse: The rite of the blood-eagle', *English Historical Review*, xcix/391, pp. 332–43

Frankfurter, D. (2011). 'Egyptian religion and the problem of the category "sacrifice"', in *Ancient Mediterranean Sacrifice*, ed. J. W. Knust and Z. Varhelyi (Oxford: Oxford University Press), pp. 75–93

Fresco, L. O. (2015). *Hamburgers in Paradise. The Story behind the Food We Eat* (Princeton, NJ: Princeton University Press)

Freud, S. (1919/1913). *Totem and Taboo: Resemblances Between the*

Psychic Lives of Savages and Neurotics, trans. A. A. Brill (London: Routledge)

Galen Last, D. van (2015). *Black Shame: African Soldiers in Europe, 1914–1922* (London: Bloomsbury Academic)

Gallace, A., and C. Spence (2014). *In Touch with the Future: The Sense of Touch from Cognitive Neuroscience to Virtual Reality* (Oxford: Oxford University Press)

Ganzeboom, K. S. et al. (2003). 'Prevalence and triggers of syncope in medical students', *American Journal of Cardiology*, 91, pp. 1006–8

Garcia-Rubio, M. A., A. J. Picazo-Tadeo and F. Gonzalez-Gomez (2011). 'Does a red shirt improve sporting performance? Evidence from Spanish football', *Applied Economics Letters*, xviii/11, pp. 1001–4

Gay, P. (1993). *The Cultivation of the Hatred: The Bourgeois Experience: Victoria to Freud*, vol. iii (New York: Norton)

Gelstein, S. et al. (2011). 'Human tears contain a chemosignal', *Science*, 6014, pp. 226–30

Genschow, O., L. Reutner and M. Wänke (2012). 'The color red reduces snack food and soft drink intake', *Appetite*, 58, pp. 699–702

Gerson, A. (1920). 'Die Menstruation: ihre Entstehung und Bedeutung', *Zeitschrift für Sexualwissenschaft*, vii/2, pp. 18–88

Gilders, W. K. (2004). *Blood Ritual in the Hebrew Bible: Meaning and Power* (Baltimore, MD: Johns Hopkins University Press)

—— (2007). 'Blut, "Leben" und Opferritual in der hebräischen Bibel', in *Mythen des Blutes*, ed. C. von Brain and C. Wulf (Frankfurt: Campus), pp. 31–42

Girard, R. (1977). *Violence and the Sacred*, trans. Patrick Gregory (Baltimore, MD: Johns Hopkins University Press)

Glaister, J., and E. Rentoul (1966). *Medical Jurisprudence and Toxicology*, 12th edn (Edinburgh and London: Livingston)

Goethe, J. W. von (1982/1806). *Faust*, Parts i and ii (Poetry in Translation: www.poetryintranslation.com/PITBR/German/FaustIScenesIVtoVI.php)

Golan, T. Tai (2004). *Laws of Men and Laws of Nature: A History of Scientific Expert Testimony* (Cambridge, MA: Harvard University Press)

Goldstein, J. H. (1998). *Why We Watch: The Attraction of Violent Entertainment* (Oxford: Oxford University Press)

Goodale, E., and J. C. Nieh (2012). 'Public use of olfactory information associated with predation in two species of social bees', *Animal Behaviour*, 84, pp. 919–24

Graf, F. (1997). *Magic in the Ancient World*
(Cambridge, MA: Harvard University Press)

—— (2012). 'One generation after Burkert and Girard: Where are the
great theories?', in *Greek and Roman Sacrifice: Ancient Victims,
Modern Observers*, ed. C. A. Faraone and F. Naiden
(Cambridge: Cambridge University Press, 2012), pp. 32–51

Grandin, T. (ed.) (1993). *Livestock Handling and Transport*
(Wallington: CAB International)

Grintz, J. (1966). 'Do not eat on the blood', *Zion*, XXXI/1 and 2,
pp. 1–17

Groot, J.H.B. de et al. (2012). 'Chemosignals communicate human
emotions', *Psychological Science*, 23, pp. 1417–24

Grumett, D., and R. Muers (2010). *Theology on the Menu: Asceticism,
Meat and Christian Diet* (London: Routledge)

Guéguen, N. (2012). 'Color and women hitchhikers' attractiveness:
Gentlemen drivers prefer red', *Color Research and Application*,
37, pp. 76–8

——, et al. (2012). 'When drivers see red: Car color frustrators and
drivers' aggressiveness', *Aggressive Behavior*, 38, pp. 166–69

Guizard-Duchamp, F. (2009). *Les terres du sauvage dans le monde
franc* (Rennes: Presses universitaires de Rennes)

Guthrie, W.K.C. (1950). *The Greeks and Their Gods* (London: Methuen)

Haak, H. L. (2012). 'Blood, clotting, and the four humours', in *Blood,
Sweat, and Tears: Changing Concepts of Physiology from Antiquity
to Early Modern Europe*, ed. M. Horstmanshoff, H. King and
C. Zittel (Leiden: Brill), pp. 295–305

Hagemann, N., B. Strauss and J. Leissing (2008). 'When the referee
sees red', *Psychological Science*, XIX/8, pp. 769–72

Halna du Fretay, M. (1891). *Mes chasses de loups*
(Saint-Brieuc: Prud'homme)

Haring, B. (2011). *Plastic panda's: Over het opheffen van de natuur*
(Amsterdam: Nijgh & Van Ditmar)

Harl, K. W. (1990). 'Sacrifice and pagan belief in fifth- and sixth-century
Byzantium', *Past and Present*, 128, pp. 7–27

Harrington, A. (1996). *Reenchanted Science: Holism in German Culture
from Wilhelm II to Hitler* (Princeton, NJ: Princeton University Press)

Hart, D., and R. W. Sussman (2009). *Man the Hunted: Primates,
Predators, and Human Evolution*, expanded edn
(Boulder, CO: Westpoint Press)

Hayes, B. (2005). *Five Quarts: A Personal and Natural History of Blood* (New York: Random House)

Hayes, J., et al. (2010). 'A theoretical and empirical review of the death-thought accessibility concept in terror management research', *Psychological Bulletin*, 136, pp. 699–739

Hell, B. (1997). *Le sang noir: chasse et mythes du sauvage en Europe* (Paris: Flammarion)

Hellwig, A. (1914). *Ritualmord und Blutaberglaube* (Minden in Westfalen: Bruns)

Henrichs, A. (1970). 'Pagan ritual and the alleged crimes of the early Christians: A reconsideration', in *Kyriakon: Festschrift Johannes Quasten*, ed. P. Granfield and J. A. Jungmann (Munich: Aschendorff), pp. 18–35

—— (1978). 'Greek maenadism from Olympias to Messalina', *Harvard Studies in Classical Philology*, 82, pp. 121–60

Hering, S., and G. Maierhof (2002/1991). *Die unpässliche Frau: Socialgeschichte der Menstruation und Hygiene* (Frankfurt: Marbuse)

Hersey, G. L. (1988). *The Lost Meaning of Classical Architecture: Speculations on Ornament from Vetrivius to Venturi* (Cambridge, MA: MIT)

Hill, R. A., and R. A. Barton (2005). 'Red enhances human performance in contests', *Nature*, 435, p. 293

Hoffner, C. A., and K. J. Levine (2005). 'Enjoyment of mediated fright and violence: A meta-analysis', *Media Psychology*, 7, pp. 207–37

Hornbuckle, P. A., and T. Beall (1974). 'Escape reactions to the blood of selected mammals by rats', *Behavioral Biology*, 12, pp. 573–6

Hufeland, C. W. (1795). *Ideeën über Pathogenie und Einfluß der Lebenskraft auf die Entstehung und Form der Krankheiten* (Jena: Academischen Buchhandlung)

—— (1837). *Enchiridion medicum, oder Anleitung zur medizinischen Praxis: Vermächtnis einer funfzigjährigen Erfahrung. Dritte Auflage* (Berlin: Jonas)

Ilie, A., et al. (2008). 'Better to be red than blue in virtual competition', *Cyber Psychology and Behavior*, 3, pp. 375–7

Jacob. W. (1974). 'Die Zellentheorie des Blutes', in *Einfuhrung in die Geschichte der Hämatologie*, ed. K. G. von Boroviczény, H. Schipperges and E. Seidler (Stuttgart: Thieme), pp. 58–73

Jacolliot, L. (1884). *Les animaux sauvages* (Paris: Librairie illustrée)

Jahoda, G. (2009). *Images of Savages: Ancient Roots of Modern Prejudice in Western Culture* (London: Routledge)

James, W. (1890). *The Principles of Psychology* (London: Macmillan)

— (1904). 'Speech to the World Peace Congress', in W. James (1982). *Essays in Religion and Morality* (Cambridge, MA: Harvard University Press)

— (1910). 'The Moral Equivalent of War', in *The Writings of William James: A Comprehensive Edition*, ed. J. J. McDermott (Chicago, IL: University of Chicago Press), pp. 660–71

Jeong, E. J., F. A. Biocca and C. J. Bohil (2012). 'Sensory realism and mediated aggression in video games', *Computers in Human Behavior*, 28, pp. 1840–48

Jerome, K. J. (1900). *Three Men on the Bummel* (London: Arrowsmith)

Johnston, S. I. (2002). 'Sacrifice in the Greek Magical Papyri', in *Magic and Ritual in the Ancient World*, ed. P. Mirecki and M. Meyer (Leiden: Brill), pp. 344–58

Jones, C. P. (2014). *Between Pagan and Christian* (Cambridge, MA: Harvard University Press)

Jones, R. B., and A. J. Black (1979). 'Behavioral responses of the domestic chick to blood', *Behavioral and Neural Biology*, 27, pp. 319–29

Jori, A. (2005). 'Blut und Leben bei Aristoteles', in *Blood in History and Blood Histories*, ed. M. B. Gadebusch (Florence: Sismel – edizioni del galluzzo), pp. 19–38

Jouanna, J. (2012). 'At the Roots of Melancholy: Is Greek Medicine Melancholic?', in *Greek Medicine from Hippocrates to Galen: Selected Papers by Jacques Jouanna*, ed. Philip van der Eijk (Leiden: Brill, *Studies in Ancient Medicine*, vol. XL), pp. 229–58

Kadletz, E. (1978). 'The Cult of Apollo Deiradiotes', *Transactions of the American Philological Association*, 108, pp. 93–101

Kaenel, G. (2013). 'Gaulois et sacrifices humains: des textes antiques aux observations archéologiques', in *Sacrifices humaines: Dossiers, discours, comparaisons*, ed. A. A. Nagy and F. Prescendi (Turnhout: Brepols, *Bibliothèque de l'école des hautes études sciences religieuses*, vol. CLX), pp. 109–16

Kant, I. (2007/1790). *Critique of Judgement*, trans. James Creed Meredith (Oxford: Oxford University Press)

King, C. (1987). 'The veracity of Ammianus Marcellinus' description of the Huns', *American Journal of Ancient History*, 12, pp. 77–95

Kirwan, J. (2005). *Sublimity: The Non-rational and the Irrational in the History of Aesthetics* (London: Routledge)

Klawans, J. (2001). 'Pure violence: Sacrifice and defilement in ancient Israel', *Harvard Theological Review*, xciv/2, pp. 133–55

Klimsley, P. A. (2013). *The Biology of Sharks and Rays* (Chicago, il: University of Chicago Press)

Knight, C. (1991). *Blood Relations: Menstruation and the Origins of Culture* (New Haven: Yale University Press)

Knight, H., and M. Hunter (2007). 'Robert Boyle's "Memoirs for the Natural History of Human Blood" (1684): Print, manuscript and the impact of Baconianism in seventeenth-century medical science', *Medical History*, 51, pp. 145–64

Knust, C. (2010). 'Von Armsündertüchlein und Liebestränken: Blut als Heil- und Zaubermittel in Volksmedizin und Volksglauben', in *Blut: Die Kraft des ganz besonderes Saftes in Medizin, Literatur, Geschichte und Kultur*, ed. C. Knust and C. Gross (Kassel: Kassel University Press), pp. 209–28

Kolakowski, M., N. N. Nagy and F. Prescendi (2013). 'L'Essai historique sur le sacrifice d'Alfred Loissy: La confession de foi d'un humaniste', *Mythos*, 7, pp. 97–109

Kolb, K. (1980). *Vom Heiligen Blut: eine Bilddokumentation der Wallfahrt und Verehrung* (Würzburg: Echter)

Koolmees, P. A. (1997). *Symbolen van openbare hygiëne: Gemeentelijke slachthuizen in Nederland 1795–1940* (Rotterdam: Erasmus Publishing)

Krcmar, M., and K. Farrar (2009). 'Retaliatory aggression and the effects of point of view and blood in violent video games', *Mass Communication and Society*, 12, pp. 115–38

Kuper, A. (2005). *The Reinvention of Primitive Society: Transformations of a Myth* (London: Routledge)

Lambert, W. G. (1993). 'Donations of Food and Drink to the Gods in Ancient Mesopotamia', in *Ritual and Sacrifice in the Ancient Near East*, ed. J. Quaegebeur (Leuven: Peeters, Orientalia Lovaniensa 55), pp. 191–201

Lanzillotta, L. R. (2007). 'The Early Christians and Human Sacrifice', in *The Strange Way of Human Sacrifice*, ed. J. N. Bremmer (Leuven: Peeters), pp. 81–102

Laurent, E. (1903). *Le sadisme et le masochisme (les perversions sexuelles, physiologie, psychologie, thérapeutique)* (Paris: Vigot)

Lawrence, C., and G. Weisz (1998). *Greater than the Parts: Holism and Biomedicine, 1920–1950* (Oxford: Oxford University Press)

Le Bon, G. (1896/1895). *The Crowd: A Study of the Popular Mind* (London: Fisher Unwin)

Lee, P. Y. (2008). 'Siting the Slaughterhouse: From Shed to Factory', in *Meat, Modernity, and the Rise of the Slaughterhouse*, ed. P. Y. Lee (Durham: University of New Hampshire Press), pp. 46–70

Lenhardt, F. (1986). 'Blutschau: Untersuchungen zur Entwicklung der Hämatoskopie', *Würzburger medizinhistorische Forschungen*, 22, pp. 19–42

Lestel, D. (2016). *Eat This Book: A Carnivore's Manifesto* (*Critical Perspectives on Animals: Theory, Culture, Science and Law*), trans. Gary Steiner (New York: Columbia University Press)

Lilliencreutz, C., and A. Josefsson (2008). 'Prevalence of blood and injection phobia among pregnant women', *Acta Obstetricia et Gynecologia*, 87, pp. 1276–9

Lin, H. (2014). 'Red-colored products enhance the attractiveness of women', *Displays*, 35, pp. 202–5

Linke, U. (1999). *Blood and Nation: The European Aesthetics of Race* (Philadelphia, PA: University of Pennsylvania Press)

Livingston, P. (2013). 'Du Bos' paradox', *British Journal of Aesthetics*, LIII/4, pp. 393–406

Lockhart, K. L., F. C. Keil and J. Aw (2013). 'A bias for the natural? Children's beliefs about traits acquired through effort, bribes, or medicine', *Developmental Psychology*, XLIX/9, pp. 1669–92

Lombroso, C. (1895). *L'homme criminel: Criminel-né, fou moral, épileptique, criminel fou, criminel d'occasion, criminel par passion: étude anthropologique et psychiatrique* (Paris: Alcan)

——, and R. Laschi (1892). *Le crime politique et les révolutions par rapport au droit, à l'anthropologie criminelle et à la science du gouvernement* (Paris: Alcan)

Lorrain, J. (1898). 'Le verre de sang', *La Vie Litteraire*, 65, pp. 385–91

Lovecraft, H. P. (1973/1927). *Supernatural Horror in Literature* (New York: Dover Publications)

Lowenstein, A. (1998). 'Films without a face: Shock horror in the cinema of Georges Franju', *Cinema Journal*, XXXVII/4, pp. 37–58

Loy, T. H. et al. (1990). 'Accelerator radiocarbon dating of human blood proteins in pigments from Late Pleistocene art sites in Australia', *Antiquity*, 64, pp. 110–16

Lubbock, J. (1865). *Prehistoric Times, as Illustrated by Ancient Remains and the Manners and Customs of Modern Savages* (London: William and Norgate)

McCarthy, D. J. (1969). 'The symbolism of blood and sacrifice', *Journal of Biblical Literature*, 88, pp. 166–76

—— (1973). 'Further notes on the symbolism of blood and sacrifice', *Journal of Biblical Literature*, 92, pp. 205–10

McClintock, M. (1995). *Imperial Leather: Race, Gender, and Sexuality in the Colonial Contest* (London: Routledge)

McClintock, M. K. (1971). 'Menstrual synchrony and suppression', *Nature*, ccxxix/5282, pp. 244–5

Macht, D. J., and D. Lubin (1924). 'A phytopharmacological study of menstrual toxin', *Journal of Pharmacology and Experimental Therapy*, 22, pp. 413–66

MacKay-Sim, A., and D. G. Laing (1980). 'Discrimination of odors from stressed rats by non-stressed rats', *Physiology and Behavior*, 24, pp. 699–704

Mahieu, V. (2012). 'Le meurtre ritual dans la littérature hérésiologique antique (2e–5e S. apr. J.-C.): Analyse de la christianisation d'un topos', *Revue d'Histoire Ecclésiastique*, cvii/3–4, pp. 801–29

Maluf, N.S.R. (1954). 'History of blood transfusion', *Journal of the History of Medicine and Allied Sciences*, 9, pp. 59–107

Mangan, J. A. (2013). *'Manufactured' Masculinity: Making Imperial Manliness, Morality and Militarism* (London: Routledge)

——, and C. C. McKenzie (2010). *Militarism, Hunting, Imperialism: 'Blooding' the Martial Male* (London: Routledge)

Mann, T. (1924). *The Magic Mountain*, trans. H. T. Lowe-Porter (London: Secker & Warburg)

Mant, A. K. (1984). *Taylor's Principles and Practice of Medical Jurisprudence*, 13th edn (Edinburgh and London: Livingston)

Marcandier-Colard, C. (1998). *Crimes de sang et scènes capitals: Essai sur l'esthéthique de la violence* (Paris: PUF)

March, K. (1980). 'Deer, bears, and blood: A note on nonhuman animal response to menstrual odor', *American Anthropologist*, 82, pp. 125–7

Marks, I. (1988). 'Blood-injury phobia: A review', *American Journal of Psychiatry*, cxlv/10, pp. 1207–13

Maurer, K. (1856). *Die Bekehrung des Norwegischen Stammen zum Christentums* (Munich: Christian Kaiser)

Méniel, P. (1992). *Les sacrifices d'animaux chez les Gaulois* (Paris: Errance)

Meyer, M. L. (2005). *Thicker than Water: The Origins of Blood as Symbol and Ritual* (London: Routledge)

Milgrom, J. (1991). *The Anchor Bible: Leviticus 1–16* (New York: Doubleday)

Mirecki, P., and M. Meyer, eds (2002). *Magic and Ritual in the Ancient World* (Leiden: Brill)

Mitro, S. et al. (2012). 'The smell of age: Perception and discrimination of body odors of different ages', *PLOS ONE*, vii/5, e38110

Mohr, A. (2005). *Das Wissen über die Anderen: Zur Darstellung fremder Völker in den Fränkischen Quellen der Karolingerzeit* (Munster: Waxmann)

Mole, R. H. (1948). 'Fibrolysin and the fluidity of blood post mortem', *Journal of Pathology and Bacteriology*, 60, pp. 413–27

Mommsen, H. (1934). 'Zur Frage des Menstruationsgift', *Municher Medizinische Wochenschrift*, 36, pp. 1458–60

Monk, S. (1935). *The Sublime: A Study of Critical Theories in Eighteenth-century England* (New York: Modern Language Association of America)

Moog, F. P., and A. Karenberg (2003). 'Between horror and hope: Gladiator's blood as a cure for epileptics in ancient medicine', *Journal of the History of the Neurosciences*, xii/2, pp. 137–43

Moore, J. Howard (1933/1916). *Savage Survivals* (London: Watts & Co., The Thinker's Library, 36)

Moriceau, J.-M. (2011). *L'homme contre le loup: Une guerre de deux mille ans* (Paris: Fayard)

Morreall, J. (1985). 'Enjoying negative emotions in fictions', *Philosophy and Literature*, 9, pp. 95–103

Moshkin, M. et al. (2012). 'Scent recognition of infected status in humans', *Journal of Sexual Medicine*, 9, pp. 3211–18

Nagy, A. A., and F. Prescendi (2013). *Sacrifices humaines: Dossiers, discours, comparaisons* (Turnhout: Brepols, *Bibliothèque de l'école des hautes études sciences religieuses*, vol. clx)

Newton-Fisher, N. E. (2007). 'Chimpanzee hunting behavior', in *Handbook of Paleoanthropology*, ed. W. Henke and I. Tattersall (Berlin: Springer), pp. 1295–320

Nilsson, S., et al. (2014). 'Behavioral responses to mammalian blood odor and a blood odor component in four species of large carnivores', *PLOS ONE*, ix/11, e1122694

Novalis (1997). *Philosophical Writings*, trans. Margaret Mahony Stoljar (New York: State University of New York Press)

Nunley, M. C. (1981). 'Response of deer to human blood odor',
  American Anthropologist, 83, pp. 630–34

Nye, R. (1993). *Masculinity and Male Codes of Honor in Modern France:
  Studies in the History of Sexuality* (Oxford: Oxford University Press)

Nye, R. A. (1975). *The Origins of Crowd Psychology: Gustave Le Bon and
  the Crisis of Mass Democracy in the Third Republic* (London: Sage)

Oaten, M. J., R. J. Stevenson and T. I. Case (2009). 'Disgust as a disease-
  avoidance mechanism', *Psychological Bulletin*, 135, pp. 303–21

Olsen, M. J., et al. (2014). 'The scent of disease: Human body odor
  contains an early chemosensory cue of sickness', *Psychological
  Science*, xxv/3, pp. 817–23

Orfila, M., J.-P. Barruel and J.B.A. Chevallier (1835). 'Taches de sang:
  Rapport medico-légal', *Annales d'Hygiène Publique et de Médecine
  Légale*, 14, pp. 349–70

Ortega y Gasset, J. (1972/1942). *Meditations on Hunting*,
  trans. H. B. Westcott (New York: Charles Scribner's Sons)

Otis, L. (1994). *Organic Memory: History and the Body in the Late
  Nineteenth and Early Twentieth Centuries* (Lincoln, NE, and
  London: University of Nebraska Press)

Overvliet, K. E., and S. Soto-Faraco (2011). 'I can't believe this isn't
  wood! An investigation in the perception of naturalness', *Acta
  Psychologica*, 136, pp. 95–111

Owen, C. (2001). *A History of Blood Coagulation* (Rochester: Mayo
  foundation for medical education and research)

Pachirat, T. (2011). *Every Twelve Seconds: Industrialized Slaughter and
  the Politics of Sight* (New Haven, CT, and London: Yale University Press)

Parmentier, A. A., and N. Déyeux (1791). *Mémoire sur le sang*
  (Paris: Boiste)

Pelis, K. (1997). 'Blood clots: The nineteenth century debate over the
  substance and means of transfusion in Britain', *Annals of Science*,
  54, pp. 331–60

Peskov, V. N. (1898). 'Un cas de manie sexuelle pendant les règles avec
  sadisme', *Archives d'Anthropologie Criminelle*, 13, pp. 568–73

Pettersson, H., M. Amundin and M. Laska (2018). 'Attractant or
  repellent? Behavioral responses to mammalian blood odor and
  to a blood odor component in a mesopredator, the meerkat
  (Suricata suricatta)', *Frontiers in Behavioral Neuroscience*, 12, p. 152

Phillips, F. (1906). 'Ancestral memory: A suggestion', *Nineteenth
  Century and After*, 59, pp. 977–93

Pick, D. (1989). *Faces of Degeneration: A European Disorder, c. 1848 –*
c. 1918 (Cambridge: Cambridge University Press, 1989)

Pollan, M. (2006). 'The modern hunter-gatherer', *New York Times Magazine*

—— (2013). *Cooked: A Natural History of Transformation* (London: Penguin)

Ponsold, A. (1957). *Lehrbuch der gerichtlichen Medizin*
(Stuttgart: Thieme, 1957)

Quinche, N. (2009). *Le théâtre du crime (1875–1929): Rodolphe A.*
Reiss (Lausanne: Presses polytechniques et universitaires Romandes)

Rapisarda, T. et al. (2013). 'Variability of volatile profiles in milk from
the PDO Ragusano cheese production zone', *Dairy Science and*
Technology, 93, pp. 117–34

Reiss, R. A. (1916). Report Upon the Atrocities Committed by the
Austro-Hungarian Army During the First Invasion of Serbia
(London: Simpkin, Marshall, Hamilton, Kent & Company)

Ribot, Th. (1875). *Heredity: A Psychological Study of its Phenomena,*
Laws, Causes, and Consequences (New York: S. Appleton & Company)

Rice, A. (2008/1976). *Interview with the Vampire* (London: Sphere)

Riha, O. (2005). 'Die mittelalterliche Blutschau, in *Blood in History and*
Blood Histories, ed. M. B. Gadebusch (Florence: Sismel – edizioni
del galluzzo), pp. 49–68

Rives, J. (1994). 'Tertullian on child sacrifice', *Museum Helveticum*, LI/1,
pp. 54–63

—— (1995). 'Human sacrifice among pagans and Christians', *Journal*
of Roman Studies, 85, pp. 65–85

Robertson, R. (2006). 'Sacrifice and sacrament in *Der Zauberberg*',
Oxford German Studies, XXXV/1, pp. 55–65

Röckelein, H. (1996). 'Hexenessen im Frühmittelalter, in *Kannibalismus*
und europäische Kultur, ed. H. Röckenlein (Tübingen: discord,
Forum Psychohistorie, Bd. 6), pp. 29–60

Rogers, L. L., G. A. Wilker and S. S. Scott (1991). 'Reactions of
black bears to human menstrual odors', *Journal of Wildlife*
Management, LV/4, pp. 632–6

Romswinkel, H. J. (1974). 'De sanguine humano destillato', *Medizinisch-*
alchemistische Texte des 14. Jahrhunderts über destilliertes
Menschenblut (dissertation Bonn)

Rothschuh, K. E. (1974). 'Von der Viersäftenlehre zur Korpuskeltheorie
des Blutes', in *Einfuhrung in die Geschichte der Hämatologie*,
ed. K. G. von Boroviczény, H. Schipperges and E. Seidler
(Stuttgart: Thieme), pp. 31–43

Rousseau, V. (2005). *Le goût du sang: Croyances et polémiques dans la chrétienté occidentale* (Paris: Armand Colin)

Roux, J.-P. (1988). *Le sang: Mythes, symboles et réalités* (Paris: Fayard)

Rozin, P. (2005). 'The meaning of "natural": Process more important than content', *Psychological Science*, XVI/8, pp. 652–8

—— (2006). 'Naturalness judgments by lay Americans: Process dominates content in judgments of food or water acceptability and naturalness', *Judgment and Decision Making*, I/2, pp. 91–7

Rubin, M. (1991). *Corpus Christi: The Eucharist in Late Medieval Culture* (Cambridge: Cambridge University Press)

Rüsche, F. (1930). *Blut, Leben und Seele: Ihr Verhältnis nach Auffassung der griechischen und hellenistischen Antike, der Bibel und der alten Alexandrinischen Theologen* (Paderborn: Schöningh)

Salzman, M. R. (2011). 'The End of Public Sacrifice', in *Ancient Mediterranean Sacrifice*, ed. J. W. Knust and Z. Varhelyi (Oxford: Oxford University Press), pp. 167–83

Samson, V. (2011). *Les Berserkir: Les guerriers-fauves dans la Scandinavie ancienne, de l'âge de Vendel aux Vikings (VIe–XIe siècle)* (Villeneuve d'Ascq: Presses universitaires du Septentrion)

Sandnabba, K. N. (1997). 'The effect of blood signals on aggressive behavior in mice', *Behavioral Processes*, 41, pp. 51–6

Sarazin, P. (2007). 'Feind in Blut: Die Bedeuting des Blutes in der Deutschen Bakteriologie, 1870–1900', in *Mythen des Blutes*, ed. C. von Brain and C. Wulf (Frankfurt: Campus), pp. 296–312

Schacter, D. L. (2001). *Forgotten Ideas, Neglected Pioneers: Richard Semon and the Story of Memory* (Philadelphia, PA: Psychological Press)

Schank, J. C. (2006). 'Do human menstrual-cycle pheromones exist?', *Human Nature*, XVII/4, pp. 448–70

Scheid, J. (2007). 'Le status de la viande à Rome', in *Sacrifices, marchés de la viande et pratiques alimentaires dans les cités du monde romain*, ed. W. Van Andringa, *Food & History*, V/1, pp. 19–28

Schellmann, J. (1997). *Joseph Beuys: Die Multiples. Werkverzeichnis der Auflagenobjekte und Druckgraphik* (Munich: Schellmann)

Schick, B. (1920). 'Das Menstruationsgift', *Wiener Klinische Wochenschrift*, 19, pp. 377–9, 416

Schild, W. (2007). 'Das Blut des Hingerichteten', in *Mythen des Blutes*, ed. C. von Brain and C. Wulf (Frankfurt: Campus), pp. 126–54

Schipperges, H. (1974). 'Blut in Altertum und Mittelalter', in *Einführung*

in die Geschichte der Hämatologie, ed. K. G. von Boroviczény,
H. Schipperges and E. Seidler (Stuttgart: Thieme), pp. 17–30

Schmidt, K. (1848). *Die Diagnostik Verdächtiger Flecke in Criminalfällen* (Leipzig: Mitau)

Schrenk, M. (1974). 'Blutkulte und Blutsymbolik', in *Einführung in die Geschichte der Hämatologie*, ed. K. G. von Boroviczény,
H. Schipperges and E. Seidler (Stuttgart: Thieme), pp. 1–16

Schury, G. (2001). *Lebensflut: Eine Kulturgeschichte des Blutes* (Leipzig: Reclam)

Seeman, B. (1962). *The River of Life: The Story of Man's Blood from Magic to Science* (London: Museum Press)

Segal, C. (1973–4). 'The raw and the cooked in Greek literature', *Classical Journal*, 69, pp. 289–308

Seidler, E. (1974). 'Medizin und Hämatologie im ausgehenden 18. und beginnenden 19. Jahrhundert', in *Einführung in die Geschichte der Hämatologie*, ed. K. G. von Boroviczény, H. Schipperges and E. Seidler (Stuttgart: Thieme), pp. 44–57

Shabani, S., M. Kamio and C. D. Derby (2008). 'Spiny lobsters detect conspecific blood-borne alarm cues exclusively through olfactory sensilla', *Journal of Experimental Biology*, 211, pp. 2600–608

Shepherd, G. M. (2012). *Neurogastronomy: How the Brain Creates Flavor and Why It Matters* (New York: Columbia University Press)

Shlosser, F. E. (1991). 'Pagan into magician', *Byzantinoslavica*, xl/2, pp. 49–53

Siems, H. (1980). *Studien zur Lex Frisionum* (Ebelsbach: Gremer)

Sighele, S. (1892). *La foule criminelle: Essai de psychologie collective* (Paris: Alcan)

Silverstein, A. M. (1979). 'Cellular versus humoral immunity: Determinants and consequences of an epic 19th century battle', *Cellular Immunology*, 48, pp. 208–21

Singer, P. (2011). *Practical Ethics*, 3rd edn (New York: Cambridge University Press)

Smith, P. et al. (2013). 'Age estimations attest to infant sacrifice at the Carthago Tophet', *Antiquity*, lxxxvii/338, pp. 1191–8

Smuts, A. (2007). 'The paradox of painful arts', *Journal of Aesthetic Education*, xli/3, pp. 59–76

—— (2009). 'Art and negative affect', *Philosophical Compass*, iv/1, pp. 39–55

Solomon, S., J. Greenberg and T. Pyszczynski (2015). *The Worm at the Core: On the Role of Death in Life* (London: Allen Lane)

Spier, I. (1916). 'Atavismen und Kriegexzessen', *Die Gegenwart*, xlv/1916, pp. 153–5, 171–4

Spörri, M. (2005). '"Giftiges Blut": Menstruation and Menotoxin in den 1920er Jahren', in *Blood in History and Blood Histories*, ed. M. B Gadebusch (Florence: Sismel – edizioni del galluzzo), pp. 311–29

—— (2013). *Reines und gemischtes Blut: Zur Kulturgeschichte der Blutgruppenforschung 1900–1933* (Bielefeld: Transcript)

Stanford, C. B. (1998). *Chimpanzee and Red Colobus: The Ecology of Predator and Prey* (Cambridge, MA: Harvard University Press)

—— (1999). *The Hunting Apes: Meat-eating and the Origins of Human Behavior* (Princeton, NJ: Princeton University Press)

Starr, D. (2000). *Blood: An Epic History of Medicine and Commerce* (London: Warner Books)

Steigerwald, J. (2013). 'Rethinking organic vitality in Germany at the turn of the nineteenth century', in *Vitalism and the Scientific Image in Post-Enlightenment Life Science, 1800–2010*, ed. C. T. Normandin and C. T. Wolf (Berlin: Springer), pp. 52–75

Steiner, R. (1982/1906). *Blut ist ein ganz besonderer Saft. Vortrag* (Berlin: Steiner Verlag)

Steintrager, J. (2012). *Cruel Delight: Enlightenment Culture and the Inhuman* (Bloomington, IN: Indiana University Press)

Stevens, D. A., and D. A. Gerzog-Thomas (1977). 'Fright reactions in rats to conspecific tissue', *Physiology and Behavior*, 18, pp. 47–51

Stevens, D. A., and N. J. Saplikoski (1973). 'Rats' reactions to conspecific muscle and blood: Evidence for an alarm substance', *Behavioral Biology*, 8, pp. 75–82

Stocking, G. W. (1987). *Victorian Anthropology* (London: Macmillan)

Stoker, B. (1986/1897). *Dracula* (Oxford: Oxford University Press, Oxford World's Classics)

Stowers, S. K. (1995). 'Greeks who sacrifice and those who do not: Toward an anthropology of Greek religion', in *The Social World of the First Christians: Studies in Honor of Wayne A. Meeks*, ed. L. M. White and O. L. Yarbrough (Minneapolis, MN: Fortress), pp. 293–333

—— (1998). 'On the Comparison of Blood in Greek and Israelite Ritual', in *Hesed Ve-Emet: Studies in Honor of Ernest S. Frerichs*, ed. J. Magness and S. Gitin (Atlanta, GA: Scholars), pp. 179–94

Strack, H. (1900). *Das Blut im Glauben und Aberglauben der Menschheit* (Munich: Beck'sche Verlagsbuchhandlung)

Straten, F. T. van (1995). *HIERA KALA: Images of Sacrifice in Archaic and Classical Greece* (Leiden: Brill)

Stratton, G. M. (1923). 'Cattle, and excitement from blood', *Psychological Review*, xxx/5, pp. 380–87

Stroumsa, G. G. (2009). *The End of Sacrifice: Religious Transformation in Late Antiquity* (Chicago, IL: University of Chicago Press)

Sussman R. W. 1999. 'The myth of man the hunter, man the killer and the evolution of human morality', *Zygon*, 34, pp. 453–71

Tarde, G. (1892). 'Les crimes des foules', *Archives d'Anthropologie Criminelle*, 7, pp. 353–86

Tardieu, A., J.-P. Barruel and J.B.A. Chevalier (1853). 'Expériences sur l'odeur du sang', *Annales d'Hygiène Publique et de Médecine Légale*, 49, pp. 413–17

Tauber, A. I., and L. Chernyak (1991). *Metchnikoff and the Origins of Immunology: From Metaphor to Theory* (Oxford: Oxford University Press)

Terlouw, C.E.M., A. Boissy and P. Blinet (1998). 'Behavioural responses of cattle to the odours of blood and urine from conspecifics and to the odour of faeces from carnivores', *Applied Animal Behaviour Science*, 57, pp. 9–21

Thoinot, L. (1898). *Attentats aux moeurs et perversions du sens génital: Leçons professées à la faculté de médecine* (Paris: Doin)

Thomas, K. (1991). *Man and the Natural World: Changing Attitudes in England, 1500–1800* (London: Penguin)

Thorndike, L. (1934). *A History of Magic and Experimental Science*, vol. III (New York: Colombia University Press)

Three, F.C.R. (1984). *Julius Africanus and the Early Christian View on Magic* (Tübingen: Mohr, *Hermeneutische Untersuchungen zur Theologie*, 19)

Tran, N. (2007). 'Le status de travail de bouchers dans l'Occident romain de la fin de la République et du Haut-Empire', in *Sacrifices, marchés de la viande et pratiques alimentaires dans les cités du monde romain*, ed. W. Van Andringa, *Food & History*, v/1, pp. 151–67

Trotter, W. (1916). *Instincts of the Herd in Peace and War* (London: Fisher Unwin)

Turner, J. (1980). *Reckoning with the Beast: Animals, Pain, and Humanity in the Victorian Mind* (Baltimore, MD: Johns Hopkins University Press)

Ullucci, D. (2012). *The Christian Rejection of Animal Sacrifice* (Oxford: Oxford University Press)

Van Gennep, A. (1960). *The Rites of Passage* (Chicago, IL: University of Chicago Press)

Vandenberg, V. (2014). *De chair et de sang: Images et pratiques du cannibalisme de l'Antiquité au Moyen Âge* (Rennes: Presses universitaires de Rennes)

Varhelyi, Z. (2011). 'Political Murder and Sacrifice: From Roman Republic to Empire', in *Ancient Mediterranean Sacrifice*, ed. J. W. Knust and Z. Varhelyi (Oxford: Oxford University Press), pp. 125–41

Verbeke, W., et al. (2015). '"Would you eat cultured meat?" Consumers' reactions and attitude formation in Belgium, Portugal and the United Kingdom', *Meat Science*, 103, pp. 49–58

Verbeke, W., P. Sans and E. J. Van Loo (2015). 'Challenges and prospects for consumer acceptance of cultured meat', *Journal of Integrative Agriculture*, XIV/2, pp. 285–94

Verplaetse, J. (2011). *Der moralische Instinkt: Über den natürlichen Ursprung unserer Moral* (Göttingen: Vandenhoeck & Ruprecht)

——, and D. De Smet (2016). 'Mental beliefs about blood, and not its smell, affect presence in a violent computer game', *Computers in Human Behavior*, 63, pp. 928–37

Vervenne, M. (1993). '"The blood is the life and the life is the blood": Blood as symbol of life and death in biblical tradition (Gen. 9,4)', in *Ritual and Sacrifice in the Ancient Near East*, ed. J. Quaegebeur (Leuven: Peeters, Orientalia Lovaniensa 55), pp. 451–70

Vialles, N. (1994). *Animal to Edible* (Cambridge: Cambridge University Press, translation of *Le sang et la chair: les abattoirs de pays de l'Adour*, 1987)

Vincent, N. (2001). *The Holy Blood: King Henry III and the Westminster Blood Relic* (Cambridge: Cambridge University Press)

Visak, T. (2011). *Killing Happy Animals: Explorations in Utilitarian Ethics* (Zutphen: Wöhrmann)

Vries, J. de (1958). *Altgermanische Religionsgeschichte: Band I & II* (Berlin: de Gruyter)

Wagner, M.-A. (2005). *Le cheval dans les croyances germaniques: Paganisme, christianisme et traditions* (Paris: Champion)

Ward, J. (1913). *Heredity and Memory* (Cambridge: Cambridge University Press)

Washburn, S. L., and C. S. Lancaster (1968). 'The Evolution of Hunting', in *Man the Hunter*, ed. R. B. Lee and I. DeVore (Chicago, IL: Aldine)

Watts, S. (2008). 'The *grande boucherie*, the "right" to meat, and the growth of Paris', in *Meat, Modernity, and the Rise of the Slaughterhouse*, ed. P. Y. Lee (Durham: University of New Hampshire Press), pp. 13–26

Weber, E. (1975). *Gibt es ein Menotoxin?* (Göttingen: Dissertation *Medizinische Fakultät*)

Webster, C. (1971). 'The origins of blood transfusion: A reassessment', *Medical History*, 4, pp. 387–92

Weele, C. van der, and C. Driessen (2013). 'Emerging profiles for cultured meat: Ethics through and as design', *Animals*, 3, pp. 647–62

Weele, C. van der, and J. Tramper (2014). 'Cultured meat: every village its own factory?', *Trends in Biotechnology*, XXXII/6, pp. 294–6

Weiermair, P. (2001). 'Reflections on blood in contemporary art', in *Blood: Art, Power, Politics and Pathology*, ed. J. M. Bradburne (Munich: Prestel), pp. 205–15

Wernz, C. (1993). *Sexualität als Krankheit: Der medizinische Diskurs zur Sexualität um 1800* (Stuttgart: Enke)

Whitaker, T. A., C. Simoes-Franklin and F. N. Newell (2008). 'The natural truth: The contribution of vision and touch in the categorisation of "naturalness"', *Lecture Notes in Computer Science*, 5024, pp. 319–24

White, H. (1972). 'The Forms of Wildness: Archeology of an Idea', in *The Wild Man Within: An Image in Western Thought from the Renaissance to Romanticism*, ed. E. Dudley and M. E. Novak (Pittsburgh, PA: University of Pittsburgh Press), pp. 3–38

Wrangham, R., and D. Peterson (1997). *Demonic Males: Apes and the Origins of Human Violence* (London: Bloomsbury)

Wyatt, T. D. (2015). 'The search for human pheromones: The lost decades and the necessity of returning to first principles', *Proceedings of the Royal Academy of Science B*, 282,

Xella, P. et al. (2013). 'Phoenican bones of contention', *Antiquity*, LXXXVII/338, pp. 1199–207

Young, F. M. (1979). *The Use of Sacrificial Ideas in Greek Christian Writers from the New Testament to John Chrysostom* (Cambridge, MA: Philadelphia Patristic Foundation)

Young, R. (1995). *Colonial Desire: Hybridity in Theory, Culture, and Race* (London: Routledge)

Zacharias of Mytilene (2008). *The Life of Severus* (Piscataway: Gorgias Press, Texts from Christian Late Antiquity 9)

Zika, C. (1996). 'Kannibalismus und Hexerei: Die Rolle der Bilder im frühneuzeitlichen Europa', in *Kannibalismus und europäische Kultur*, ed. H. Röckenlein (Tübingen: discord, Forum Psychohistorie, Bd. 6), pp. 75–115

Zola, E. (1895/1885). *Germinal*, trans. Havelock Ellis (London: Lutetian Society)

Zondek, B. (1953). 'Does menstrual blood contain a specific toxin?', *American Journal of Obstetrics and Gynecology*, 65, pp. 1065–8

ACKNOWLEDGEMENTS

I dedicate this book to my wife Isabelle and to Assenede, the country village in the north of Flanders, Belgium, where I live and work. The open landscape full of polders and creeks, local friends and remarkable characters, grazing animals and brushwood on the dikes, encouraged me to write this book, a work forged from a query that has preoccupied me for several decades. Assenede also encapsulates the home that I share with Isabelle. This book is an ode to her love, patience, humour, taste and philosophy of life. How many times did I restrain myself from asking her opinion on my reflections? 'Not enough,' she would respond in a flash. 'How can a philosopher hold such far-fetched expectations about happiness, while happiness is just lying here, waiting to be grasped?' That is perhaps the most concise summary of this book, since it is indeed about happiness, or what I would call 'philosophical happiness', whatever that may be.

Looking for a solid answer to a lifelong query, I had to combine insights from multiple disciplines including theology, philosophy, history, cultural studies and science – from haematology to experimental psychology. In a book about our fascination with blood, such a mix of diverse domains of knowledge is self-evident. Representing our attitudes towards blood is as multifaced as the fluid itself. Of course, since I am no expert in these areas, I had to rely on the expertise of many academic colleagues. Heartfelt thanks to those who addressed my questions and requests: Dominique Adriaens, Stephan Arntz, Jan Bremmer, André Caulier, Mark Cavaliers, Mariella Debille, Dirk de Korte, Jelle De Schrijver, Johan De Smedt, Delphine De Smet, Ellen de Visser, Theo De Vuyst, Kristin Duysters, Raf Francken, Olivier Gomme, Bas Haring, Kurt Houf, Annelies Lannoy, Matthias Laske, Geerdt Magiels, Laura Meijer, Koen Mertens, Christel Moons, Vivian Nutton, Mark Post, Monique Smeets, Paul Stengers, Stanley Stowers, Vincent Vandenberg, Soraya Vandenbroucke, Jack Van Messel, Mark Van Overveld, Lien Van Speybroeck, Wim Verbeke, Marieke von Lindern, and the many others whom I bothered with questions without thanking them for their skilful help.

I would like to express my special appreciation to my friend and colleague at Ghent University Danny Praet, who reviewed the original Dutch manuscript; Michiel Ten Raa at Nieuwezijds Publishers, who gave me the opportunity the publish this manuscript in spring 2016; and Patrick Peeters at Flanders Literature, who promoted this book among foreign publishing houses and helped to fund the English translation with a generous grant. Finally, *Blood Rush* would be a different publication altogether without the omnivorous cultural and historical interests of Andy Brown, my skilful translator, and the perfectionism of Vivian Constantinopoulos and Phoebe Colley at Reaktion Books. Undoubtedly, any remaining shortcomings are my own responsibility, but thanks to their skills, efforts and professional attitude I feel less reservation in taking this risk. Finally, I would like to thank my *alma mater* Ghent University, and especially the Faculty of Law and Criminology, for what I perceive as the best job on Earth. I owe my greatest respect to an institution that gives me the liberty to write a book on a topic that has no immediate legal or criminological importance. The freedom to explore personal fascinations is far from self-evident nowadays.

INDEX